⌐

SHADOW OF SURIBACHI

In appreciation of the gallantry of Sgt. Henry O. Hansen at Iwo Jima — Joe Rosenthal, A.P.

Rosenthal's Flag-raising Photograph. Published with permission of AP/Wide World Photos. Photograph provided by the Hansen family.

SHADOW OF SURIBACHI

RAISING THE FLAGS ON IWO JIMA

PARKER BISHOP ALBEE, JR.
AND
KELLER CUSHING FREEMAN

PRAEGER

Westport, Connecticut
London

Library of Congress Cataloging-in-Publication Data

Albee, Parker Bishop.
    Shadow of Suribachi : raising the flags on Iwo Jima / Parker
Bishop Albee, Jr. and Keller Cushing Freeman.
       p. cm.
    Includes bibliographical references and index.
    ISBN 0–275–95063–8 (alk. paper)
    1. Iwo Jima, Battle of, 1945. I. Freeman, Keller Cushing.
II. Title.
D767.99.I9A4   1995
940.54′26—dc20   94–34304

British Library Cataloguing in Publication Data is available.

Library of Congress Catalog Card Number: 94–34304
ISBN: 0–275–95063–8

First published in 1995

Praeger Publishers, 88 Post Road West, Westport, CT 06881
An imprint of Greenwood Publishing Group, Inc.

Printed in the United States of America

The paper used in this book complies with the
Permanent Paper Standard issued by the National
Information Standards Organization (Z39.48–1984).

10 9 8 7 6 5 4 3 2 1

To all who lived

in the shadow of Suribachi

Contents

Illustrations following Chapter 5.

Acknowledgments

This book is the product of the generosity of many people. But it owes a special debt of gratitude to the men of Iwo Jima who shared their memories with the authors in innumerable letters, telephone conversations, photographs, and personal interviews. In alphabetical order, they include: the late Louis R. Burmeister; Stanley E. Dabrowski; Colonel John A. Daskalakis, USMC (Ret.); Norman T. Hatch; Major General Fred E. Haynes, USMC (Ret.); Arthur J. Kiely, Jr.; Charles W. Lindberg; Arthur H. Naylor; James A. Robeson; Colonel Dave E. Severance, USMC (Ret.); Charles Tatum; Sherman B. Watson; Major Harrold A. Weinberger, USMC (Ret.); George Greeley Wells; Major John Keith Wells, USMC (Ret.); and Richard Wheeler, whose books on the Iwo Jima campaign have been a most helpful guide to the experience of the men of the 3rd Platoon, 2nd Battalion, 28th Marines.

The late Robert Lee Sherrod, Time/Life correspondent on Iwo Jima, was an invaluable source of information about the role of the press corps in reporting the Pacific war. He was especially generous in allowing us the use of his original combat notebooks. We regret that his death on February 13, 1994, prevented his seeing the fruits of his generosity. His lines (quoted from his obituary notice in the April 1994 issue of *Proceedings,* a publication of the U.S. Naval Institute) provide a useful insight into the flag-raising controversy from a man whose distinguished career moved from journalism to the writing of history: "We journalists frequently don't get things right. Sometimes we are conned into errors; other times, we surmise wrong. But correcting journalism is what history is all about."

Some of the men of Iwo Jima were no longer alive at the time we began our research for *Shadow of Suribachi.* We are grateful to their families for helping us recreate their experiences. The family of Sergeant Henry O. Hansen, especially his niece, Judith A. Garcia, made available the Hansen family papers, an important component in our research. George L. King, brother-in-law of Henry Hansen, and Ophelia Duguay Lepore, close friend of the family during the World War II years, offered their personal reminiscences, fleshing out the bare bones of documents and newspaper accounts. Louis R. Lowery, the combat photographer who documented the first flag raising, died in 1987, after an outstanding career with *Leatherneck* magazine. His widow, Doris Hippler Lowery, and their daughter, photographer Lesle Lowery Sullivan, were most generous in sharing their memories and Lou Lowery's photographs with us.

For a contemporary analysis of Iwo Jima photography, we are grateful for the trained eye of author/photographer William Hubbell.

Finally, at the top of the flagpole, we salute Pulitzer Prize-winning photographer Joseph J. Rosenthal--the indomitable Joe. It is regrettable that Joe limited himself to photography. With his balanced judgment, his capacity to organize complex data, his colorful style of expression, and his scrupulous dedication to a fair and accurate reconstruction of the past, he would have made a world-class historian. He obviously missed his calling.

An essential component in the creation of a book is the preparation of the manuscript. For technical advice, we thank former Marine major James M. Shoemaker, Jr.; for graphic design, artist David W. Clough; and for guidance through the mine fields of the publishing world, author/publisher Cami Berg. Parker Albee would like to thank the University of Southern Maine for a strategically timed sabbatical; Stephen Matoian and Gordon Robinson III for their research assistance; Christopher J. Galgay who as a history student first introduced him to the Hansen family; and Eleanor Weymouth, especially for helping to launch the project with her long hours of typing and retyping the early drafts.   In South Carolina, Wilma Dingley's keen editorial eye, indefatigable duty at the keyboard, and persistent faith in the project made her the ideal comrade-in-arms for this long campaign. Ken M. Woods served with distinction at the computer command post. The manuscript benefited from a final polishing by Furman University's Linda Julian, Ph.D., friend and grammarian extraordinaire.

Beyond gratitude is our debt to our families, and especially to our spouses, Marian Resch Albee and David Lynn Freeman. Their names deserve to be on some permanent roll of honor.   Parker Albee would like to express his appreciation for the forbearance and support of his children: Christopher Ellis Albee (dedicated research assistant), Rebecca Adams Albee, Todd Stevens Albee, and of his father, Parker Bishop Albee, Sr. Keller Cushing Freeman would like to acknowledge the aid and comfort provided by her family: Kathryn Crow Gaston, Caleb Cushing Freeman, Mary Stuckey Freeman, John Anthony Freeman, Thomas Cushing Freeman, David Gardiner Freeman, Lynn Howard Freeman, Kathryn Blake Freeman Gearing, Adam Frederick Gearing, and Robert Karl Werner Herzog.

During these past years our research has profited immeasurably from the contributions of many friends and colleagues beyond those mentioned above. We thank them for serving us so ably. Finally, we acknowledge our debt to all the men who wrote with their lives the pages of Iwo Jima's history.

Introduction: An Aerial View of Suribachi

Fifty years ago on a fly-speck island in the vast Pacific, an Associated Press photographer recorded 1/400 of a second in the 200-year flow of American history. The date was February 23, 1945. The obscure Pacific island was Iwo Jima, scene of the most elaborate amphibious landing ever staged by the United States Navy and Marine Corps. Japanese resistance was fierce. Casualties mounted at a horrific rate.

The battle for Iwo Jima had provided little for the American public to cheer about when, on the morning of the campaign's fifth day, Marines of the 28th Regiment secured the summit of Mount Suribachi. The highest point on the island, this extinct volcano towered 560 feet above the bloody chaos of the landing beaches, affording the Japanese an enviable vantage point.

So when a ragged patrol from the 2nd Battalion's Company E reached the top of the mountain and signaled its safe arrival by raising a flag, there was cause for rejoicing. The moment held symbolic as well as strategic significance: Company E's 3rd Platoon had just planted the first American flag ever to fly over Japanese home territory.

The 5th Division's unit journal recorded the time of the flag raising as 10:30. Unrecorded was a subsequent flag raising that occurred some two hours later, when the first flag was replaced by a larger, more visible banner. Six men--five Marines and a Navy corpsman--struggled with the force of a sharp winter wind and the resisting weight of a flagstaff improvised from a long piece of metal pipe. In the moment before the six men completed their upward thrust of the heavy flagpole, AP photographer Joe Rosenthal, at age 33 already a veteran of five Pacific campaigns, raised his Speed Graphic camera and shot what was hailed as the most famous war photograph of all time. Thanks to his photograph, the second flag raising on Suribachi became as symbolically significant to the American public as that episode was strategically insignificant to the course of the Iwo Jima campaign.

Rosenthal made more than a Pulitzer Prize-winning photograph on that inauspicious February day. He also created a national icon--one of America's "most charged and powerful cultural symbols."[1] The story embedded in that picture is a story the American people deserve to hear.

Many people, especially those who lived through the years of World War II, undoubtedly believe that they have already heard the full story of Iwo Jima and its famous flag. There are even professional historians who consider that the canon is complete, with all necessary pages written in this chapter of American history. We offer, in response, this admonition attributed to Will Rogers: "It's not what people don't know. It's that they know so many things that just ain't so." The American public has persisted in knowing two mutually exclusive stories about the Suribachi flag raisings. The irony lies in the fact that neither of these well-known stories is true.

Truth, we admit, is a moving target, proverbially hard to hit. We make no claim here to have cornered the market on truth--even the limited truth of the American experience on Iwo Jima. We do claim to have scraped away accumulated half-truths and to have exposed some full-blown untruths on the subject. We have tried to leave a clear trail of documentation so that interested readers can evaluate our conclusions. All are open to the corrections of that ongoing conversation, the interpretation of history.

The flag-raising story is more than the backdrop to a famous photograph. It is also the story of how two simple events were transformed into a pair of conflicting myths that reflect opposing aspects of our national character.

We Americans swing between polar extremes in our response to the realities of our shared national experience. On the one hand, we are a gullible, naive, and sentimental people. We believe in Mom and Apple Pie and the American Flag. We delight in such symbols as young George Washington and his little hatchet, embracing the myth that from earliest childhood our first president was a person who could not tell a lie, even to save himself a whipping. We want to believe in the wisdom, decency, and benevolence of our leaders, those ordinary people of whom we expect such extraordinary contributions to the public weal.

We also expect much of ourselves, knowing that "to whom much has been given, of him much will be required." So we believe Americans should stand prepared to pick up our guns when there are wrongs to right. We expect to come home from these necessary wars victorious, agreeing with Admiral Chester W. Nimitz that for ordinary Americans uncommon valor is indeed a common virtue.

There is, however, an opposite pole to our national psyche. We are also a skeptical people, given to debunking heroes and distrusting authority. Sometimes this national characteristic manifests itself in a healthy skepticism. We are, after all, the nation that founded its government on a doctrine of checks and balances. We count on the scrupulous scrutiny of the press to keep all branches of our government honest, to tell us the truth about those matters, great and small, that concern the citizens of a democratic society.

But we withhold our unqualified trust even from our Fourth Estate. "Don't believe everything you read in the papers" is a well-respected American axiom. At times our pragmatic skepticism degenerates into a cynicism that proclaims all politicians crooks and liars, all judges corrupt, all military leaders models for General Bullmoose, and all heroes mere Hollywood Marines whose exploits are scripted by a sensation-mongering press. Like Harry S Truman, our president in the final days of World War II, we're from Missouri and you've got to show us. And even when you do, we'll doubt you.

Shadow of Suribachi contends that the Iwo Jima flag raisings deserve more than a footnote in military history. The story also belongs to the social history of the United States because it tells us something about ourselves as we were half a century ago and as we are today. Two myths took root that February day on Iwo Jima, myths that reflect two persistent aspects of the American character: our sentimentality and our cynicism.

Like negatives in a tank of developing fluid, two images of the Suribachi flag raisings gradually emerged. One picture was flawed by an excess of light: the overexposed myth of the heroic American infantryman charging up the mountain through a storm of artillery fire, fighting in brutal hand-to-hand combat with a demonic foe, until at last he and his courageous companions planted Old Glory like a stake in the heart of Japan. In the midst of the raging battle, an unarmed American civilian photographer braved incredible dangers to capture that historic moment for the American people.

The second picture suffered from light deprivation. Here was a myth of underexposure, the clouded picture of fraud, greed, and lies: a conspiracy between a glory-grabbing Marine Corps and the manipulative press to hoodwink the American public. This myth contended that the flag raising was, from beginning to end, a put-up job, as fake as any drama played out on a Hollywood movie set. This script called for the Marine Corps to herd a flock of reporters and photographers up to the top of Suribachi while Marines (selected for diversity of geographic location, civilian occupation, and ethnicity) raised and lowered flags at the direction of the photographer until Rosenthal declared a "take." Then everybody trudged down the mountain and attended to the public relations chore of selling the American people a bill of goods.

Neither of these pictures can stand the reality test of comparison with the actual events on Iwo Jima. Yet both the heroic and the antiheroic myths persist to the present day, perpetuated over the years in a variety of forums.

Mythmakers continue to emerge, not only from the expected ranks of commercial television and motion picture producers, but also from the ranks of journalists and credentialed historians. If it were necessary to justify a new book to correct the flag-raising story, a recent article (published in January 1994) by nationally syndicated columnist Jack Anderson, and a widely distributed book (published in 1991 by Harvard University Press) by historians

Karal Ann Marling and John Wetenhall provide ample justification.[2] Misinformation and unsubstantiated allegations riddle the Anderson column. Marling and Wetenhall's book, despite its authors' disclaimers, gives aid and comfort to the antiheroic myth of Suribachi. Anderson's column and the Marling-Wetenhall book have produced a firestorm among veterans with firsthand knowledge of the unvarnished reality of Iwo Jima.

Those who approach the subject of the Suribachi flag raisings half a century after those events took place will not find themselves on well-cleared ground. The terrain now is as strewn with the rubble of reportings and misreportings as the literal landscape of Iwo Jima was defaced by the debris of war. Like the Seabees who came ashore to bring order to the chaos of Iwo's landing beaches, contemporary scholars must cut roadways through fifty years' accumulation of contradictions and distortions in their attempt to scrape down to the bedrock of reality.

Committed to that task, we undertook four areas of research in preparing the manuscript for *Shadow of Suribachi*. We obtained interviews from key participants who had survived the hell of Iwo Jima. Photographer Joe Rosenthal, interviewed by numerous journalists over the years, had never previously told his story to historians. His voice was one of the many we felt privileged to hear.

Our research also attended to the voices of ghosts: men who now live only in old letters and memories of family and friends. Chief among these was Sergeant Henry O. Hansen, one of the all-too-many young men who never left the island of Iwo Jima. First identified as the only man to participate in both flag raisings, Hansen was demoted posthumously from the ranks of the six flag raisers in Rosenthal's photograph following a controversial Marine Corps investigation. The unpublished papers of the investigation board and other previously classified government documents formed another important component of our book.

Considerable attention was given to a fourth area of primary research: the role played by the press in its reporting (and, at times distorting) of the Iwo Jima campaign. We feel some fraternal sympathy for these journalists, since, we must admit, the double myth of Suribachi is a complex story to grasp and to convey.

In our account we have tried to chart a course that avoids both the Scylla of sentimentality and the Charybdis of cynicism. We invite the reader to follow this course with us through the chapters of *Shadow of Suribachi*.

NOTES

1. Miles Orvell, *Winterthur Portfolio,* Vol. 27, No. 1, Spring 1992, 99.
2. Jack Anderson, "The Real Story of Iwo Jima Photo," *Albany* (Georgia) *Herald,* January 19, 1994; Karal Ann Marling and John Wetenhall, *Iwo Jima: Monuments, Memories, and the American Hero* (Cambridge, Mass.: Harvard University Press, 1991).

Chapter 1

Bringing Home the War

February 19, 1945. The Marines landed in a massive amphibious assault on the small Pacific island of Iwo Jima. The *Boston Globe* carried the news to an anxious family in the modest Boston suburb of Somerville.

Guam, Feb. 19 (AP)--American Marines, their path cleared by the most intensive neutralization campaign of the Pacific war, have landed on strategic little Iwo Jima, one of the Volcano Islands 675 statute miles south of the Japanese homeland, Adm Chester W. Nimitz announced in a special communique today.

Iwo is so close to Tokyo--750 miles--it is administered by Tokyo prefecture.

This momentous development in the fast-moving Pacific war put American troops on the logical ocean stepping-stone to Tokyo.[1]

All four sons in the family of Henry T. Hansen and his former wife, Madeline (recently remarried as Mrs. Joseph Evelley), were in uniform that season. The Hansen daughter, Gertrude, was soon to join her brothers in service with the Naval Cadet Nurse Corps. But it was their third son, 25-year-old Henry Hansen, who concerned the family most that February morning. A sergeant in the Marine Corps, Hansen had already served with a paratroop unit in the South Pacific from November 1943 to January 1944, fighting in the bloody Bougainville campaign.[2] With relief, his family had welcomed him home, only to say goodby again when he reenlisted, to be assigned to the newly formed Marine 5th Division at Camp Pendleton, Oceanside, California, in March 1944.

Then in October Gertrude Hansen had received a letter with a new return address: "Co. E. 28th Marines 5th Marine Division F.M.F. c/o F.P.O. San Francisco, Calif."

Dear Gert.

    I am now out of the states as you can see by my address. I'm on an island out here. Which one I can not say. It's not too bad here. It's cool & the country has very nice scenery. But personally who the hell likes scenery. ha! I'd rather be back in the states myself.[3]

There was no further news until a brief Christmas letter arrived: "I can't get any cards, or gifts where I'm at. So I take this time to wish you all a very Merry Xmas & a happy New Year."[4]

As the new year, 1945, rang in, World War II was lumbering into its fourth costly year. In the Pacific Theater, where Hansen and his fellow Marines faced a formidable Japanese foe, the end of the road seemed nowhere in sight. Then came the ominous news that the 5th Marine Division had landed on Iwo Jima, giving the Hansen family a concrete focus for their anxiety. But within four days heartening news was published: Marines had raised the American flag atop Mt. Suribachi, Iwo Jima's highest peak. News accounts on February 23 described that day's action as "heroic," signaling a change of fortune for the Marines. The *Boston Globe's* front page told the dramatic story.

Guam, Feb. 23 (AP)--American Marines reached the summit of Mt. Suribachi at the southern tip of Iwo today, and began a renewed drive on the central airfield after repulsing two Japanese counter-attacks.

    The Stars and Stripes were raised over the volcanic Suribachi fortress 97 hours after the costly invasion began. . . .

    Surmounting of Suribachi was the brightest spot in the entire Iwo campaign.[5]

Two days later an electrifying news photograph appeared on Sunday's front pages, a photograph depicting United States Marines raising the American flag on Suribachi. The figures, from the man on the far left with arms upstretched toward the sky to the man at the pole's base with arms thrust down toward the earth, represented a harmony of form and spirit rarely seen on film. Families with Marines on Iwo Jima might take heart from this triumphant image captured by Associated Press photographer Joe Rosenthal and immediately hailed by millions of Americans.[6] News reports conveyed the information that the flag had been raised by a unit from the 28th Marines, Henry Hansen's regiment.[7]

With the first announcement of the invasion of Iwo Jima, the Hansen family began a vigil shared by thousands of Americans. Since the rigors of the campaign left little time for letter-writing, families were dependent on the national press to bring home the war. Fortunately, the progress of the American forces was tracked in detail by military and civilian correspondents and photographers representing numerous publications and news services.

A review of newspaper and magazine accounts of the flag-raising story, however, reveals that from the earliest reports there were the seeds of what was to become the heroic myth of Suribachi. In the weeks between February 23 and the conclusion of the campaign on March 26 the American press began the process of transforming reality into myth.

In reporting the news from Iwo Jima, promptness was the order of the day. From the outset news stories appeared in papers across the country on the very day events on that remote Pacific island took place. This phenomenon occurred thanks to an efficient news-reporting system, to radio transmissions, and to the international dateline. Transmissions out of U.S. Pacific Fleet Headquarters in Guam on February 19 announcing that morning's invasion of Iwo Jima appeared, almost miraculously, in the February 19 morning headlines at home in the United States.[8]

Other accounts contributed to the uncanny sense of instantaneous reporting, accounts wired directly via Naval Radio from Vice Admiral Richmond Kelly Turner's flagship stationed off Iwo Jima. This same-day promptness was true for most events occurring early on any given day. Occurrences later in the day, or stories filed late in the day, might not make that same morning's newspapers in the States.

News pictures were another matter. And herein lay the potential for misinterpretation. Since film had to be developed, photographs could not appear in the nation's newspapers the day they were shot. Film was flown from Iwo to Guam, where it was developed and wirephotoed to the States. Typically, a two-day delay occurred before a photograph could appear in print. This delay produced a situation in which same-day news stories were not accompanied by their news pictures. The resulting hiatus set up the possibility for reader confusion on the homefront.

The February 19 headline stories proclaiming the invasion were not illustrated by photographs taken on Iwo Jima that day. Nor did the news stories appearing on February 20 contain any photographs taken on the island. During this two-day interim, newspapers were relegated to illustrating their invasion stories with maps (showing Iwo Jima's location, shape, and the point of invasion), aerial photographs (taken during the pre-invasion bombing), or photographs of the fleet gathering offshore prior to the invasion.[9]

It was not until February 21 that the first photographs actually taken on Iwo of the February 19 invasion appeared in the nation's newspapers. The *Boston Herald* on this day carried two AP wirephotos showing the difficult terrain where the Marines were forced to land. There in the morning's newspapers for the Hansens and all those with servicemen in the Pacific to see were photographs of unidentified bodies: Marines fallen on the lethal sands of Iwo Jima.[10]

The morale-lifting conquest of Suribachi on the morning of February 23, "the brightest spot in the entire Iwo campaign," was reported in the nation's newspapers that very day but without appropriate photographs. Lacking photographs of the event, the story of Suribachi's capture was left to unillustrated news accounts that relied heavily on verbal embellishment. One such account appeared on the front page of the *Boston Globe*: "The leathernecks clambered up the 45-degree cliffs despite grenades and demolition charges hurled down into their faces by the desperate defenders."[11] The climb up Suribachi was, from its first reporting, described as a hazardous mission executed under deadly fire.

The *Globe* also carried two additional stories, both received from Turner's flagship, the *Eldorado,* poised just off Iwo. One story related a saga of heroic dimensions:

Don Pryor, broadcasting from Adm Turner's flagship off Iwo Jima over C.B.S. today, said:

"This afternoon over Iwo Jima you could see the most beautiful sight in the world--the Stars and Stripes fluttering small but triumphant high on the top-most ridge of Suribachi volcano.

"Four other correspondents, a couple of Marines and I watched a small group of 28th Marines winding their way painfully up towards the crest this morning as we waited on the beach for a boat to bring us out here to the flag ship. They had fought their way against opposition that even the freshest of men would never believe they could take. Up sheer rock cliffs on ladders--and on and on and on up the steep rocky sides of the upper slope--while the Japs threw hand grenades from above, peppered them with rifle and machine gun fire.

"I understand that the flagpole is a steel rod carried in sections which each man added to his already heavy burden. . . . The first word I heard of it came from a sophisticated correspondent who came into the wardroom shouting, 'They've raised Old Glory on the top of Suribachi.' Old Glory. We all rushed to the portholes to see and there sure enough it was--tiny and wonderful standing clear against the sky above that awful mountain.

"Nobody talked about it much. But that, to all of us, was a supreme moment."[12]

The action was further amplified in a second report of heroics wired from the flagship.

Volcano Islands, Feb. 23 (AP) (Via Navy Radio)--American marines watched Japanese soldiers fling themselves from the crater of Mt. Suribachi yesterday as the leathernecks drew up the steep slopes of the dominating volcanic formation on the southern tip of battle twisted Iwo

Island.

In contrast to the fierce resistance to the north, "a number" of enemy troops chose spectacular suicide to being hunted down in caves of the 566-foot high mountain, while others defiantly heaved grenades at marines moving into position to assault the isolated fortress of lava rock.[13]

Portrayed as an act of heroic proportions, the flag raising would become a source of great pride to the families of the men ultimately identified as planting the Stars and Stripes on Suribachi.

The flag raising was hot news for the printed word, but there were no photographs to illustrate the dramatic episode. Lacking photographs, photo editors improvised. The *Globe* printed an aerial view of the island with the American flag sketched in over Suribachi, a somewhat less than inspired solution to the photo editor's problem.[14]

The *Boston Herald* chose to illustrate its front-page story of Suribachi's conquest with an enlargement of an earlier photograph of Marines digging foxholes on Iwo Jima. There was no sign of Suribachi or an American flag.[15] The *Washington Post* used the same photo to illustrate its front-page story: "The Twenty-eighth Regiment of the U.S. Marines raised the United States flag on the summit of Iwo Island at 10:35 A.M. today."[16] The *New York Times* revealed the greatest ingenuity. Under a bold-type, front-page headline, "Marines Take Suribachi," the *Times* ran the same photograph used by the *Herald* and the *Post* of Marines digging foxholes. Lacking a much-desired photo of Marines on Suribachi, the editors titled their photograph, "Marines Inch Ahead on Rugged Hills of Iwo." The terrain pictured was less mountain than mole hill, but it was the closest anyone managed to come in the photo editors' attempt to picture Marines on a mountain on Iwo Jima.[17]

A *Times* story the following day, accompanied by a map of Suribachi and by yet another early photograph of Marines racing ashore, described the fighting that had preceded the capture of that important volcanic stronghold.[18] Still glaringly absent were photographs that actually portrayed the American forces' most significant conquest.

Many an editor doubtless chafed to know whether any photographer had been present for the assault on Suribachi or for the flag raising that was the high point of the campaign to date. But the national press had to endure the usual two-day delay. The flag raising occurred on a Friday. The suspense should end on Sunday.

Sunday, February 25, 1945. Emblazoned with that day's headlines on the front page of many of the nation's thick Sunday editions was the Rosenthal flag-raising photograph, a photograph to capture the attention of the American people in a way that no photograph ever had before. Typical of the prominent treatment given the photograph was the *Boston Herald*'s placement: front page center with a caption reporting that Marines of the 5th Division planted the flag "in battle still raging."[19] The *Washington Post* also gave the photograph front-page display, as did the Sunday *New York Times*.[20]

None of these papers identified Rosenthal as the photographer. The *Times* caption, which was typical, simply read: "Associated Press Wirephoto (Navy radio from Guam)." Ironically, on page 22 the *Times* did carry a story datelined San Francisco, announcing that Rosenthal had won praise for his earlier photographs of the Iwo invasion.[21]

The national press created other possible areas of public confusion. Not only was the photographer not identified in these newspapers, but the Marines in the photo were not properly identified either. The *Times* carried a short item, buried on page 28, which identified Platoon Sergeant Ernest I. Thomas, Jr., of Tallahassee, Florida, as "the marine" who raised the flag "during the height of the battle" for the volcano. Thomas, it was reported, "broke out the ensign while his company was under enemy sniper fire." The four-sentence story also mentioned that this flag soon was replaced by a larger one that the men of Company E carried to the top of Suribachi.[22]

The American public now had access to the information that two flags had been raised on Suribachi. This news of a second flag, however, was two days late and relatively inconspicuous in its cursory mention on page 28 of the *New York Times*. Other newspapers tended to omit this dispatch. Since the first flag raising had occurred on the morning of February 23, it had been reported in the nation's headlines that same day. The second flag raising had occurred at noon (or slightly later) and went unreported in February 23's newspapers. This simple accident of timing may have prevented the second flag raising from sharing mention with the first flag raising in the front-page stories on February 23. Even though the second flag raising might not have been considered as newsworthy as the first, it might still have received timely mention, avoiding the confusion that was to plague these two events for the next fifty years.

There was one way in particular in which the immediate reporting of a second flag raising might have helped to avoid confusion. Had it been widely reported on February 23 that *two* flags were raised that day on Suribachi's summit, when Rosenthal's photograph appeared two days later it would have been incumbent on news editors to caption it properly: as a photo of the second flag raising. Instead, since only one flag raising had been widely reported, the natural assumption was that this was the one Rosenthal had photographed.

In the month following the first appearance of Rosenthal's photograph, the national press did not convey the fact that this was a photograph of a second flag raising. During the entire Iwo Jima campaign, the public was left with the impression that only one flag had been raised and that Rosenthal had photographed it.

In the brief *Times* story on page 28, there was also the seed of additional confusion, this relating to the identity of the flag raisers. The *Times* identified

Thomas as raising the first flag. But there were no names cited of the other Marines who helped him, much less of those who raised the second flag. It was to be a long and torturous route until proper identification was achieved for both sets of flag raisers. And in the minds of some, a half-century has not yet seen the task completed.

Initially, there was no mention as to which of the two flag raisings Rosenthal had photographed or the full roster of names of the men who raised the flags. These omissions would ultimately raise problems to haunt Rosenthal, the Marine Corps, and the families of the flag raisers. But in the midst of war, on the day when Rosenthal's inspiring photograph was the front-page message to millions of Americans, none of these future difficulties were foreseen.

The photo's dramatic image left a deeper impression than all the printed words that had preceded it. This impression was, however, something of a misimpression. Traditionally, flag raisings symbolize victory. The press and the American public took the photograph as a sign that victory was near. The *Times* highlighted this theme. Its front-page story accompanying the Rosenthal photograph reported that American fortunes changed with the raising of the flag on Suribachi.

> The marines are benefiting from the capture of Mount Suribachi volcano at the southern end of the island, and the advance northward. Enemy artillery fire no longer is dominating the interior area under American control. The mortar fire on the marines' landing places has been reduced and supplies are pouring ashore. . . .
> The planting of the American flag on Suribachi two days ago marked a definite change in American fortunes on Iwo.[23]

The *Times* was too quick to declare a victory. The battle for Iwo Jima was to continue for thirty-one more devastating days.

The heroic story and the dramatic photo were grist for the national newsweekly mills as well. These publications followed the lead of the dailies with similar stories as soon as they could get to press. Their first opportunity was in their March 5 issues. Sounding the same victory note, *Newsweek* carried the Rosenthal photo over the caption, "Victory on Iwo: The flag goes up on Mount Suribachi."[24]

Alongside the instantly famous photo *Newsweek* also carried an on-the-scene report by their correspondent, William Hipple, who had accompanied the Marines ashore. Hipple's account also highlighted the themes of American heroism and fierce Japanese resistance to the assault on Suribachi.

> **Rolling Stones:** On the fifth morning of the campaign, at 10:35 we saw four men standing on the highest peak of Mount Suribachi. They raised the Stars and Stripes high over the island. It was a thrilling sight

for every man on that conquered part of the island which was now new American territory. . . .

From deep interconnecting caves, . . . the Japs had fired down upon us. In many cases they must have had to lower the guns and themselves by ropes. In desperation at the end when their guns were knocked out or their ammunition was gone, they rolled boulders down on advancing Americans with little if any result.[25]

Whereas the *New York Times* story of February 25 had reported that one man, Thomas, raised the flag, Hipple's report from Iwo indicated that *four* men were involved in the flag raising. Of course, Rosenthal's photograph itself was proof that there was more than one raiser. The number of raisers had begun to multiply; it would multiply further.

Time in its March 5 issue ran the Rosenthal photograph (mistakenly dating the raising as occurring on February 24), as well as a radioed story from its correspondent on Iwo, Robert Sherrod. Sherrod's otherwise lengthy account of these first days of battle contained a mere one-sentence reference to the flag raising: "When the U.S. flag was raised over this highest point on the island, some marines wept openly."[26]

Like Hipple, Sherrod at this time had no way of knowing that Rosenthal's photograph existed. Neither could he have known that the photo would be run with his dispatch in this same issue of *Time* and that this one photograph would render the event worthy of far more than a sentence.

With such a stunning photograph available, the nation's leading photo newsweekly could be expected to jump at the chance to publish. But an unexpected development occurred in the coverage of the flag raisings when *Life* magazine, while reporting "By week's end . . . the American flag had been raised over Mt. Suribachi," inexplicably failed to run the Rosenthal photo in its March 5 edition. *Life*'s issue included stories about the battle (one by Sherrod), an acknowledgment of the flag raising, and even other Rosenthal photographs from Iwo. But strangely enough, the editors of the most widely circulating photo newsweekly in the country chose not to publish this classic photograph.[27]

None of these March 5 issues of *Newsweek, Time,* or *Life* mentioned that there had been two flag raisings. None identified Rosenthal as the photographer of the most acclaimed picture of the war. None attempted to identify the raisers pictured. Understandably, any distinction between the first and the second flag raisings was still lost on the American public. From Day One the story was that of *the* raising of *the* flag atop Suribachi, a conflation of two separate events that came to possess a life of its own.

Early on, speculation abounded as to the identity of Rosenthal's flag raisers, even before it was clear how many were represented in his photograph. The *Boston Globe* reported in mid-March that Lieutenant Colonel L. B. "Pat" Hanley, the former Boston University football coach just back from Iwo, brought word that one of his former players, Second Lieutenant Ray Whalen of Watertown, "led the platoon that raised the historic flag on Mt. Suribachi." The *Herald* also carried the Hanley story.[28] Once again, both stories were written as if there had been only one flag raising.

As to the identity of the photographer of the famous photo, the *Washington Post* again carried a copy of the photograph in its February 28 issue. In this larger reprint's caption, the *Post* this time did credit Rosenthal, "a native of Washington," as the photographer.[29] The *San Francisco Chronicle*, on the other hand, had identified Rosenthal as the photographer from the start. Its caption for the photograph on February 25 read: "Another in the remarkable series snapped by AP Cameraman Joe Rosenthal of S.F." The caption identified the photograph as depicting "hoisting the American Flag at the peak of Mt. Suribachi on the south tip of Iwo island at 10:35 A.M. last Friday."[30] The *Chronicle* clearly stated what other publications implied: the Rosenthal photograph had captured the reported 10:35 A.M. flag raising--in other words, the first flag raising on Iwo Jima.

By this time many other American cities, in addition to San Francisco and Washington, would have been happy to claim Rosenthal as a native son. Surprisingly, however, the other major San Francisco daily, the *San Francisco Examiner*, failed to print Rosenthal's famous photograph in any of its February editions.[31] Three days later, the *Examiner* did publish a second Rosenthal photograph of Marines around a flag on top of Suribachi. In this printing of what would become known as Rosenthal's "gung-ho" photo, several Marines stood shouting and waving helmets and rifles in front of a flagstaff flying the Stars and Stripes. The *Examiner* was one of the first newspapers to publish this second Rosenthal photograph, a picture that understandably received little circulation relative to his famous scene of the flag raising.[32]

On March 25 the *New York Times* reported that the Rosenthal flag-raising photo would receive a special honor: "The famous photograph of marines raising the flag on Mount Suribachi has been chosen as the official symbol of the Seventh War Loan, which starts May 14."[33] The *Times* explained that to get the photo Rosenthal "followed a heroic band of marines up the slope of Mount Suribachi while the battle raged."[34] Again, there was no mention of two flag raisings, both of which the *Times* itself had reported weeks earlier. For a month now accounts in the nation's presses had been written as if there had been a single flag raising, the one that Rosenthal immortalized. Then came *Life* magazine's exposé that claimed to set the record straight.

Life abruptly ended its strange month-long shutout when it ran Rosenthal's photograph in a March 26 article titled "The Famous Iwo Flag-Raising." The purpose of the story in *Life* was a bit of journalistic one-upmanship: a deflating jab at the bubble of fame swelling around Rosenthal's flag-raising photo. The *Life* article revealed that there were *two* flag raisings on February 23 and that the Rosenthal photo was not actually taken at the time of the *first* flag raising.

"The only pictures of that historic event," the story claimed, "were made by S/Sgt. Louis R. Lowery of *Leatherneck,* the Marine's magazine."[35] Lowery's name had never been mentioned in any of the earlier news stories.

Along with the Rosenthal photograph, *Life* printed a previously unpublished photo by Lowery of what was revealed as being the *first* flag raised on Suribachi. The article went on to quote a Marine correspondent's dispatch to *Leatherneck* magazine.

> ". . . Lieut. Harold Schrier, executive officer of E Company, led a platoon to the top.
>
> "This platoon took over the peak, meeting little resistance on the way up. At 10:30 these marines raised the first American flag over Iwo Jima, a ship's flag from an assault transport, brought ashore in a map case by Lieut. George Wells, 2nd Battalion Adjutant. A length of Jap pipe was the flagpole.
>
> "With the platoon as it climbed Suribachi was S/Sgt. Louis R. Lowery, staff photographer for *Leatherneck.* No other photographer came up until after the flag was raised and Lowery got a clean scoop on pictures of the ceremony and the climb up the volcano. . . ."
>
> Later that day, while the peak was still under enemy fire, Joe Rosenthal went up with another group of marines. Standing on rocks and a Jap sandbag at the edge of the volcano crater, he photographed them raising a second and larger flag. This picture, far more dramatic than Lowery's, was the one published throughout the U.S. and hailed by Secretary of the Navy Forrestal as "that unforgettable photograph."[36]

Life had revealed for the first time in a nationwide story that the Rosenthal photograph did *not* represent the first flag raising. It was also now clear that on February 23 there had been not one but two photographers on Suribachi. As in the case of the flag raisers, the number of photographers would multiply.

Time in its March 26 issue also carried the story of two Suribachi flag raisings, with Rosenthal's photo clearly captioned "Second Flag Raising."[37] *Newsweek,* on the other hand, did not carry that news on this date, nor did it publish the Lowery photograph of the first flag raising. The scoop about the two flag raisings, including the Lowery photograph and the background to the famous Rosenthal photograph, seemed to belong exclusively to Time/Life.

In one respect, however, both *Time* and *Life* had been scooped by Rosenthal's hometown newspaper the week before--without the local reporter's appreciating what he had unearthed. Interviewing Rosenthal fresh upon his return from Iwo on March 17, a reporter for the *San Francisco Chronicle* asked the inevitable question: How had Rosenthal gotten his heralded shot? In responding, Rosenthal clearly indicated that his photo was not taken at the time of the first flag raising:

Well when we got to the brow of the hill, I saw they had a small
flag on a short pole which they were taking down and they were about
to put up a large flag on a tall pole.

I guess I was about three quarters of an hour behind the original
group that first scaled the mountain."[38]

Appearing in the *Chronicle* the following day, this fact was reported with no
fanfare, and it was apparently not picked up by other newspapers. So *Time* and
Life a week later appeared to have a scoop with the revelation that Rosenthal's
photo was not taken at the first flag raising.

How had *Life* magazine obtained Lowery's photograph? How had it learned
that Rosenthal's photo was of a *second* flag raising? Both *Time* and *Life* clearly
possessed a source other than Rosenthal's interview in the *Chronicle*. The *Life*
article implied that its revelation had come via *Leatherneck*, the Marines'
magazine. Yet curiously enough the April 1 issue of *Leatherneck* carried no
word of two Suribachi flag raisings and no copy of the photo by their own
photographer, Lowery. Instead, a full-page reproduction of the Rosenthal
photograph occupied the issue's back cover.[39]

A peculiar situation emerged. *Life,* a regular client of AP, had refrained
for weeks from running AP's spectacular Rosenthal photo, only to publish it in
tandem with the Lowery photo. *Leatherneck*, whose staff photographer,
Lowery, had captured the first flag raising in an exclusive series of photographs,
chose not to run his pictures. The Marines' magazine featured the Rosenthal
photograph instead.

Publication of the Lowery photograph in the March 26 issue of *Life* produced
a private revelation to the Hansen family at home in Somerville, Massachusetts.
Prominently displayed in that photo was Henry Hansen grasping an erect
flagpole. Although unidentified in the photo's caption, Hansen was immediately
recognized by his mother and sister.[40]

During the past month, it had been largely thanks to Joe Rosenthal's widely
published photograph that the Hansens, along with millions of other Americans,
were aware that a flag had been raised on Suribachi. Now, suddenly, the flag
raising took on an acutely personal significance for Mrs. Evelley and her
daughter, Gertrude. For anxious weeks they had had no news of Hansen. Then
the Lowery photograph appeared in *Life* magazine, picturing him alive and well
on top of Suribachi.

On March 26, the welcome news was announced that the long, costly
campaign for Iwo Jima was at last over. The victorious Marines were
withdrawing their three divisions, leaving the island's future occupation to the
Army. The following day a telegram from Washington was delivered to "Mrs.
Madeline E. Evelley, 39 Madison St., Somerville, Massachusetts."

DEEPLY REGRET TO INFORM YOU THAT YOUR SON
SERGEANT HENRY O HANSEN USMC WAS KILLED IN ACTION
1 MARCH 1945 AT IWO JIMA VOLCANO ISLANDS IN THE
PERFORMANCE OF HIS DUTY AND SERVICE OF HIS COUNTRY.
WHEN INFORMATION IS RECEIVED REGARDING BURIAL YOU
WILL BE NOTIFIED. TO PREVENT POSSIBLE AID TO OUR
ENEMIES DO NOT DIVULGE THE NAME OF HIS SHIP OR
STATION. PLEASE ACCEPT MY HEARTFELT SYMPATHY.
LETTER FOLLOWS=A A VANDEGRIFT LIEUT GENERAL USMC
COMMANDANT[41]

There was an eerie logic in the juxtaposition of the two events: the
telegram, dated March 27, announcing Hansen's death on Iwo Jima, and the
arrival of the issue of *Life* magazine, dated March 26, displaying a photograph
of Hansen, very much alive at the summit of Suribachi.

In the first week of April, a story broke confirming what the Hansen family
had already concluded for themselves from the evidence of the Lowery
photograph published by *Life:* Hansen had participated in the first flag raising.
The *Boston Herald* confirmed the report, basing their story on an article in
Collier's.

Sgt. H. O. Hansen of 39 Madison street, Somerville, was one of three
Marine Corps members who led 42 other Marines up the last leg of Mt.
Suribachi on Iwo Jima, 750 miles from Tokyo, and hoisted the American
flag. . . .[42]

The full *Collier's* story elaborated on the nature of the battle for Suribachi
and specifically mentioned Hansen's prominent role.

Later on the narrow path to Mount Suribachi, three Marines were
surrounded at the mouth of a cave. There was not room to use rifles.
One Marine made a flying tackle at the nearest Jap and, when felled,
twisted the Jap's neck and broke it. Another plunged feet first on a Jap
lieutenant catching him in the groin. The third Marine leaped Tarzan-
like from atop the cave, his jungle knife flashing. The Jap he landed on
was stabbed in the heart before they hit the ground. There were no
rules, no quarter and no surrender.

It was in that manner that we took Mount Suribachi, and Lieutenant
Colonel Chandler W. Johnson of Highland Park, Illinois, commander of
the second battalion, 28th Marines, handed a folded American flag to
Lieutenant Harold G. Schrier, and said: "Put that on top of the hill."

"Okay," the lieutenant said, and with Platoon Sergeant Ernest I.
Thomas of Tallahassee, Fla., and 42 tired Marines, went up the battered

hill, 750 miles from Tokyo. Japs were still in the caves but the Marines used grenades, flame throwers and rifles on them, and Schrier, Thomas and Sergeant H. O. Hansen of Boston, put the flag up early on February 23, just as the colonel had ordered.[43]

Once again, journalism attempted to improve on reality by providing a lurid depiction of the fierce fighting required to raise the American flag on Suribachi. Even at this late date, however, there was no mention that two flags were raised on that heroic day.[44] Similar accounts, featuring only a single flag raising, persisted in dominating press coverage, despite their incompatibility with the March 26 stories in *Life* and *Time,* to say nothing of their incompatibility with the account given by Rosenthal himself. The *Time* and *Life* editors had claimed to set the record straight, but the record seemed to defy correction. Subsequent publications, seemingly oblivious to the March 26 exposé and to Rosenthal's account, continued to tell the story of a single flag raising, a story that would gather momentum in the weeks, months, and years ahead.

The sensational reports in the national press presented this composite to the American public as to what Suribachi's conquest had entailed: 42 Marines, bearing heavy steel flagpole sections, climbed sheer rock cliffs on ladders while Japanese hurled grenades and demolition charges into their faces, peppered them with rifle and machine gun fire, and rolled boulders down on the advancing Marines before finally, in desperation, flinging themselves to their death from the volcano.

This composite contained basic ingredients of the heroic myth of Suribachi. To discover the reality behind that myth, it is necessary to move away from the headlines on the homefront in the spring of 1945 and retrace the steps Hansen and the men of the 28th Marines took as they prepared for an unimagined destination: Iwo Jima.

NOTES

1. *Boston Globe*, February 19, 1945.
2. Service Record, June 29, 1944, Henry O. Hansen papers in the possession of the authors (hereafter cited as Hansen MSS).
3. Hansen to Gertrude Hansen, letter dated October 1, 1944, Hansen MSS.
4. Hansen to Mrs. Evelley, letter dated December 9, 1944, Hansen MSS.
5. *Boston Globe*, February 23, 1945.
6. *Boston Herald*, February 25, 1945.
7. Ibid., February 23, 1945.
8. *Boston Herald*, February 19, 1945.
9. Ibid., February 19, 20, 1945; *Washington Post*, February 20, 1945.
10. *Boston Herald*, February 21, 1945.
11. *Boston Globe*, February 23, 1945.

12. Ibid., CBS Inc. 1945. All rights reserved. Originally broadcast on February 23, 1945 on CBS Radio.

13. Ibid.

14. Ibid.

15. *Boston Herald*, February 23, 1945.

16. *Washington Post*, February 23, 1945.

17. *New York Times*, February 23, 1945.

18. Ibid., February 24, 1945.

19. *Boston Herald*, February 25, 1945.

20. *Washington Post*, February 25, 1945; *New York Times*, February 25, 1945.

21. *New York Times*, February 25, 1945. Within days, however, it was widely reported that Rosenthal had taken the famous photograph.

22. Ibid.

23. Ibid.

24. *Newsweek*, March 5, 1945, 38.

25. Ibid.

26. *Time*, March 5, 1945, 25.

27. *Life*, March 5, 1945, 36-38, 41-42, 44.

28. *Boston Globe*, March 16, 1945; *Boston Herald*, March 16, 1945.

29. *Washington Post*, February 28, 1945.

30. *San Francisco Chronicle*, February 25, 1945.

31. *San Francisco Examiner*, February 25-28, 1945.

32. Ibid., February 28, 1945.

33. *New York Times*, March 25, 1945.

34. Ibid.

35. *Life*, March 26, 1945, 17-18.

36. Ibid., 18. The Army magazine, *Yank*, had published a heavily cropped version of the Lowery flag-raising photograph, omitting two of the flag raisers, neglecting to mention that this was the first of two flags raised that day, and failing to identify Lou Lowery as the photographer. See *Yank* (Central Pacific ed.), March 9, 1945, 4.

37. *Time*, March 26, 1945, 60.

38. *San Francisco Chronicle*, March 18, 1945.

39. *Leatherneck* (Pacific edition), April 1, 1945, 40.

40. *Life*, March 26, 1945, 18. Judy Seawell to Gertrude Hansen, letter dated May 1, 1945, Hansen MSS.

41. Vandegrift to Mrs. Evelley, telegram dated March 27, 1945, Hansen MSS.

42. *Boston Herald*, April 6, 1945.

43. *Collier's*, April 14, 1945, 53-54.

44. Ibid., 26 ff.

Chapter 2

Surrounding Suribachi

The tides that carried Henry Hansen, his comrades, and their flags to a microscopic Pacific island had their origins many miles and many months removed from the D-Day landing on Iwo Jima, February 19, 1945. Hansen's Marine division, the 5th, came into existence on Armistice Day 1943, when orders were dispatched from Washington to activate another division to flesh out the four already committed to the war in the Pacific.

On February 4, 1944, Major General Keller E. Rockey left Washington and his post as assistant commandant of the Marine Corps to assume command of the fledgling 5th Division, which was still in the process of being assembled at Camp Pendleton, California. His was a heterogeneous unit of more than 20,000 men garnered from boot camps at San Diego, California, and Parris Island, South Carolina, from Camp Pendleton itself, and from East Coast bases at Quantico, Virginia, and Camp Lejeune, North Carolina, where Hansen had been stationed for a time.[1] At the core of the division were Marines from combat units in the Pacific, already veterans of battles with the Japanese.

On February 8, 1944, Hansen's old paratroop unit, with some veterans of former raider units, joined the 5th Division's last infantry regiment to be formed, the 28th Marines. Quartered in Tent Camp No. 1 in Las Pulgas Canyon, since Pendleton's barracks were by then full to overflowing, Hansen came under the command of Colonel Harry B. Liversedge, a strapping officer nicknamed "Harry the Horse," from his days on the football team at Quantico.[2] Liversedge was seasoned by service in the South Pacific as commander of a raider battalion in the New Georgia campaign. He began the months of rigorous training designed to weld his mixed bag of Marines into combat teams capable of working effectively with each other and with their artillery, tank, pioneer, and engineer support units.[3]

In 1944, Fred E. Haynes, now a retired Marine major general with a distinguished record, was a captain, serving as operations officer (S-3) for the 28th Regiment under Liversedge, an officer he described as "a very quiet,

pleasant, considerate man."[4]   Haynes outlined his commanding officer's
philosophy in a 1953 article in the *Marine Corps Gazette*:

>   In developing the combat team, primary effort was put into small
> unit training. The colonel's idea of training was based on the philosophy
> that if you had eighty-one good rifle squads you had the makings of a top
> notch regiment. . . . This paid off handsomely, because Iwo was a battle
> in which the lower units did most of the maneuvering. In fact, maneuver
> was largely limited to the company and below.[5]

This was the philosophy that would enable the men of Liversedge's regiment
first to surround and then to capture Suribachi.

Liversedge's 28th was composed of three battalions. The 2nd, to which
Henry Hansen was assigned, was commanded by Lieutenant Colonel Chandler
W. Johnson, an Annapolis graduate noted for being a stern disciplinarian. Of
the three companies in Johnson's thousand-man battalion, Hansen was a member
of Company E, commanded by Captain Dave E. Severance. The tall captain,
like Hansen a former Marine paratrooper, had the responsibility for this 250-
man unit composed of a headquarters platoon, a machine gun platoon, a mortar
platoon, and three rifle platoons. Hansen was in the 3rd Rifle Platoon, a forty-
six-man unit led by an energetic Texan, First Lieutenant John Keith Wells.
Wells pronounced himself profoundly pleased to have under his command
seasoned men, such as Hansen, from former raider and paratroop units.

>   I had great admiration for the raiders. They were first-class fighting
> men. I really admired them. The paratroopers, as a whole, seemed to
> be much sharper. This colonel told me that he picked his paratroopers,
> especially the young ones, out of boot camp, on their high I.Q., and not
> on their Physical. Thank goodness we had the combination.[6]

Wells's second in command was Platoon Sergeant Ernest I. Thomas, Jr.,
whose service as a boot camp drill instructor earned him the name "Boots." At
age 20, Thomas was one of the youngest platoon sergeants in the Corps. The
platoon guide was Sergeant Henry O. Hansen, usually known as "Hank." He
was also nicknamed "The Count" by his Camp Pendleton tentmates because,
according to his platoon mate, Corporal Richard Wheeler, "he had a way of
looking natty, even in fatigue clothes."[7] Wells recalled a slightly different
explanation for Hansen's nickname:

> We called him "The Count." I didn't really ever know his nationality.
> He would make some home brew in camp, and I'd go down and we'd
> have a few, and it seems like whenever he'd get a little bit more than he
> normally could use, why he'd lay down. And when somebody'd try to

wake him, he'd talk in--I don't know *what* language. And he'd put on
the air of a dignitary. Don't think that he wasn't first-class. He'd fight
a circle saw off, I mean to tell you.[8]

Gradually, Hansen settled in to his new platoon, which represented a
geographic and occupational cross section of America, including bank clerks,
farmers, electricians, plumbers, truck drivers, ranchers, merchant seamen,
newspapermen, a five-and-dime store manager, and an art student. The dozen
men who came to the platoon from service in raider or paratrooper units,
although mostly under 25 years of age, were considered seasoned veterans.
Two Navy hospital corpsmen were also attached to the platoon: Pharmacist's
Mate Second Class John H. Bradley and Pharmacist's Mate Third Class Clifford
R. Langley.[9] These Navy corpsmen trained alongside the Marines, and,
according to Wheeler, "they thought of themselves as Marines, too. They
played a very important role, and they had a great deal of respect from the
Marines. They actually showed more courage than anybody. They matched the
Marines for courage, and then some."[10]

In the autumn of 1944 Hansen and his mates got a change of scene. Leaving
Camp Pendleton behind, they sailed for Hawaii and Camp Kamuela. The troops
of the 5th Division had taken a giant leap closer to their ultimate destination:
Iwo Jima. Only the company commanders were privy to the name of the
battleground for which Hansen's platoon was so strenuously preparing.
Severance, then Company E's commander, recalled his emotions at the briefing
where he first learned of his company's mission. Prior to mid-December, there
had been rumors but no official confirmation.[11]

We were briefed that we were to land in the shadow of Suribachi, move
one battalion directly across the island, and follow it with two battalions
who would execute a left turn and face, on line, toward Suribachi. I felt
a sense of despair for myself and my company. The indicated slope and
height of the mountain indicated there could be a slaughter and the only
way to take it would be to send wave after wave of troops crawling up
the slopes. I suspect my brother company commanders felt much the
way I did.[12]

In such a manner, the 2nd Battalion's company commanders learned that
they were en route to Iwo Jima and that their focus in the mission was the
island's most physically imposing feature and perhaps its most strategic
fortification: Suribachi.

Haynes, former operations officer in the 28th Regiment, explained that in
Hawaii, "as part of our training, we took a tape, and we taped an imaginary tip
of an island. And then we organized. We landed in a column of battalions over
Green One [beachhead], and we lined our boat teams up just as they would be

for the landing. And this bubble [a small mountain that Haynes pointed out on a map] looked just like Mount Suribachi. It was about 450 or 500 feet high."[13]

In January 1945 the Marines left Hawaii. Lieutenant General Holland M. ("Howlin' Mad") Smith, commander of the Expeditionary Troops, described himself as "full of confidence in the force I commanded but acutely aware of the difficulties of the mission" when he sailed from Pearl Harbor on Vice Admiral Richmond Kelly Turner's new command ship, the USS *Eldorado*.[14]

Before departing Pearl in January, an item in the local press unnerved the handful of Marine officers who had been informed about their destination. The *Honolulu Advertiser* on Sunday morning, December 24, published an aerial photo of an island being bombed by 7th AAF Liberators. There, clearly identified in the photo's caption, was Iwo Jima. The physical characteristics of this island labeled "Iwo Jima" were all too similar to "Island X" where the Marines had been training in Hawaii. The intelligence officers of the 5th Division were deeply concerned when they saw the newspaper story. They feared their troops would put two and two together and come up with their destination. Then the inevitable information leaks could alert the Japanese to the target planned for the invasion force gathering momentum in the Pacific. But the well-disciplined troops apparently kept their speculations to themselves.[15]

Wheeler, Company E's unofficial historian, asserted he did not know where his unit was bound until he was on board the *Missoula* and at sea:

> When they started to give us the details about the Japanese defenses--they had all sorts of sketches and photos--I thought "Good Lord! This is going to be pretty bad."
> Then I wrote a little note home: "Dear Mom and Dad, I am finally going into combat. Don't worry. I will be o.k."[16]

If it had been the style of the Marines "to reason why," instead of simply "to do or die," they might well have asked why so many ships and men were traveling so many miles to invade a mote of an island four-and-a-half miles long by two-and-a-half miles wide. Iwo Jima, whose name means Sulfur Island, was just that: eight square miles of volcanic ash, rock, and noxious sulfur. One of the island's original Japanese garrison officers, Major Yokosuka Horie, considered the place an abomination: "only an island of sulfur, no water, no sparrow, and no swallow."[17]

Iwo Jima's charm was all in its location. The small island was, in a sense, the key to the aerial invasion of Japan. Smith justified the campaign on these grounds: "Any attempt to invade Japan would run afoul of this island. . . . It threatened our occupation of Okinawa, to the northwest, which, by 1945, was part of our grand strategy for closing in on Japan."[18]

As military historian Robert Leckie put it: "Seldom before had an objective been so obviously necessary, and perhaps never before had so much counted on such a no-account place."[19]

Leaving Pearl, the convoy bearing the 5th Division undertook a 4,000-mile journey across the Pacific, a journey that would end in Japanese waters off Iwo Jima's coast. On February 11 the ships reached Saipan, captured from Japan just the previous summer. Relentlessly, the clock was ticking: D-Day was a mere eight days away.[20]

At Saipan there was celebrity excitement in store for Smith and his Marines. The *Eldorado* boarded a distinguished passenger, Secretary of the Navy James V. Forrestal. As Smith recorded, "I believe this was the first time in the history of the Marine Corps that a Secretary of the Navy went to war with his amphibious troops."[21]

On February 16, after final maneuvers that included a simulated amphibious landing on the west coast of Tinian, the invasion fleet set out for Iwo Jima. "Tension began to mount now. This was the 5th Division's first combat assignment, and everyone was keyed up as the convoy approached the objective."[22] Hansen and his platoon mates sailed in an armada that was the largest Navy-Marine operation ever mounted. It consisted of 485 vessels (including eight battleships) carrying 70,647 Marines of the 4th and 5th Divisions, with the 3rd Division in reserve.[23]

The Japanese were fully aware that the Americans had their sights set on Iwo Jima.[24] Arrayed against the vast American air, sea, and land force was Lieutenant General Todamichi Kuribayashi, some 22,000 troops, and the elaborate defensive fortifications of Iwo Jima. Commander of Iwo Jima and architect of its defenses, Kuribayashi the previous June had been made commanding general of the Japanese Army's 109th Infantry Division and assorted naval troops attached to the Bonins-Volcano Defense Sector. The command was considered a great honor because Iwo Jima and its sister islands in the Bonin chain were part of the Prefecture of Tokyo, the outer defense ring of the Japanese home islands.

Kuribayashi knew that the orders that sent him to Iwo Jima in the summer of 1944 also sent him into inevitable confrontation with the formidable forces of the United States. Despite his misgivings, he planned to be ready. In eight months he drove the 22,000 men in his command to superhuman efforts. He sent all civilians on the island back to Japan, not even providing women from the "comfort troops" for his men. There was to be no comfort, not even a ration of *sakē* on that bleak, inhospitable island. All Iwo Jima had to offer was a network of over 1,500 caves from which Kuribayashi created an incredible labyrinth, consisting of sixteen miles of interconnecting tunnels. Working conditions were ferocious, and Korean labor troops bore the brunt. Gas masks had to be worn for protection from the island's sulfur fumes, and the heat at 30 feet below the surface was obliterating.[25] But the merciless discipline of Kuribayashi allowed no quarter. By February 1945, the Iwo Jima garrison inhabited an underground citadel, in places five levels deep, stocked with ammunition, medical supplies, food, electricity, and a communications system linking the bunkers to blockhouses, pillboxes, and gun positions throughout the island. Kuribayashi was truly "Lord of the Underworld."[26]

Admiral Chester W. Nimitz, commander in chief of the Pacific Fleet based on Guam, gave Iwo Jima top bombing priority in November 1944.

Probably no island in World War II received as much preliminary pounding as did Iwo Jima. For ten weeks, until 16 February when the intensive pre-landing bombardment began, the island was hit by land-based aircraft almost every day, and the total tonnage of bombs dropped was not far from 6800. . . . Under ordinary circumstances, so heavy and prolonged a bombardment would have been more than sufficient to pulverize everything on an island of that size.[27]

The Japanese resilience was uncanny. After each American bombing raid, Iwo Jima's indefatigable garrison began reconstruction almost before the smoke cleared. Airfield runways seemingly devastated by attacks were patched up and serviceable within twenty-four hours.[28]

In his effort to defend Iwo Jima, Kuribayashi also had a powerful psychological weapon in his arsenal: the samurai warrior code of Bushido, which inculcated courage, loyalty, unquestioning obedience, reverence for the emperor, and contempt for death--useful characteristics as the invasion drew near.[29] Kuribayashi exhorted his men to embrace the high calling of the samurai, to become true *kamikazes*.

We are here to defend this island to the limit of our strength. We must devote ourselves to that task entirely. Each of your shots must kill many Americans. We cannot allow ourselves to be captured by the enemy. If our positions are overrun, we will take bombs and grenades and throw ourselves under the tanks to destroy them. We will infiltrate the enemy's lines to exterminate him. No man must die until he has killed at least ten Americans. We will harass the enemy with guerilla actions until the last of us has perished. Long live the emperor![30]

Copies of the "Courageous Battle Vow" were posted on the walls of bunkers and pillboxes. Kuribayashi's men would obey to the letter, as Hansen and the men of the 28th Marines would soon discover.

D-DAY: FEBRUARY 19, 1945

The invasion of Iwo Jima was an organizational tour de force of no mean proportions. Time/Life correspondent Robert Sherrod, in his eyewitness account of the campaign, explained that an amphibious landing involved considerably more than ordering the Marines to climb down their ships' nets to be transported ashore in small boats. Sherrod described the commander in chief of the undertaking, the formidable Vice Admiral Kelly Turner.

"Nobody but Kelly could get away with running a show big as this by himself," said a friend at Iwo Jima as he watched Turner pace the bridge of the *Eldorado* during 0500 General Quarters. The admiral wore an old bathrobe. He barked orders like a chief bosn's mate, stopping now and then to growl at the stupidity of slow-thinking people in general.[31]

Equally irascible, and especially on this occasion, was Turner's Marine partner in the amphibious landing, "Howlin' Mad" Smith, described by Sherrod as "always demanding, and often profane," a man who "looked and talked as Wallace Beery might, in the role of a Marine general."[32] Turner and Smith had briefed Sherrod and the more than seventy other correspondents aboard the *Eldorado*. Secretary of the Navy James V. Forrestal also had addressed the gentlemen of the press:

You news correspondents have a responsibility somewhat like my own-- to the public. The tremendous scale and scope of this war can best be conveyed to the people by the press. . . . Back home there is a great tendency to count the victory as already won, to have the turkey on the table before it is shot. The people should understand that we are fighting a fanatical enemy who can be beaten only by death.
My hat is off to the Marines.[33]

Forrestal was more accurate than flattering when he told the correspondents that theirs was a significant responsibility: to report clearly and objectively to the American public just what its military was accomplishing in the war against Japan, and at what cost. Thanks to Sherrod, a member of that press corps sailing toward Iwo Jima, it is possible to re-create from his combat notebooks the raw data of the invasion. His journal entries are like staccato bursts of gunfire.

Feb 19
up at 0500
some fire-red balls

0645 now daylight. Ships stopped.
Suribachi looks like slightly melted ice
cream cone. . . .

0720 sun 5° above horizon & here come 10

B24's--their bombs walk down the island
like twinkling Xmas lights, followed by
smoke rising from ground.

0735 a heavy cruiser is in close--looks like
300 yards--firing stuff into caves. Pall
of smoke & dust (mostly) now covers whole
island except north end. Only very peak
of Suribachi is visible.[34]

John P. Marquand, who witnessed the invasion as a correspondent for
Harper's, gave this memorable description of the island looming just in front of
the men aboard the LVTs:

Anyone who has been there can shut his eyes and see the place
again. It never looked more aesthetically ugly than on D-day morning,
or more completely Japanese. Its silhouette was like a sea monster with
the little dead volcano for the head, and the beach area for the neck, and
all the rest of it with its scrubby, brown cliffs for the body. It also had
the minute, fussy compactness of those miniature Japanese gardens. Its
stones and rocks were like those contorted, wind-scoured, water-worn
boulders which the Japanese love to collect as landscape decorations.[35]

The men of the 5th Division aboard amphibious tractors zigzagging toward
their line of departure 4,000 yards offshore were unlikely to have expended
much energy reflecting on metaphors of landscape design.   Their island
destination evoked more malevolent associations:

"You'd look out across this particular expanse of no man's land and
it was bubbling and seething with steam coming up out of the ground."
"The entire vegetation was gone, completely."
"As we hit the beach, we saw the ash, and nothing living."
"You'd think: if there is a hell, I'm living through it now."[36]

As the amber parachute flares lofted over the landing beaches to signal that
the first assault troops were safely ashore, there was only light enemy artillery
fire.

The Japanese opposition to Marine advances up the sloping sides of
the island continued light until the attack had carried inland about three
hundred yards. Here the troops were sprinkled, then showered, and
finally deluged by mortar and artillery fire from Suribachi and the north.
Men began to claw the gray, coarse sand with their hands and feet in an

effort to get under the surface.[37]

The 28th Regiment's 2nd Battalion hit Green Beach on the left flank of the landing force. It was an unenviable position, too close for comfort to the heavily fortified volcano, Suribachi. Captain Arthur H. Naylor, who led the 2nd Battalion's Company F, described those first critical minutes in the surf.

My company was the extreme left-hand flank going in, so that we stretched from the ocean as far up toward the middle of Suribachi as we could. We faced Suribachi.

We kind of caught it there on the beach. When our landing craft hit, mortars were falling all around. We weren't quite ashore, but there was no way I was going to let the people in my landing craft stay on board. I ordered everybody to jump out and go ashore and I jumped out the back and went into about 12 feet of water. I lost my rifle; I lost my helmet.

I saw so many men being killed and wounded as we were going in that first day. And shells flying all over the place. I can remember seeing so many men in my company dead.[38]

Naylor's brother company in the 2nd Battalion, Company E, also arrived on Green Beach in one of the early assault waves. Hansen's 3rd Platoon landed to the far left of the entire force, closest to Suribachi. The platoon had been divided into two boats: one under the command of Thomas, the other commanded by Wells. The men in Thomas's boat had better luck in their landing than Wells's companions, according to Wells's recollection: "They landed over on our left, and they got up high and dry. A big wave came and washed my men and equipment out. The very thing I didn't want to happen."[39]

Hansen splashed ashore from Wells's boat. His friend Wheeler arrived dryshod with Thomas. Wheeler later remarked that "the first waves actually had it easier than later ones. Less fire. I actually thought it would be worse than it was. Men weren't getting killed every minute. There's an awful lot of fire that misses, even with the shell fire, the mortars."[40]

Company E's First Sergeant John A. Daskalakis, a former paratrooper who had served with Hansen at the battle of Bougainville, recalled the daunting problem of getting his troops through the sand piled high into terraces.

Rough. Oh boy, they were terrible! It was hard going. Three terraces. Then turn left. Toward Suribachi. Then we got hung up there with their [the Japanese] mortar positions--five-inch mortars. You could see them coming through the air. They'd explode. Fascinating. You kept your eye on those mortars [fired from emplacements], at the base of the mountain. We couldn't see them. They had them camouflaged. When I got my troops across I'd make them wait until the thirty-round belts [of ammunition] expired, and then I'd move my troops. They [the Japanese] had thirty-round belts for their machine guns. That's the only way I got my men across.[41]

There was, however, no choice but to advance. Ahead were the virtually invisible defenses of the entrenched Japanese. Behind on the beaches was chaos.

Tanks and halftracks lay crippled where they had bogged down in the coarse sand. Amphibian tractors, victims of mines and well aimed shells, lay flopped on their backs. Cranes, brought ashore to unload cargo, tilted at insane angles, and bulldozers were smashed in their own roadways. . . .
And scattered amid the wreckage was death.[42]

The 1st and 2nd Battalions of the 28th Regiment at Green Beach were ordered directly across the island at its narrowest point, in order to secure the western beaches and to isolate Suribachi. This strategic Japanese vantage point had to be taken in order to protect the landing beaches.
The 1st Battalion began its charge across the island's neck. The 2nd Battalion landed just behind the 1st, "its mission to support the 1st and prepare for the main event, the regiment's attack on Mount Suribachi."[43]
Hansen's 3rd Platoon, having landed the closest to Suribachi, had the farthest to travel along the beach northward before turning inland toward their designated assembly area. There, as the regimental reserve force, they took up their position near the proposed command post.

Many occupied themselves by studying Suribachi, perhaps half a mile away. They were seeing it for the first time from the angle at which it would have to be assaulted. Its flanks dropped to meet the sea, but the near side was semicircled by brush-covered approaches that held a 1,300-yard belt of blockhouses, bunkers, pillboxes, mortar pits, caves, tunnels, trenches, and other defenses.[44]

Here, in the shadow of Suribachi, Company E suffered no casualties. Such a charmed life could not last long on Iwo Jima, however. The 1st Battalion in its race across the island's neck had been "badly shot up and scattered." So after about an hour in its assembly area, Company E was ordered "to spread out and retrace the steps" of the 1st Battalion.[45] It was Company E's turn to move out and cross Iwo Jima. Later, Johnson's battalion faced south, toward the volcano, in a position constituting the left flank of the 28th Regiment's line across the island. To the 2nd Battalion's immediate right was the 3rd Battalion, and to the far right (extending to the west beach) was the 1st Battalion. Liversedge, the regimental commander, decided to move his lines closer to the base of the mountain, since "enemy fire was increasing in intensity each hour and it was hoped that more ground could be gained before the full power of the Japanese was brought to bear."[46]

Late in the afternoon of D-Day, Liversedge ordered the attack toward Suribachi. The three battalions jumped off. "Despite a naval gunfire and air preparation, the attack stalled. Heavy resistance, the open terrain, and the disorganizing effects of rapid advance made early in the day combined to crush this attempt to push on." At 1700 "button up" orders were issued, and the troops began digging in for their first night on Iwo Jima.[47] It had been a long day; it would prove to be a long night.

By the end of D-Day, the 28th Marines had successfully isolated Suribachi from the rest of the island. Yet this feat had not decreased the volcano's deadly artillery fire. From the guns at its sprawling base to the batteries on its commanding heights, the volcano and its garrison under Colonel Kanehiko Atsuchi still held fast.

D-DAY + 1: FEBRUARY 20, 1945

Dawn broke on the second day of battle with the Marines having secured less than 10 percent of Iwo Jima's land area, an achievement far short of their commanders' projections. This sinister little island would take more time and more lives than even the most pessimistic had predicted.

The campaign at this point was divided into two separate operations: the 26th and 27th Regiments, along with the entire Fourth Division, confronted the murderous terrain to the north; the 5th Division's 28th Regiment faced south toward Suribachi. That death-dealing mountain seemed to possess an almost palpable malevolence.

> On this day, and increasingly as days went by, Suribachi seemed to take on a life of its own, to be watching these men, looming over them, pressing down upon them. When they moved, they moved in its shadow, under its eye. To be sure, there were hundreds of eyes looking at them from the mountain, but these were the eyes of a known enemy, an enemy whose intent was perfectly clear. In the end, it is probable that the mountain represented to these Marines a thing more evil than the Japanese.[48]

Kuribayashi, the formidable Japanese commander of Iwo Jima, knew that the Marines would concentrate their first efforts on Suribachi. He had garrisoned the mountain with approximately 2,000 men under Atsuchi. The advantage the Marines held, however, was not in the slim numerical superiority of their infantry but in the support provided from the air and sea. Navy and Marine fighter planes strafed and bombed Suribachi, "dropping Napalm until its steep sides appeared to burst into flame."[49] Still, conditions continued hazardous at the base of Suribachi, where the Argus-eyed Japanese garrison could observe every move of the advancing Marines.

At sundown on D + 1 Johnson called a halt to the day's costly progress. The Marines of the 2nd and 3rd Battalions had paid dearly for the meager 200 yards wrested from the Japanese: "eight officers and 158 men killed or wounded—twenty per cent of the regiment's effective strength."[50] The mountain was still in Japanese hands as the men of the 28th dug in for another cold and anxious night.

D-DAY + 2: FEBRUARY 21, 1945

On the morning of D + 2, Liversedge recognized that he could ill afford another day of devastating casualties in exchange for minimal yardage gained from the enemy entrenched at the base of Suribachi. His men of the 28th Marines were giving all they had. What they needed was more softening up of the Japanese defenses before the infantry moved forward against the mountain. There was still room between the regiment's lines and Suribachi's base for air, navy, and artillery support. "Ask for all of it, Pete," Liversedge told his operations officer, Major Oscar F. Peatross, "and tell those planes to drop it close—we can't use air tomorrow."[51]

D + 2 would prove to be a fateful day for the 28th Marines and especially for the men of the 2nd Battalion's Company E. Hansen, Wheeler, and their comrades moved up to the regimental line, directly facing the mountain at a point only 200 yards from Suribachi's main defenses. Johnson's 2nd Battalion comprised the regiment's left flank. Severance's Company E constituted the right flank of the 2nd Battalion, placing his men just to the left of the island's center "where the terrain leading to the defenses was entirely open."[52] Until this time, Company E's casualties had been relatively light, but this new deployment placed them at serious risk.

To further compromise their plan of advance, the tanks expected to support the unit were nowhere in sight. Problems of rearming and refueling kept them in the rear. "H-Hour was delayed while we waited for the tanks," Severance explained. "When they didn't show up by about 9:00 A.M. we were ordered to advance without them."[53] Severance described the intimidating objective of his company's assault:

> The troops faced a solid wall of reinforced concrete pill boxes and infantry trenches extending across the narrow neck of the island, and probably some 30 yards in depth. The positions were "mutually supporting," that is, their firing ports were so situated that one could see

another and cover it by fire . . . this network of support extending across the entire position. Without tanks, it was necessary for the riflemen and machine gunners to fire at as many ports as they could identify, to keep the enemy's heads down, while our assault squads with demolitions and flame throwers attack one at a time.[54]

These were desperate conditions, and heroic acts were demanded of the men of the 3rd Platoon. Wheeler, the platoon's chronicler, sustained significant injuries on this day when a fragment from a mortar shattered his jaw. While one of the platoon's Navy corpsmen was treating this wound, a second shell exploded into the shallow depression where Wheeler had taken shelter, lacerating his leg. He was evacuated to an aid station and then to the beach for transportation to a hospital ship offshore.[55]

Wheeler's evacuation prevented him from observing an extraordinary act of self-sacrifice in which Private First Class Donald Ruhl, a 21-year-old cattle rancher from Montana, saved the life of Wheeler's good friend, Hansen. With uncanny vividness of detail, Wheeler's platoon leader, J. K. Wells, recalled the episode that earned Ruhl the Medal of Honor and cost him his life.

Ruhl came to me on the first day on the island and wanted to be my runner. We always talked about him being a renegade. Listen, there was not one ounce of fear in him.

They ordered us to attack without *any, anything*. We had absolutely no help from anybody. We had no tank support, had no artillery support, had *no* support, *period*. And we were attacking this chain of concrete blockhouses.

Well, I was not about to tell the men to follow me. I just raised up, and waved my tommy gun toward the field and took off running. I just thought it was pure suicide, if you want to know.

Well, I think, when it was all over with, it was a lifesaver, because the Japs had expected a preparation. We attacked without any help, any preparation, anything. And we ran in on top of them. We ran on by those blockhouses and there was a trench that ran along behind. I stopped at the edge to see how the men were coming from behind.

I turned back around just in time to see Hansen and Ruhl run over and lay down side by side and look over in the trench. They must have almost bumped heads with the Japanese. They pulled back fast. Then just at that time I saw this [explosive]--it looked larger than their grenades. I saw it land right between them. I heard Ruhl say: "Look out, Hank!" And he flopped over on it and it went off and he ballooned up in the air. I was afraid they were going to get Hansen, too, before he could get in a little shelter.[56]

Nearly fifty years after Iwo Jima, Wheeler, who knew both Ruhl and Hansen well, confided to the authors that he had often reflected on the motivations for this sort of heroism. "I've tried to analyze what makes a man do a thing like that. Of course, he [Ruhl] was a very courageous fellow. It seems to me that these things are more like a reflex action, to confine or contain the damage."[57]

There was plenty of damage to contain on D+2. And some of it descended on the leader of the 3rd Platoon. A Japanese mortar shell burst into the shallow hole where Wells had briefly taken cover. Wells vividly remembered the explosion: "I had no feeling below the waist and a burning sensation in my neck. When I reached down and felt my legs I found them all wet. I thought it was all blood, but a piece of shrapnel had exploded one of my canteens. My clothes were nearly all blown off me from the waist down, and I was full of shrapnel."[58]

Thomas assumed command after his lieutenant was finally persuaded to seek medical attention. A few days, later the soft-spoken sergeant described the conditions his unit had run into while charging Suribachi:

> I guess you could say we caught hell. We lost 17 men out of 46 in about 45 minutes. That was when our platoon leader was wounded and I had to take over.
>
> After that, I don't remember much. I think I and some other Marine led some tanks up there to fire into pillboxes and caves.[59]

The 2nd Battalion's commander, Johnson, was an officer who exemplified, as well as admired, the reckless courage of men like Ruhl, Wells, and Thomas. Wheeler described him as "a blustery, gruff, stern fellow." Wheeler confessed, "I was scared to death of him. Once he gave me the dickens about not properly using the concealment on the site, and then he'd walk out in the open. It takes two kinds of Marines: cautious men and reckless men. I was one of the cautious ones."[60]

It was just turning dark when the men of Company E broke through the enemy's defenses. "We had moved so fast," Severance recalled, "that we had by-passed some of the Jap forces, and spent the night cut off from our Battalion."[61] The company was in a difficult spot as it buttoned up for the night: it was isolated, it was low on ammunition and rations, and it had sustained several critical casualties.[62]

D+2 had been a costly day for the Marines. Officially, the battle's total casualty count now read: "644 United States Marines were killed, 4,168 wounded and 560 were missing."[63] At her home in Massachusetts, Hansen's mother received these first news reports of the catastrophic dimensions of the campaign in which her son was engaged. "Watching the Marines cross that island reminded me of the charge of Pickett at Gettysburg," Howlin' Mad Smith later remarked.[64] The campaign was only fifty-eight hours old and already the

United States Marines were engaged in one of America's bloodiest battles since the Civil War.

D-DAY + 3: FEBRUARY 22, 1945

There was certainly no doubt in the minds of the Marines as to the nature of the war they were waging when February 22 dawned cold and rainy on Iwo Jima. Back in the States the nation was celebrating George Washington's birthday. On this Pacific island there was little to celebrate. A 20-knot gale churned up a 9-foot surf. Storm clouds hung like premonitions over Suribachi, obscuring the mountain's crest. But war is played by rules different from those of baseball: the game is not called on account of rain.

At eight o'clock the men of the 28th Regiment were back at work, all three battalions in action against the Suribachi garrison. Company E, isolated on the volcano's southeastern side, had made it through the night. Severance reported that his company spent the day "mopping up the remaining resistance, and clearing out or destroying caves on the south and west sides of the mountain."[65]

The Iwo Jima campaign was primarily an infantry operation, and D+3 was no exception. At the base of Suribachi it was a matter of small units of Marine riflemen engaged in direct assaults on the enemy fortifications. By day's end the volcano had been surrounded, except for a 400-yard gap on the west coast.[66] Although an undetermined number of the volcano's Japanese defenders were still alive, concealed in the mountain's network of caves, the logical next move was for the Marines to assault Suribachi.

During the night of February 22, some of Suribachi's Japanese garrison escaped to the northern part of the island, in obedience to the command of their mortally wounded leader, Atsuchi.

Led by a Navy lieutenant, about 20 of them made it. After locating Captain Samaji Inouye, commander of Iwo's Naval guard, the lieutenant reported that Suribachi was lost. But Inouye was a traditionalist to the core. "You traitor, why did you come here?" he shouted. "You are a coward and a deserter. I shall condescend to behead you myself."

The lieutenant knelt and meekly bowed his head. Inouye drew his sword and raised it. But it never fell--Inouye's junior officers tore it out of his grip. Captain Inouye began to weep. "Suribachi's fallen," he moaned. "Suribachi's fallen."[67]

NOTES

1. "In those days all Marine Corps recruits were assigned to one of the Corps' two boot camps. Those enlisting west of the Mississippi River were sent to San Diego; those who joined up east of the Mississippi went to Parris Island, South Carolina, an isle whose reputation was just marginally better than those of Alcatraz and Devil's Island." See William Manchester, *Goodbye, Darkness* (Boston: Little, Brown and Co., 1979), 119.

2. Hatch interview with the authors, December 28, 1992.

3. "The triangular nature of a reinforced marine division was carried through companies and platoons to assault squads and teams. . . . their normal composition at Iwo . . . represents the highest perfection reached in organizing the men who did the bulk of the fighting." See Jeter A. Isely and Philip A. Crowl, *The U.S. Marines and Amphibious War* (Princeton, N.J.: Princeton University Press, 1951), 456-457.

4. Haynes interview with the authors, December 29, 1992.

5. Fred E. Haynes, "Left Flank," *Marine Corps Gazette*, March 1953, 49.

6. J. K. Wells interview with the authors, May 21, 1993. The authors have eliminated certain repetitions and digressions in the transcripts of taped oral interviews. Ellipses have not been used to indicate these omissions.

7. Richard Wheeler, *The Bloody Battle for Suribachi* (New York: Thomas Y. Crowell Co., 1965), 9.

8. J. K. Wells interview with the authors, May 21, 1993. Hansen probably spoke a few words learned from his father's Scandinavian background. But his own preferred identity was Irish, from his maternal origins. He even good-humoredly called himself "Henry O'Hansen," a play on his middle initial, "O." for "Oliver" (George King interview with the authors, January 2, 1993).

9. Wheeler, *The Bloody Battle for Suribachi*, 12-13.

10. Wheeler interview with the authors, February 5, 1993.

11. Severance interview with the authors, October 27, 1993.

12. Severance to Wetenhall, letter dated July 24, 1989, courtesy of Mr. Severance, who sent a copy of this extensive letter to Albee. Severance to Albee, letter dated November 10, 1992.

13. Haynes interview with the authors, December 29, 1992.

14. Holland M. Smith and Percy Finch, *Coral and Brass* (Washington, D.C.: Zenger Publishing Co., 1948), 249.

15. *Honolulu Advertiser*, December 24, 1944; Haynes interview with authors, November 20, 1992; Howard M. Conner, *The Spearhead: The World War II History of the 5th Marine Division* (Nashville, Tenn.: Battery Press, 1987 reprint), 26-27.

16. Wheeler interview with the authors, February 5, 1993.

17. Robert Leckie, *Delivered from Evil* (New York: Harper and Row, 1987), 865.

18. Smith and Finch, *Coral and Brass*, 240-241.

19. Leckie, *Delivered from Evil*, 865.

20. Conner, *The Spearhead*, 26, 29.

21. Smith and Finch, *Coral and Brass*, 251.

22. John C. Chapin, *The Fifth Marine Division in World War II* (Washington, D.C.: Historical Division, Headquarters, U.S. Marine Corps, 1945), 8.

23. *WW II Time-Life Books History of the Second World War* (New York: Prentice Hall Press, 1989), 397.

24. Conner, *The Spearhead,* 36.

25. Leckie, *Delivered from Evil,* 865.

26. *WWII Time-Life* Books, 397-399. "General Kuribayashi's own command post in the northern part of the island was located in a cave 75 feet under-ground, one of several linked by over 500 feet of tunnels." Ronald H. Spector, *Eagle Against the Sun* (New York: Free Press, 1985), 495.

27. Samuel Eliot Morison, *Victory in the Pacific: 1945* (Boston: Little, Brown, and Co., 1975 ed.), 12-13.

28. Conner, *The Spearhead,* 37.

29. Bernard Millot, *Divine Thunder* (New York: McCall Publishing Co., 1971), 5, 22.

30. Ibid., 112.

31. Robert Sherrod, *On to Westward* (Baltimore, Md.: Nautical and Aviation Publishing Co. of America, 1990 ed.), 254-255.

32. Ibid., 256.

33. Ibid., 160-161.

34. Sherrod Notebook 6, 1-3, courtesy of Mr. Sherrod. Sherrod died in February 1994. In October 1993 he reviewed and approved the authors' transcripts of his interviews.

35. John Marquand, "Iwo Jima before H-hour," *Harper's,* May 1945, 499.

36. Quotations of anonymous Marines in the British television series, *The World at War,* Vol. 23, Thorn EMI Video, Thames Television, London, 1982, script by David Wheeler.

37. Conner, *The Spearhead,* 47.

38. Naylor interview with the authors, April 16, 1993.

39. J. K. Wells interview with the authors, May 21, 1993.

40. Wheeler interview with the authors, February 5, 1993.

41. Daskalakis interview with the authors, December 29, 1992.

42. Carl W. Proehl, ed., *The Fourth Marine Division in World War II* (Washington, D.C.: Infantry Journal Press, 1946), 153.

43. Richard Wheeler, *Iwo* (New York: Lippincott and Crowell, Publishers, 1980), 92.

44. Ibid., 94.

45. Severance to Wetenhall, letter dated July 24, 1989.

46. Conner, *The Spearhead,* 50-55, passim.

47. Ibid.

48. Ibid.

49. Ibid.

50. Ibid.

51. Ibid.

52. Wheeler, *Iwo,* 132.

53. Severance to Wetenhall, letter dated July 24, 1989.

54. Ibid.

55. Wheeler interview with the authors, February 5, 1993.

56. J. K. Wells interview with the authors, May 21, 1993.

57. Wheeler interview with the authors, February 5, 1993.

58. Wheeler, *Iwo,* 132.

59. Keyes Beech, *Leatherneck*, May 1945, 62. By the battle's end, the 3rd Platoon had received more medals on Iwo Jima than have ever been won by any other infantry platoon in any branch of service for a single engagement (J. K. Wells interview with the authors, May 1, 1994).

60. Wheeler interview with the authors, February 5, 1993.

61. Severance to Wetenhall, letter dated July 24, 1989.

62. Wheeler, *Iwo*, 132.

63. *Boston Globe*, February 23, 1945. Eventually, casualties from the 36 days of battle on Iwo Jima would claim 5,931 Marines killed, and 17,372 wounded. Statistics from the USMC Historical Center.

64. *Boston Herald*, March 20, 1945.

65. Severance to Wetenhall, letter dated July 24, 1989.

66. Severance interview with the authors, October 27, 1993.

67. *Time-Life History of World War II*, 399.

Chapter 3

First Flag at the Summit

"The story of Suribachi is too familiar to be repeated. The world knows how the Marine patrol scaled the mountain face and planted the Stars and Stripes on the summit, producing the greatest photograph of this war and, perhaps, of any war."[1]

In his memoirs, published three years after the battle for Iwo Jima, Lieutenant General Holland M. Smith appears to undercut any future historian's justification for recounting the American capture of Suribachi on the morning of February 23, 1945. His assumption that the world knew all the relevant facts about this dramatic episode was more than a little premature. At the time of this writing (1994), there is still considerable confusion as to how many flags were raised on Suribachi, by whom, at whose command, under what circumstances, and for what reasons.

February 23 was not a propitious day to launch an assault on Iwo Jima's volcanic fortress. Robert Sherrod, who went ashore with the 4th Division's commander, Major General Clifton B. Cates, recorded in his combat notebook the morning's discouraging weather: "up at 0700 to go ashore with Cates at 0800. . . . Weather today again stormy, cold, prohibits much landing of supplies. 9th Marines can't get ashore. . . . Choppy, mean water."[2]

Conditions were mean on land as well as on the seas. Despite the naval and aerial bombardments and the efforts of the infantrymen of the 5th Division to destroy the defenses girdling Suribachi's base, there was by no means any certainty that the Japanese garrison had been rendered incapable of resistance. The most feasible route of assault lay up the north face of the mountain, the zone of the 2nd Battalion, 28th Regiment. Two days earlier, on D+2, Operations Officer Major Oscar F. Peatross had received orders to set in motion plans for the capture of Suribachi. In 1986 Major General Oscar Peatross, USMC (Ret.), wrote a letter revealing the origins of the assault plan:

On D+2, the Twenty-eight RLT (Regimental Landing Team) Headquarters, for which I was the Operations Officer, received a message to the effect that it was imperative that the Twenty-eight seize Mt. Suribachi immediately. At that time, we had our arms practically wrapped around Suribachi. Complete seizure meant to us sending a patrol to the top of the mountain and cleaning out the caves at the base of the volcano.[3]

Peatross reported that the 2nd Battalion, "since it was in the middle of the mountain (i.e., at the north face)," was directed to send a patrol up Suribachi. Colonel Harry B. Liversedge, the regimental commander, went to the 2nd Battalion command post to discuss details of the plan's execution.[4]

Col. Liversedge and I went to the Second Battalion CP and talked with its commander, Lt. Col. Chaney Johnson, his Executive Officer Maj. Tom Pearce and the Operation Officer Capt. Martin Reinemann. We emphasized the need to let the rest of the troops know that the mountain had been secured. Consequently, we talked smoke pots and other things and finally decided on Col. Johnson's idea of taking a flag up; raising it on the spot where it could be seen over the entire island.[5]

So it was the 2nd Battalion's commander, Lieutenant Colonel Chandler W. Johnson, whose idea was ultimately adopted. Suribachi would get a flag, not a smoke pot, as the symbol of the American conquest of this stronghold. But it was Liversedge himself who chose the man to lead the historic patrol up the mountain.

Col. Liversedge selected the officer from the Second Battalion who was to be the leader of the patrol: 1st Lt. Harold G. Schrier. He was selected because all of the weapons available in the regiment were to be turned over to the patrol leader and the Col. wanted to make certain the officer knew how to use them. (Lieutenant Schrier was the only Second Battalion Company Executive Officer with prior combat experience.) Air, artillery, naval gunfire, mortars, and rockets--all of the firing needed--would be controlled by the man leading the patrol. Liversedge had faith in Schrier because the latter had led patrols under his own command at New Georgia (Solomon Islands), while in the Raider Battalion.[6]

The choice of which patrol Schrier would lead was left to the commander of Company E, Captain Dave E. Severance. According to Severance, it was the luck of the draw that targeted the 3rd Platoon. Severance had not learned that a platoon was to be sent up Suribachi until the morning of February 23 (although his battalion commander, Johnson, had evidently gotten the order the night before). "I was told to provide a platoon and a machine gun section (about 40 men), to be led by my Executive Officer, 1st Lt. Harold George Schrier. I selected my third platoon purely because of their position. I would have been confident sending any of the three platoons."[7]

Richard Wheeler described the reaction of the men of his old unit to the news of the honor thrust upon them: "The twenty-five men of the 3rd Platoon were by this time very dirty and very tired. They no longer looked nor felt like crack combat troops. . . . They hardly yearned for the distinction of being the first Marines to tackle the volcano. But the colonel didn't bother to ask them how they felt about it."[8]

"It is a military aphorism," Wheeler observed, "that men who perform well in battle are rewarded with further assignments." On the morning of D+4, Schrier assembled the men of the 3rd Platoon. The platoon's thin ranks were now bolstered to some forty men by the addition of a machine gun section. Led by Schrier, the patrol started its trek back around the volcano to Johnson's battalion headquarters at the mountain's northeast base.[9]

Meanwhile, a scouting party from the 2nd Battalion's Company F was sent out to test the temper of the Japanese defenders of Suribachi. According to the 28th Regiment's Action Report (filed by Landing Team 228, the 2nd Battalion), this scouting party was one of two sent up Suribachi that chill winter morning: "D and F Companies were ordered each to send a three-man Reconnaissance patrol about half way up the mountain in their sectors. These patrols did not receive any hostile fire."[10]

No additional details about the activities of the Company D patrol have come to light. Severance of Company E commented in a recent interview: "I've heard some weird tales about the Dog Company patrol. How somebody got a Silver Star for a pitched battle where somebody was badly wounded. As far as I know, Dog Company's patrol didn't get to the top."[11]

The patrol whose activities are of greater significance for the Suribachi story was one led by Sergeant Sherman B. Watson of Company F. Watson was accompanied by Private First Class Theodore White, Private First Class George Mercer, and Private First Class Louis C. Charlo.[12] In a recent interview Arthur H. Naylor, the former commander of the 2nd Battalion's Company F, reconstructed the activities of Watson's patrol.

Naylor's company command post was located about 60 yards from Johnson's battalion command post, near the base of Suribachi. Naylor recalled that he "ran back and forth between the two posts," admitting that at age 23, a 60-yard dash through Iwo's volcanic sands was somewhat taxing but still within his capacity. He had joined the Marines in December 1941 and served in the paratroops before joining the 5th Division at Camp Pendleton in February 1944. He had known Liversedge, the commander of the 28th Regiment, as well as

Johnson, long before they all landed on Iwo Jima. He described his commanding officers as "fearless--real Marines." In the case of Johnson, he modified his judgment a bit to say Johnson was perhaps "more reckless than fearless."[13]

At a battalion commanders' briefing during the night of February 22, Liversedge had told Johnson and his brother officers: "tomorrow, we climb."[14] Pursuant to that command, at eight o'clock on the morning of February 23, Johnson ordered Naylor to send a patrol halfway up the north face of Suribachi to see what the Japanese were up to. Naylor, in turn, ordered one of his platoon leaders, Second Lieutenant Raymond Whalen, to take a patrol halfway up, but not to proceed to the summit.[15]

Although Whalen (who should not be held accountable for the misreporting) was later touted in the Boston newspapers (he was from Massachusetts) as having raised the first flag on Suribachi, Naylor said that Whalen himself did not go up the mountain. Instead Whalen sent the four-man patrol led by Watson. Naylor was certain that Company F sent no other patrols that morning, but he could not speak for patrols possibly sent by Company D or E. He stated that in his observation of Watson's patrol, clearly visible from his post, he did not see any other Marines scaling Suribachi until nine o'clock.[16]

> I had George Haynes, who was in charge of my machine gun patrol, set up machine gun fire to cover this patrol up Mount Suribachi halfway up. And I watched them all the time. We were only a hundred yards from the base of Mount Suribachi where they were going up, so we could see it all very clearly. And nothing happened.[17]

Watson reconstructed his patrol's climb up Suribachi--the very first made by the U.S. forces on Iwo Jima. Especially vivid was his recollection of the machine gun cover provided by Haynes's patrol.

> There was a guy from the machine gun company. He called us and said, "I'll let this machine gun fire right over the top of you." It sounded pretty good, as long as he was spraying right in front of us. But we got so high, the damned gun choked up. We were running under this thing. "Tutt-tutt-tutt!" They finally shut it off. We almost ran into our own damned fire. Machine guns, you know, are on a little tripod. You can only tilt them so far. I don't know what degree of incline, but it was pretty steep most of the way [up Suribachi]. It was pretty much of a crawl-scramble deal to get up there. We went straight up, like a bunch of dummies. Those other people [the later patrol led by Schrier], they switched back, so they weren't climbing straight up.[18]

Watson said that it was Naylor himself who ordered him to "take whatever men you need and reconnoiter all the way to the top. Don't get in a fire fight, if you can keep from it."[19] The four-man patrol had no radio contact with Naylor's command post at the base of Suribachi, and they met no one on their climb to the summit. It was, Watson remarked, "much, *much*" quieter than they had expected. "There was nobody shooting at us. The only guy shooting at us was this guy [with a machine gun] down on the bottom of the hill."[20]

Well, we went to the top, right to the lip of the volcano. We just went up there, looked around, and nobody fired at us. They [the Japanese] had some gun emplacements up there. We turned right back down. As we were coming down, we met Schrier. He had about a company of guys--a platoon, at least. They were in single file. I'd say we were pretty well down at the bottom. At least three-quarters of the way, when we met Schrier.[21]

After reporting to Naylor, Watson and Mercer went down to the beach.

You know, there wasn't nothing to do. Stand around. So we kind of wandered off to scrounge up some food. And on the way we stopped and saw Johnson. He was a great old guy. He court-martialled me a couple of times. He was a real old-time Marine.
    We went down to the beach and went aboard an LST and had breakfast. The Navy was good enough to feed us. Soon as we did that, we went back up to work.[22]

Based on the unchallenged climb by Watson's patrol, Johnson decided it was now time to send Company E's 3rd Platoon up Suribachi.
    When the men of the 3rd Platoon circled back to 2nd Battalion headquarters, they found its commander exhibiting the same fearlessness and contempt for Japanese shelling that he had since landing on the beach on D-Day. Johnson was standing before an improvised pup tent at ground level rather than in a protected sand-bagged dugout. He was "sipping from a cup of steaming coffee, wearing his fatigue cap with its visor bent upward, and smiling. He was apparently pleased with the way things were going."[23] While Johnson and Schrier consulted, Sergeant Henry Hansen and some forty battle-weary Marines prepared for the unenviable task of climbing Suribachi, uncertain as to what awaited them from caves that harbored the lethal weaponry of the Japanese.
    Schrier's patrol was given the radio call sign "Hot Rocks."[24] Staff Sergeant Louis R. Lowery, a photographer for *Leatherneck* magazine, joined Schrier and his men to record their climb. Just as Schrier prepared to leave the 2nd Battalion command post at the mountain's base, Johnson turned to his adjutant, First Lieutenant George Greeley Wells, with a request for a flag Wells carried in his map case. Wells had obtained the flag from the attack transport ship,

Missoula, the ship that had taken the battalion to its staging point at Saipan. In a recent interview, Wells recalled the episode:

> I gave the flag to him [Johnson] or I gave it to Schrier, I don't remember which it was, but I think probably I gave it to the colonel. He did say "Go up there and do your best but don't get a bunch of people killed." So that's how the patrol started out. It was just as tense as if somebody had been shooting at them all the time, although there wasn't a lot of gunfire.
>
> Everybody was standing there below the mountain just watching them go up. And then when they finally went over the top we didn't know what happened.[25]

It was from the survivors of the 3rd Platoon that the story of what happened would be learned. Wheeler, whose earlier evacuation to a hospital ship prevented his accompanying his platoon up Suribachi that foggy grey morning, suggested two of his former platoon-mates as reliable sources for latter-day historians: James A. Robeson and Charles W. Lindberg. "There's Chick Robeson. He's a real hero. He was just a kid on Iwo. He's not full of baloney. He'll tell the straight dope. He went through it all. And Chuck Lindberg. He's another hero. Not too chesty. You can trust him, too."[26]

Private First Class James A. "Chick" Robeson was described by his former platoon leader, First Lieutenant John Keith Wells: "He'd just turned eighteen, but looked like he was about thirteen. I don't think he'd been away from Mother very long. But then he turned into being just one hell of a warrior. I guess you'd say he was my little brother, my baby brother."[27]

When interviewed, Robeson did not recall any talk about putting a flag up on Suribachi until the morning of February 23 when his platoon assembled at Johnson's command post, but he readily recalled his climb up the volcano:

> Lieutenant Wells, leader of my platoon, had already been wounded. We'd lost quite a few. Sergeant Snyder and Corporal Keller and I were the first three up there, I know that. And then we fanned right on through, and right behind us was Lieutenant Schrier, and I'm not sure who else. I know Hansen was right close there. He might have been about the fourth, but I'm not sure about that. We went on through.
>
> We were wary, because we expected something. But there wasn't a shot fired.[28]

Lindberg, burdened that morning with a 72-pound flamethrower, confirmed that the greatest challenge in climbing Suribachi was provided by the mountain itself, and not by its Japanese defenders. As the patrol scrambled up Suribachi, Lowery, the photographer from *Leatherneck* magazine, asked to have the small flag unfolded for a quick picture. Lindberg, who was slightly ahead of Lowery in the line of ascent, recalled that "he wanted a picture of the flag on the way up, in case we didn't get all the way."[29] Lowery reported that he "took pictures all the way, up--including one of the guys displaying the flag . . . just in case we didn't make it."[30]

There were few other opportunities for an action shot. Although Schrier had sent flankers out to protect his column, the only Japanese sighted were already dead. Despite the fact that Schrier's men zigzagged up to the crest of the volcano under conditions considerably less harrowing than those described in the press, the assault patrol had the complete attention of the Marines left at the base of Suribachi.[31] Five hundred sixty feet below, binoculars were trained on the 3rd Platoon. One Marine quipped: "Those guys ought to be getting flight pay."[32]

It took less than half an hour for the patrol to reach the rim of the crater. Schrier halted his men to evaluate the situation. Lindberg commented that at this point "we thought we were going to be in for a lot of trouble."[33] Still there were no Japanese in sight, just a few battered gun emplacements and the silent entrances to what appeared to be unoccupied caves. Schrier signaled his men to file over into the crater. Lindberg described the scene at the summit:

> When we reached the top Schrier said, "Let's get this flag up." A couple of the guys [Corporal Robert Leader and Private First Class Leo J. Rozek][34] found this piece of pipe, about 12 or 14 feet long--a piece of water pipe. It had a bullet hole in it. Somebody claimed our men put it in it, but they didn't.[35]

The pipe was passed up to a point about 35 feet from the summit of the mountain, where Platoon Sergeant "Boots" Thomas waited with Hansen, Schrier, and Lindberg.[36] Photographer Lowery was on the spot, with Robeson standing armed beside him. "The idea," Robeson explained, "was for me to more or less guard him."[37]

While Robeson stood watch, Lowery took a remarkable series of photographs, documenting almost every aspect of that first flag raising on Suribachi. The four men most actively involved, according to eyewitness accounts corroborated by Lowery's photographic evidence, were Schrier, Thomas, Hansen, and Lindberg. There are photos of Schrier kneeling and holding the triangularly folded flag in his lap while Hansen rigged a rope through the hole in the Japanese pipe, and of Hansen, Schrier, and Lindberg lashing the flag to its metal pipe flagstaff, with Thomas crouched nearby, cradling his gun.[38]

Once the flag and its pole were assembled, Schrier gave the terse order to get the flag up. Lindberg recalled that "because it was small, we carried it to the highest spot we could find."[39]

At the volcano's crest Lowery photographed the four Marines, assisted by two others, as they lifted the heavy flagpole parallel to the ground. Just as they were about to plant the flagstaff, Lowery asked the men "to wait a moment before they embedded the flagstaff in the volcanic ash while he changed film in his camera." He loaded the fourth and last roll of film he had packed.[40] Then the flagpole was secured. One shot in his flag-raising sequence shows Hansen and Schrier steadying the pole, with Lindberg and Thomas looking on. For a few seconds the only sound was the flag snapping in a stiff breeze. Lindberg recalled: "That's when all the troops down below started to cheer. And the ships whistled, and we had kind of a very proud moment."[41]

It was not only Lindberg and the men of Schrier's patrol on top of Suribachi who were having a proud moment. Down on the landing beach, Howlin' Mad Smith was having one, too. He described the experience in his memoirs:

Secretary Forrestal said he would like to go ashore next morning. . . .

Our boat touched shore just after the flag was raised. The cry went up from all quarters, "There goes the flag!"

The flag was raised at 1037 on February 23 and this vision of triumph had an electrifying effect on all our forces ashore and afloat. We were in a mood for victory and this glorious spectacle was the spark.

The raising of the flag high atop Suribachi was one of the proud moments of my life. No American could view this symbol of heroism and suffering without a lump in his throat. By a happy circumstance, I was standing beside Secretary of the Navy Forrestal when the tiny speck of red, white and blue broke and fluttered on the gaunt crest of the volcano. Turning to me, the Secretary said gravely, "Holland, the raising of that flag on Suribachi means a Marine Corps for the next 500 years."[42]

Forrestal's account in his diary was considerably briefer and less dramatic than Smith's: "Went aboard PCS 1403 (Lt. Cherry in command); closed the shoreline of Iwo Jima and went ashore in a Higgins boat about 1030. On the way in we saw the American Flag being raised by the Marines who had scaled the heights of the Suribachi volcano."[43]

It was not just the top brass, like Smith and Forrestal, who viewed the Suribachi flag with deep emotion that morning. A former Marine from the Iwo campaign, Charles Tatum, remembered the moment when a comrade slapped him on the back and pointed toward Suribachi. "The Stars and Stripes were clearly visible from the peak of the ancient volcano. The 28th Marines were now 'King of the Hill.'" To this day, whenever Tatum hears "The Star-Spangled Banner," it calls up the image of that small flag waving in the wind.[44]

Robert Sherrod, aboard an LSM, was also struck by the distant sight of the Stars and Stripes as he approached the beach that morning. "Look, they've got the flag up on Mount Suribachi!" someone yelled. "It was a dramatic moment. It seemed that we could do anything if we could capture that vertical monstrosity at the south end of Iwo. Tears welled in the eyes of several Marines as they watched the little flag fluttering in the breeze."[45]

At approximately 10:30 on February 23, 1945, Sergeant Henry O. Hansen of Massachusetts and members of the 3rd Platoon raised the first American flag ever to fly over Japanese home territory. It was more than just a proud moment; it was also an historic one.[46]

Wheeler gives this account of how the news passed from land to sea:

> The electrifying news began spreading at once to the units all around the base and to those fighting the main battle to the north. Men sprang from their foxholes under fire to pass the word along.
>
> On the beach near the center of the two-mile landing zone, Gordon Hebert's signalman ran up to him and said, "They've just raised the flag on Suribachi!" The beachmaster verified the statement with a quick use of his binoculars, then turned his public address system to its highest volume and announced the event up and down the beach."[47]

If the sight of the Stars and Stripes raised the spirits of the American troops on shipboard and ashore, it caused some legitimate concern to the men of the 3rd Platoon still patrolling the crest of Suribachi. Not only could the flag be seen by the Marines and sailors of the fleet, but it also was visible to enemy artillerymen operating unchallenged at the northern end of Iwo Jima. Up to the point of the flag's being raised, not one shot had been fired, journalistic fabrications to the contrary notwithstanding.[48] There remained, however, the potential threat from Japanese believed to be still lurking in the volcano's caves.

First to experience this threat was Robeson. His attention was suddenly diverted from Lowery photographing the flag raising by the unexpected emergence of a Japanese soldier who had been hiding in a cave down in the bowl of the volcanic crater. "From a cave right near us I saw something, and I said, 'Hey, fellows!' I wheeled around and I grabbed the first guy. I had a Browning Automatic Rifle. And that's when a grenade, or something, came out. And then a Jap came out with a broken-off sword and he went charging out of there."[49]

Robeson, unlike his Japanese attackers, lived to tell the tale. Lindberg, another survivor, reported that the flag raising was immediately followed by a firefight: "Right away: boom! I think the Japanese started to come out of the caves. So then we had to go after them. Right away."[50] Concealed in the crater's cave were other Japanese. Shortly after the first skirmish, they made their presence known with a shower of hand grenades.

Lowery was caught in the line of fire. As he approached the entrance to a cave that one of the flamethrowers had just torched, a Japanese soldier stuck his head out. Seeing the photographer, "he rapped a grenade against his helmet to start the fuse, then lobbed it at me."[51] "There wasn't much choice at the time," Lowery recalled. "I dove over the side of the mountain, rolling and sliding about 40 feet."[52] Although he successfully avoided the grenade, his camera was smashed in his tumble. Miraculously, the film was not ruined. This lucky fluke preserved invaluable documentation of the capture of Suribachi. And his timely leap over the crater's rim preserved the life of the photographer responsible for that documentation.

As Lowery, skinned and bleeding, limped down the steep slope toward the beach, where he hoped to locate another camera, he encountered no further challenges from Suribachi's Japanese defenders. All he met was a stream of Marines, some carrying electronic equipment to set up an American observation post at the mountain's summit. Then, as he neared the bottom, he passed three photographers slogging up the slope. Two of the group were acquaintances and fellow Marines: 5th Division motion picture photographer Sergeant William H. Genaust and still photographer Private First Class Robert R. Campbell. The third, a slender man with a jaunty mustache, was a civilian. Lowery told the trio he already had pictures of the flag raising. The civilian, whom he did not know, "sort of looked disappointed." To encourage him, Lowery quickly added: "You should go up there. There is a hell of a view of the harbor."[53] It was not an occasion for formal introductions, so Lowery did not get the civilian photographer's name.[54] That would come later, and under circumstances utterly unimaginable to the parties concerned.

Coming ashore from the *Bayfield*, Sherrod jotted these details in his small combat notebook:

> 1140 approaching control boat in LSM. Can see troops standing on Suribachi & flag flying.
> Walked on to 5th Div CP. Young, blue-eyed Lt Col Bob Williams, exec. of the 28th came by--is congratulated on taking Suribachi. Took it with little opposition.[55]

Then on page 50 of Sherrod's notebook, this entry, recorded later that afternoon at two o'clock:

> "Is Suribachi worth story?"[56]

NOTES

1. Smith and Finch, *Coral and Brass*, 259.

2. Sherrod Notebook 6, 45-46.

3. Peatross to Hemingway, letter dated March 31, 1986, quoted in Albert Hemingway, *Ira Hayes, Pima Marine* (Lanham, Md.: University Press of America, 1988), 99.

4. Ibid.

5. Ibid.

6. Ibid. Company E's former commander, Severance, agreed that it was Liversedge who selected Schrier "because he'd worked with him in the raiders; he knew he understood how to call in artillery. He was my company exec. All three of my platoon leaders were out of commission" (Severance interview with the authors, October 27, 1993).

7. Severance to Wetenhall, letter dated July 24, 1989. "As I recall, they [the 3rd Platoon] were closest to the battalion command post" (Severance interview with the authors, October 27, 1993).

8. Wheeler, *Bloody Battle for Suribachi,* 126-127.

9. Wheeler, *Iwo,* 155.

10. Annex to CT 28 Action Report, D+4. See Appendix A of this book.

11. Severance interview with the authors, October 27, 1993.

12. Ibid.

13. Naylor interview with the authors, April 16, 1993.

14. Severance interview with the authors, October 27, 1993.

15. Naylor interview with the authors, April 16, 1993. Severance was also on alert. He feared that the Japanese "would shoot the hell out of the four-man patrol. But when they didn't, I thought they were waiting for a larger unit" (Severance interview with the authors, October 27, 1993).

16. Naylor interview with the authors, April 16, 1993.

17. Ibid.

18. Watson interviews with the authors, May 28, 1993, and June 30, 1993.

19. Watson interview with the authors, May 28, 1993.

20. Ibid.

21. Ibid.

22. Ibid.

23. Wheeler, *Iwo,* 155.

24. Conner, *The Spearhead,* 65; Bernard C. Nalty, *The United States Marines on Iwo Jima* (Washington, D.C.: Historical Division, Headquarters, U.S. Marine Corps, 1970 ed.), 5.

25. G. G. Wells interview with the authors, October 15, 1992. Severance reports that he didn't know his 3rd Platoon was carrying a flag up Suribachi (Severance interview with the authors, October 27, 1993).

26. Wheeler interview with the authors, February 5, 1993.

27. J. K. Wells interview with the authors, May 21, 1993.

28. Robeson interview with the authors, June 8, 1993. In neither the authors' interview with Robeson nor any other interviews with the survivors of Suribachi is there evidence to support the claim that a flag raising had long been the focus of attention for Marines on Iwo Jima.

29. Lindberg interview with the authors, May 25, 1993.

30. *The Pensacola* (Florida) *Journal,* February 21, 1985.

31. Lindberg interview with the authors, May 25, 1993; Watson interview with the authors, May 28, 1993.

32. Conner, *The Spearhead,* 65.

33. *Blade-Tribune* (Oceanside, Calif.), May 29, 1988.

34. Raymond Henri et al., *The U.S. Marines on Iwo Jima* (New York: Dial Press, 1945), 72.

35. Lindberg interview with the authors, May 25, 1993.

36. *Los Angeles Times*, March 3, 1983.

37. Robeson interview with the authors, June 8, 1993.

38. From the photographic evidence provided by Lowery, it is evident that Thomas did not raise the first flag on Suribachi as a solo act, nor did he raise it "during the height of battle" as originally reported in the *New York Times*. *Newsweek*'s account was equally misleading when it attributed the flag raising to "a small patrol" later followed by a "40-man patrol."

39. Lindberg interview with the authors, May 25, 1993.

40. *Pensacola* (Florida) *Journal*, February 21, 1985. It is interesting to note, in light of subsequent false charges that Rosenthal posed or staged the second flag raising, that Lowery, as a photographer, actually interacted with the Marines raising the first flag. Lowery thereby influenced the precise timing of that original flag raising. As a fellow Marine, Lowery was free to do so; his conduct was in no sense improper. Rosenthal, a civilian, did *not* order or direct the raisers of the second flag, and in no way influenced that event.

41. Lindberg interview with the authors, May 25, 1993; *Los Angeles Times*, March 3, 1983.

42. Smith and Finch, *Coral and Brass*, 261-262.

43. Walter Millis, ed., *The Forrestal Diaries* (New York: Viking Press, 1951), 30.

44. Tatum interview with the authors, October 8, 1993.

45. Sherrod, *On to Westward*, 191-192.

46. See Appendix A.

47. Wheeler, *Iwo*, 159. It was ironic that Wheeler, destined to be the chronicler of the 3rd Platoon, was not with his unit on its historic ascent of Suribachi. Evacuated two days earlier, Wheeler had no idea his old platoon had scaled the mountain. When he heard the commotion that followed the first flag raising, he was in his berth below deck on a hospital ship. He feared the noise was in response to another Japanese *kamikaze* attack. Finally, someone came and told him the good news. But he still didn't know his platoon was involved. He never saw either flag fly from the summit of Suribachi, and he only learned of his platoon's role a month later when his ship reached San Francisco. Wheeler interview with the authors, February 5, 1993.

48. Robeson interview with the authors, June 8, 1993; Lindberg interview with the authors, May 25, 1993.

49. Robeson interview with the authors, June 8, 1993.

50. *Blade-Tribune* (Oceanside, Calif.), May 29, 1988.

51. Wheeler, *Iwo*, 161.

52. *Los Angeles Times*, March 3, 1983.

53. Ibid.

54. Rosenthal interview with the authors, November 5, 1992.

55. Sherrod Notebook 6, 47-48 and 53.

56. Ibid., 50.

Chapter 4

A Second Flag for Suribachi

When Robert Sherrod made his notebook query at 2:00 on February 23, 1945, he was unaware that the flag he saw flying at Suribachi's summit was not the same one he had observed that morning at 11:40. In this ignorance, he was not alone. Most of the men on Iwo Jima that day knew nothing about the raising of a second flag, although this event would produce half a century of debate, much of it acrimonious. The American public has been a silent and, for the most part, ill-informed partner in this debate.

Some of the public's misinformation can be explained by the desire of the press to tell a good story. The battle for Iwo Jima, however, should have been a story that required no embellishment. There was blood and glory in sufficient quantity to satisfy even the most demanding reader. But as the news accounts indicate, in the eyes of some members of the American press, the *realities* of the first flag raising on Suribachi were just the jumping-off point.[1]

It was quite a leap from the facts of that tense but uneventful climb up Suribachi (made, according to Corporal Harold Keller, a member of the 3rd Platoon, under conditions "about as dangerous as a Sunday School picnic") to the versions published in newspapers and news weeklies during that early spring of 1945.[2] Sergeant Henry Hansen and the members of his platoon would hardly have recognized themselves in the lurid accounts fed to their families at home by a sensationalizing press.

Years later, Company E's commander, Dave Severance, would reflect: "To this day I can't imagine why the Japanese did not defend Suribachi. They could have tied up a whole regiment for days with a small defending force and a number of grenades!"[3]

The passive behavior of Suribachi's Japanese defensive troops was equally unimaginable to some members of the press. So they imagined a scenario more in keeping with their expectations and with those of their American public back home.

But all the inaccuracies and distortions connected with the first flag raising would pale to insignificance in comparison with the confusion wrought by misreportings of the second flag raising. It was, perhaps, the very fact that a second flag was raised that would seem suspicious to those not privy to the reasons for the decision to add a flag to Suribachi. What follows is an attempt to lay out those reasons: to tell who gave the orders and why. Most likely, had it not been for one photograph, it would have made little difference to the American public just how two flags came to be raised on Suribachi and it surely would be of little interest to anyone today.

So half a century after the events of February 23, 1945, here are the facts, insofar as they can be established. To Sherrod's question: "Is Suribachi worth story?" the answer still seems to be "yes."

D DAY + 4: FEBRUARY 23, 1945

The brief firefight with those few Japanese who came out of their caves on Suribachi soon subsided into that tedious yet dangerous work called mopping up. For Private First Class James A. Robeson this meant descending from the volcano's rim, where the small American flag snapped in a stiff wind, to the bowl of the crater, where protection from the weather was exchanged for potential exposure to whatever Japanese were still concealed in the volcano's caves. "After we put the first flag up, they sent my platoon down in the crater, because they could see barrels and stuff down there and they didn't know what they were."[4]

Robeson's 3rd Platoon, Company E, was soon reinforced by what was left of Company F, commanded by Captain Arthur H. Naylor.

It was later in the day. It may have been the noon hour, or eleven o'clock, for all I know. Colonel Johnson ordered me to take up my own company, what was left of them. To go up on the top and to search out around the perimeter. I was down inside the crater, throwing hand grenades down into the caves.[5]

Sergeant Sherman Watson, who had led the first scouting party up Suribachi, returned from his brief breakfast break to climb the mountain for the second time, now in the company of his commanding officer. "I'd guess we were back up there before noon; quite a bit before noon. Mostly we went around the rim. Then another group of guys went around the bottom [of the crater], just clearing it out, looking for stuff. But there was no stuff that I ever saw."[6]

Naylor, in the three or four hours he and his men spent securing the summit, also recalled seeing very little "stuff," and no real action. "I only saw two Japanese come out of caves, and I didn't have a rifle. I only had my .45, so there was no way I could hit them. I saw them come out and look, and then run back into their cave. There were still a lot of caves out of which they were trying to get Japanese to surrender."[7]

The Marines had virtually no success in convincing the Japanese to abandon their underground fortress. So demolition teams with explosives and flamethrowers were ordered to seal off the caves. Contrary to some accounts, Naylor had *not* been sent up Suribachi to carry the congratulations of Vice Admiral Richmond Kelley Turner, Lieutenant General Holland M. Smith, Colonel Harry Liversedge, or anybody else to First Lieutenant Harold George Schrier and his men.[8] Naylor never even spoke to Schrier: "I don't recall talking with any officer in either unit on either side of me during the whole operation."[9] Suribachi was still a potentially dangerous location, and Naylor had been sent there to help secure the mountain, not to engage in social pleasantries with his brother officers.

Meanwhile, down at the base of the volcano at the 2nd Battalion's command post, Lieutenant Colonel Chandler Johnson was making preparations to send another flag up the mountain. It was this flag that would, both literally and figuratively, supplant the flag raised earlier that morning by the men of Schrier's platoon.

The man who had carried the first flag for Suribachi ashore in his map case, 2nd Battalion Adjutant George Greeley Wells, provided this explanation for Johnson's decision to send a second flag to the top of Suribachi:

> Now, about the second flag. The story that I remember very distinctly is that the Colonel got a call from Regiment which said that Forrestal wanted the flag and wanted to congratulate everybody. And the Colonel said to me, "The hell with it! This battalion earned this flag! Get *another* flag." He ordered me to put it [the first flag] in my safe and keep it, and the hell with Forrestal.[10]

In a CNBC television special for Veterans' Day, 1991, Wells was interviewed by Cassandra Clayton. She commented: "When Secretary of the Navy James Forrestal saw the Stars and Stripes waving on Mount Suribachi he knew that history was in the making and he sent word that he wanted that flag for posterity." Wells affirmed: "That was the message that *we* got. And our colonel turned to me and said 'Dammit, we're not going to give up *our* flag! Our people have fought for it and we're going to keep it. Go down and get another flag and we'll raise that, and that's the one we'll give Forrestal.'"[11] Other accounts have suggested that the greater visibility of a larger flag was Johnson's primary consideration in ordering a second flag, since the first flag measured only 28 inches by 54 inches.[12]

Whatever Johnson's personal reasons might have been for sending a second flag up Suribachi, he soon had substantial encouragement from a higher level of command: Major General Keller E. Rockey. Warrant Officer Norman T. Hatch, assigned to the 5th Division as chief photo officer on Iwo Jima (with about thirty photographers under his command), recounted this conversation with Lieutenant Colonel George Roll, head of Division Intelligence (D-2), to whom Hatch and all other division photo and public information officers reported. On the morning of February 23, shortly after the first flag was raised, Roll came up to Hatch at the 5th Division command post and said: "Norm, the general has decided that flag is not large enough up there for the rest of the island to see. He wants to put up an official flag which will be much larger. This will also give the ships at sea an opportunity to see that we own part of the island now. You'd better have some photographers go up there ready to shoot it."[13]

Hatch speculated that Rockey thought it was worth the effort to put up a larger flag because "he figured it would be a good morale factor."[14] In any case, two commanding officers, one at the battalion level and one at the division level, each arrived spontaneously at the same conclusion: that a second flag was required for Suribachi.

So Hatch assigned one of his division still photographers, Private First Class Robert Campbell, and one of his motion picture photographers, Sergeant William Genaust, to head up Suribachi and get some pictures of the second flag.[15] Technical Sergeant Louis R. Lowery, who had photographed the first flag raising, was not a member of Hatch's divisional photo pool. Lowery, although a good friend and a regular visitor to Hatch's desk at the division command post, worked directly for *Leatherneck* magazine and did not report to Hatch. No photographers from the division pool had been specifically assigned to accompany Schrier's patrol up Suribachi for the first flag raising. This fact rather undercuts the credibility of writers who have claimed that the Marine Corps all along planned to stage a flag raising on Suribachi as some sort of elaborate public relations ploy.[16]

Correcting much of the misinformation as to why a second flag was sent up Suribachi, who procured that flag and from what source, as well as the especially fraught issue of who actually *carried* the flag up the mountain, is the research of Colonel Dave E. Severance, USMC (Ret.), former commander of Company E. Severance, concerned about all the inaccuracies surrounding the second flag raising, including some false statements by putative participants, began collecting statements to forward to the commandant of the Marine Corps in 1986.[17]

Among the statements in Severance's files was one from the 2nd Battalion's former Assistant Operations Officer, Albert Theodore Tuttle.

Most of the articles I have read about the flag raising on Mount Suribachi state that an "unknown Marine" went aboard LST 779 and asked for a large battle flag. I am that "unknown" Marine. . . . When the first flag was raised, which Lieutenant Schrier had carried up the hill, all of us at the base of Suribachi joined Lieutenant Colonel Johnson in three "hurrahs." He then turned to me and said, "Go down to one of the ships on the beach and get a large battle flag--large enough so that the men on the other end of the island can see it. It will lift their spirits also." Obedient to that command I walked down to the beach and went aboard LST 779. I asked the on-duty officer for a large battle flag. He was surprised by such a request and asked why I wanted it. I told him that if he wanted to see his flag up on top of Mount Suribachi, he should go and get one for me. Shortly he returned with the large battle flag.[18]

The next piece of the puzzle was found in a letter to the editors of *Time* magazine, a letter from Mrs. H. Randolph Wood quoting her son, Ensign Alan S. Wood, USNR, the communications officer of LST 779. Wood was the officer who had given Tuttle the flag.

A . . . marine came on board asking for a larger flag, so I gave him our only large flag. . . .
    The now famous flag was one I ran across one day at Pearl Harbor while I was rummaging around the salvage depot. It was in a duffle bag with some old signal flags--probably from a decommissioned destroyer or destroyer escort. It looked brand new and was folded neatly.[19]

Tuttle described the next step in the large flag's journey to the summit:

When I returned to the command post with the flag I asked Colonel Johnson if I should take the flag up to Lieutenant Schrier. He said, "Yes." After going only a few yards he called me back. "We have just received word from Lieutenant Schrier to send up some batteries for their SCR-300 radio because messages are coming in very faintly." Since the Colonel's runner from Company E, Private First Class Rene Gagnon, was headed up the hill with the batteries, the Colonel suggested that Gagnon carry the flag; whereupon I gave the flag to him. He carried it up the hill and helped to raise it as he has said.[20]

Still another piece in the puzzle of the second flag for Suribachi was supplied as recently as November 1991 by a letter from Norman F. Boas. Boas quoted an account given to him by Joseph Hopkins, captain of LST 779 from which the large flag was procured: "When we had stopped over in Pearl Harbor someone had given us a rather torn and battered flag that had flown over a heavy cruiser, that we stored in our flag locker. . . . [At Iwo Jima] a marine came aboard my ship and asked for the largest Navy flag we had."[21]
So the second, larger flag (weighing in at 4 feet 8 inches by 8 feet) was fetched from LST 779 by Tuttle and carried to Johnson's battalion command post.[22]
The next stage in the flag's journey was its conveyance up the mountain to

Schrier. Tuttle was not the only man who expected to carry the larger flag up to the summit. Company E's First Sergeant, John A. Daskalakis, had also anticipated making that trek. On February 10, 1986, he wrote this account to his former company commander:

> Lt Col C.W. Johnson, CO, 2-28, called me back to the Bn CP on D+4, 23 February 1945. When I arrived, our patrol 3rd Platoon + 3d MG Section, under Lt. H.G. Schrier's command, was climbing Mount Suribachi. We watched as they made the climb and eventually flew a flag which was barely visible. Lt Col Johnson instructed me that I was to wait for a larger flag which he had sent for and then take it to Lt. Schrier. He then went to his radio and had a lengthy transmission with the patrol leader. During this time, Lt A. Tuttle arrived with a flag. Lt Col Johnson finished his transmission, turned to me and said he had changed his mind. A radio battery was needed by the patrol. Lt Col Johnson said our runner, PFC Rene Gagnon could take both to Lt. Schrier. I then returned to my unit and reported to my Company Commander, Capt. Dave E. Severance.
>
>   The above is a true account of the "second flag."[23]

In December 1992, Daskalakis reconfirmed his 1986 statement in an interview with the authors. Daskalakis said Johnson did not discuss with him *why* he wanted a second flag taken to the volcano's crest; he just handed the flag to Daskalakis and said, "Take it up to George Schrier." He also instructed Daskalakis to tell Schrier to keep the first flag. (This story corroborates Greeley Wells's account.) Daskalakis already had the larger flag bundled up inside his jacket and was preparing to leave the command post when Johnson remanded his order. He told Daskalakis to give the flag to one of the runners from Company E, Private First Class Rene Gagnon. Daskalakis explained that Gagnon was a company runner, assigned to carry information between battalion and company command posts. Runners were needed as backup for radio communications between the units. As Daskalakis put it, "You couldn't depend on transmission to get through. We sent the company runners (we had at least two) in relays back and forth, so one runner was there all the time. He [Gagnon] just happened to be there."[24] So it was by the purest chance that Gagnon carried the second flag up Suribachi and into the spotlight of publicity that was to dazzle the lives of everyone connected with that flag.

At some point Gagnon, carrying fresh radio batteries and the new flag to Schrier, made contact with four men from Company E's 2nd Platoon: Sergeant Mike Strank, Corporal Harlon Block, Private First Class Franklin Sousley, and Private First Class Ira Hayes.[25] Severance, having received a request "to send a detail to lay a sound power telephone wire up the volcano," had ordered Strank to collect a small patrol and lay the wire.[26]

It was mere coincidence, then, that the four-man patrol running communication wire and Gagnon, carrying a large American flag tucked in his jacket, were all headed up Suribachi at approximately the same time that morning. Strank's patrol had not been ordered to deliver a flag, although once all five men had arrived at the summit, Strank reportedly took the flag from Gagnon and presented it to Schrier with these orders: "Colonel Johnson wants this big flag run up high so every son of a bitch on this whole cruddy island can see it."[27]

Private First Class Wayne Bellamy and several men of Company A, 1st Battalion, were exploring the outer surface of the volcano's north slope when they heard a shout from the crest that a pole was needed to raise the newly arrived larger flag. Bellamy reported: "There was a large tangle of steel and debris just in front of us. It looked like an emplacement that had been blown apart. We found a length of pipe but had to move a lot of other steel to get it. I helped to take the pipe within a hundred feet of the summit, then sat down and rested."[28] Schrier, presumably unwilling to have even a moment elapse in which there was no American flag flying on top of Suribachi, ordered that the second flag, once attached to Bellamy's pipe, be raised simultaneously with the lowering of the first flag on its pole.[29] Raising the second flag on its improvised staff was not as simple a procedure as might be supposed. The large flag itself was heavy and cumbersome. The metal pipe had not been designed to carry a flag. The rocky, rubble-strewn ground at the volcano's rim was no more cooperative than the sands of Iwo's landing beaches. And, like an insult added to an injury, there was the wind--tearing at the flag, snatching words from the mouth, and scattering them like volcanic ash.[30] The summit of Suribachi, despite the fact that Japanese opposition was far less formidable than anticipated, was not a hospitable place to be that winter February day.

When the second flag went up to replace its predecessor, it was an event of no importance to the Marines engaged in securing the mountaintop for American occupation. There was no cheering from the troops down below. Most didn't even notice that there had been a changing of the guard. Down at the 2nd Battalion command post, Daskalakis, who himself had come within an inch of carrying the second flag to the summit, paid the matter no attention. As he recalled years later: "We didn't think it was a big deal at all. We thought it was run-of-the-mill stuff."[31] Severance recently commented that "most of the regiment didn't even know there was a second flag up there."[32] He believed that about an hour and a half separated the two flag raisings. The first flag was reported as being raised at various moments from 10:20 to 10:37 that morning. By Severance's calculations, that would place the second flag raising at about noon. Other sources contend that the flag went up as late as 2:00 that afternoon.[33] The problem of pinning down the time arises from the fact that there are no entries in the journals of the 2nd Battalion, the 28th Regiment, or the 5th Division that record the event or its time. The second flag raising was, at the time it occurred, a *non*event. A photograph would soon change all that.

So when Time/Life correspondent Sherrod, unaware that he was looking up at a second flag, wrote in his notebook at 2:00 on February 23: "Is Suribachi worth story?" it was not an unreasonable question. There was even room to doubt whether the *original* flag raising deserved more than a few lines. After all, at this point the battle for Iwo Jima was far from won.

Only later would the irony of Sherrod's notebook entry become apparent. In the margin of the page, Sherrod added (at a later date): "We didn't know yet about Rosenthal (Joe) picture."[34]

But the world soon would.

NOTES

1. The authors have no desire to detract from the courage and integrity of many newsmen who, at great personal risk, accurately reported the Iwo Jima story.

2. Corporal Harold Keller, quoted in Richard Wheeler, *A Special Valor* (New York: Harper and Row, 1983), 381.

3. Severance to Wetenhall, letter dated July 24, 1989.

4. Robeson interview with the authors, June 8, 1993.

5. Naylor interview with the authors, April 16, 1993.

6. Watson interview with the authors, May 28, 1993.

7. Naylor interview with the authors, April 16, 1993.

8. Henri et al., *The U.S. Marines on Iwo Jima*, 73: "Captain Art Naylor (Port Jervis, N.Y.), a chunky, blond man with no hat or helmet and a tear in the seat of his pants, appeared on the rim of the crater to shout the congratulations of Vice Admiral Turner and Lieutenant General Smith. The men paused to listen and went on with their work."

9. Naylor interview with the authors, April 16, 1993.

10. G. G. Wells interview with the authors, October 15, 1992.

11. "The Real Story," November 11, 1991, CNBC telecast.

12. William S. Bartley, *Iwo Jima: Amphibious Epic* (Washington, D.C.: Historical Branch, G-3 Division, Headquarters, U.S. Marine Corps, 1954), 76.

13. Hatch interview with the authors, December 28, 1992.

14. Ibid.

15. Ibid.

16. For example: "Marine publicists readied flag raisings"; "Suribachi and the flag were routine publicity." See William Bradford Huie, *The Hero of Iwo Jima* (New York: Signet Books, 1962), 32.

17. Severance was acting in response to claims by former Master Sergeant Carl Jackel that it was Jackel himself who had carried the second flag up Suribachi, "a claim that Jackel has been making for over ten years and which is false" (Severance to commandant, letter dated March 14, 1986, USMC Historical Center).

18. Tuttle to Severance, statement dated February 13, 1986, USMC Historical Center.

19. Mrs. Wood, letter to *Time* magazine, July 9, 1945, 4.

20. Tuttle to Severance, statement dated February 13, 1986, USMC Historical Center. In the December 7, 1986, issue of the Mormon Church periodical, *Church News*, an obituary notice for the November 28, 1986, death of Theodore A. Tuttle describes him

as "the marine who went back to get the flag to give the men who planted it atop Mt. Suribachi." Even so minor a role as that played by Tuttle in connection with the second flag raising was sufficient to cast a beam of public recognition forty-one years after the event.

21. Boas, letter to *New York Times*, November 16, 1991. The flag, as can be seen in photos taken at the time of its raising, was, as Ensign Wood stated, a new one. The winds of Suribachi tattered it.

22. Bartley, *Iwo Jima*, 76. Considerable misinformation has been disseminated about the procurement of the second flag. Bill Ross, in *Iwo Jima*, does not credit Tuttle with obtaining the second flag from LST 779. He designates LST 799 as the ship, calls the flag which Wood obtained from the Pearl Harbor salvage depot "the ship's rarely used ceremonial flag," and says that (instead of Tuttle) "a runner, a lisping corporal called 'Wabbit'" got the flag from Ensign Wood. Ross does not further identify "Wabbit" or give the source for this version of the story. See Bill D. Ross, *Iwo Jima* (New York: Vanguard Press, 1985), 99 and 101. Richard Newcomb, in *Iwo Jima* (New York: Holt, Rinehart and Winston, 1965), conveys the same misinformation on pages 166 and 169.

The authors were able to track down a partial identification of "Wabbit" through an interview with former 2nd Battalion Adjutant G. Greeley Wells, who described "Wabbit" as a runner from Company F, given that nickname because he lisped (Wells interview with the authors, October 15, 1992). This information was confirmed by Company F's former commander, Arthur Naylor (Naylor interview with the authors, April 16, 1992).

23. Daskalakis to Severance, letter dated February 10, 1986, USMC Historical Center.

24. Daskalakis interview with the authors, December 29, 1992. This account differed slightly from Tuttle's, which indicated that Tuttle gave Gagnon the flag.

25. Severance interview with the authors, October 27, 1993. Huie incorrectly identified Hayes (and, presumably, the other three patrol members) as belonging to Schrier's *3rd* Platoon, which had raised the first flag earlier that morning (Huie, *The Hero of Iwo Jima*, 32).

26. Severance to Albee, letter dated December 2, 1992; Severance interview with the authors, October 27, 1993.

27. Wheeler, *A Special Valor*, 383. There are discrepancies between this version of the flag's conveyance up Suribachi and that of Hayes, as reported by Hy Hurwitz in the *Boston Globe*, May 16, 1945. In the Hurwitz article, Hayes credits his patrol leader, Strank, with carrying the flag up Suribachi and with revealing their flag-raising duties to Hayes and his patrol mates "halfway up" the mountain.

28. Wheeler, *Iwo*, 162.

29. Rosenthal interview with the authors, November 5, 1992.

30. Burmeister interview with the authors, January 21, 1993. "High atop the mountain the wind velocity was terrific." See James E. Fisk, "Mass on a Volcano," *Catholic World*, Vol. 168, January 1949, 316.

31. Daskalakis interview with the authors, December 29, 1992.

32. Severance interview with the authors, October 27, 1993.

33. Harold Evans, editor of the *London Sunday Times*, gives 12:15 as the time in his 1978 book, *Pictures on a Page* (Belmont, Calif.: Wadsworth, 1978), 145. Joe Rosenthal estimates the time as about noon (Rosenthal interview with the authors, November 5, 1992).

34. Sherrod Notebook 6, 50.

Chapter 5

The Photograph

For half a century he has told this story. Told it with remarkable consistency and vividness. Told it first on Guam to his fellow war correspondents and photographers. Told it with some trepidation to his Associated Press employers in New York. Told it to a flood of journalists in 1945, then to a gush of them as each anniversary rolled around: the tenth, the twenty-fifth, the fortieth. He has told it to the Marines and to the American public: making speeches, writing letters to all sorts of editors, trying to set the record straight once and for all.

Now he's outlived current events and become a part of history. So he tells this story to a generation of historians for whom Iwo Jima constitutes research, not memories. This aging, near-blind photographer, living alone in a small San Francisco apartment cluttered with boxes of the past: Joe Rosenthal, who took a photograph one February day in 1945 of six men raising a flag on top of an extinct volcano in the Pacific, and in that 1/400 of a second created the most famous war image of all time.

He was, as he himself affirms, an improbable candidate for a brush with immortality: five feet four-and-one-half inches tall, 140 pounds, eyesight so poor--1/20 of normal vision--that he wore thick-lensed glasses. The Army, Navy, and the Marine Corps all had rejected him for active service when, after the 1941 bombing of Pearl Harbor, he tried to volunteer. Joe Rosenthal, 4-F.[1]

It was only by a bit of stringpulling that the Maritime Service was induced to waive the eye test and admit Rosenthal to its ranks, where he served as a warrant officer, taking pictures of life aboard an American convoy bound for England in July 1943. He was teamed with a New York writer, Bill Donoghoe, documenting U.S. convoy activities in the Atlantic. He spent seven months in the Maritime Service, traveling from England to the North African theater, where he developed colitis. Returning to the States in 1944, he joined the Associated Press with the hope of seeing the war in the Pacific. He more than got his wish. On March 27, 1944, he left San Francisco, the city he had called home since 1930, for an assignment with the Wartime Still Pictures Pool, a collaborative organization of the civilian photo services covering the war. He photographed the invasions of New Guinea, Hollandia, Guam, Peleliu, and Angaur. Then, at age 33, more than ten years older than most of the Marines whose actions he was recording, he found himself involved in their amphibious landing on Iwo Jima.[2]

Rosenthal's preferred arrival time on the beach at Iwo Jima was H-Hour plus 1 (ten o'clock in the morning): "At Saipan I . . . told the public relations officer that I had to get onto the beach earlier. 'It's the difference between getting the pictures I want,' I said, 'and not getting them.' . . . at Guam I had learned that the best time to shoot landing pictures is from H-Hour + 1 to H + 3. If you land earlier you are only pinned down and in the way."[3]

Rosenthal attached himself to the 4th Marine Division, leaving his ship at 6:30 on D-Day to load into an LCVP landing boat with fifteen Marines carrying mortar ammunition to the beach. He was in the boat for more than five hours, that time spent circling about, waiting for the chaos on shore to subside so that his boat could land. Their tidy landing schedule had been seriously disrupted by the heavy surf swamping the Higgins boats, by the volcanic sands paralyzing the amtracs, and by the Japanese mortar fire strewing the beaches with the debris of machinery and men. Rosenthal recalled his first minutes on Iwo Jima and his first photographs of the Marines as they struggled to get off the lethal beaches.

> No man who survived that beach can tell you how he did it. It was like walking through rain and not getting wet, and there is no way you can explain it.
>
> I remember clearly the deep, loose, dark-gray volcanic sand terracing up about 15 feet at a time, and the parts of bodies and the large darker patches of blood seeping into that sand. I remember shooting some pictures of the Marines plowing across the beach, and then I moved off to the left behind a smashed blockhouse.[4]

Rosenthal survived the hazards of D-Day and spent the next ten days on Iwo, taking a total of sixty-five pictures. Much of his time was devoted to getting back and forth from ship to shore. One day it took him nineteen hours, moving from one landing craft to another, to get to the command ship just three miles offshore.[5]

It was on board the command ship, *Eldorado,* that he wrote the captions for his photographs and prepared his film package for the daily transmission by seaplane to Guam. There all film was processed, reviewed by the military censors, approved (or rejected) by the picture-pool coordinator, Murray Befeler, and radiophotoed back to San Francisco to be retransmitted over the wire service for possible publication in newspapers all over the country.[6]

Rosenthal left Iwo Jima the evening of February 22, taking a load of film out to the *Eldorado* for transmission to Guam. He described the events of the following day in an extensive interview with the authors at his San Francisco apartment on November 5, 1992.   His account provides the frame of circumstances for the Pulitzer Prize-winning photograph that has become the most widely reproduced and re-created photograph of all time.[7]

I was on the command ship overnight, and in the morning I was going to catch whatever boat was available from the command ship that would carry me back to the beach. Then we got the word that Howlin' Mad Smith [Lieutenant General Holland M. Smith, commander of Marine Expeditionary Troops] and the Secretary of the Navy, James V. Forrestal, were going to view the beach from another boat. They had gone ahead to this boat. Bill Hipple [correspondent for *Newsweek]* and I, with one or two other guys (I think there might have been a military correspondent) went down this long gangway, just like on a big passenger ship. The sea was quite heavy, about ten-foot swells, and the small boat (we had to get on the small boat which would carry us to the larger boat where Forrestal and Smith were) was bobbing up and down. The gangway at the bottom of a little platform was dipping down into the waves, and we had to time this.

I had a bag over my shoulder with my film and other things: extra pair of socks, package of rations. I also had a Rolleiflex, a smaller camera. I took this for the lesser shots, personal shots. For the action stuff I depended on my larger camera, which was a press-type camera, 4 X 5 Speed Graphic, that I was used to, accustomed to for years. It was dependable.

As we bobbed up and down, I passed over my large camera and the bag. I swung it by the strap. As the boats bobbed up and down, I swung it over, and we were close enough [to the other boat] that someone simply grabbed that. I still had, hanging over my shoulder, the waterproof bag that contained my Rolleiflex. That *did* go in the drink. It was waterproofed, but still a couple of drops did get into the mechanism, and the following pictures showed that. I didn't clean it out, because I had film in it.

But the Speed Graphic was not in the waterproof bag. If it had been, it probably would have sunk and I'd have lost it. In which case, I'd go around trying to beg another from the Navy supply of cameras. I was fortunate in saving it and the film. The film packs were in the same bag. And a dry pair of socks.

The steps that I was on were slippery, and I just misjudged the step. I slid and fell into the water. My helmet came off.

Now, I used to smoke a lot, and I would smoke with a holder, leaving my hands free to talk. I remember bobbing up and down as the

huge waves would go up and up. The boat rolled over and I looked up
at it, and I said, "Joe, this is the way to go." The boat hung there. I
could see the tilt of the tillerman on the raised aft platform. He was
furiously spinning that wheel. I looked up and said, "I hope it works."
It hung above me by five or six feet. I could easily have been crushed
between the two boats, because they came this close--five feet. He was
trying to get that tiller to engage with the water, but it just hung there.
It hung there, and then the boats drifted apart.

When I was pulled over to the other boat, the cigarette holder was
still in my mouth, with a bedraggled cigarette.[8]

What would become the most significant day of Rosenthal's professional life
had almost ended before it began. But undeterred by his near-fatal accident,
Rosenthal, now soaking wet, joined his friend Hipple for the interview with
Smith and Forrestal. At the conclusion of the interview, Rosenthal saw a photo
opportunity, and asked them:

"Do you mind if I take a photo of the two of you, so that I can get
Suribachi in the background?" They were quite congenial about it, and
I took the picture. Then Hipple and I left.

We got into a boat that took us closer to shore and then we
transferred to still another boat--that was a larger boat; I think an LCT,
large enough to land tanks. And from that we made our way in to the
shore. It was on *that* boat that we heard a sudden noise. It has been
reported that there was very loud cheering and whistles blowing, and all
that. To tell you the truth, *I* didn't hear *that* kind of commotion. What
I heard was what I thought was normal front-line action. There was
cheering and all. But not enough for me to think that something
explosive was going on. The boatswain told us that he'd heard over the
radio that a patrol was going up there [Suribachi]. Hipple took his
glasses to look up there, then he passed them on over to me. What I
thought I was looking for was actually to see a group of men on the side
of the mountain going up. But apparently they had already reached the
top and spread out.[9]

One of the first things that we did when we came ashore (Bill
Hipple and I), we went by a kind of dump of rifles and helmets. It was
like a field of helmets about 20 feet square, belonging to people who
were killed or wounded. I went over there and picked out one, because
I'd lost mine in the sea. The fascinating thing about this helmet was
there was an indentation, like from shrapnel or a bullet, I couldn't tell
which.

Bill and I started to go toward the rise of ground at the base of
Suribachi. It's at the narrow neck of the island, only about 800 yards all

the way across there.

We passed over an area that had some tiny white flags, little strips of cloth which were markers for possible land mines. Some of them were knocked over, kicked accidentally or otherwise. But they were still markers of a pathway. We started to go softly, tippy-toe, and suddenly we looked at each other. The same thought: "What the hell difference is it if we walk softly or we just walk normally?" We guessed that if some of the markers had been knocked over, they had already been tested. As we walked another 50 feet or so a couple of Marines came up and said to us, "Hey, we got a couple of Japs trapped around the base of Suribachi."

Around that base apparently some of the Japanese who had hidden in these very intricate caves had come out and were trying to escape by sea. They had been noticed by these Marines, who were going to capture them, surround them. We both almost decided to go to the top [of Suribachi] later, and go see [the capture]. Bill said, "You better watch it, Joe." I forget now how he put it--almost to suggest I should be very careful. I said, "Yeah, well, I think between the two stories, I better go off and see about this flag." Bill went on with the Marines. So he never went up to the top [of Suribachi] that day.

After parting from Bill, one of the things I was looking for was Bob Campbell, whom I knew before the war. I knew he was out there. I was a little bit worried about him, you know, as a friend. I went over to the command post and checked there. I saw Johnson while I was bumming some rations. They were pretty awful. I wouldn't eat the whole ration. I would see cast-off cans. Guys wouldn't like this hash, so they'd throw it away. It was all I needed. That hash, cold hash. Boy, it was good. Even Spam. I don't eat Spam now.

I didn't really talk except a grunt or two with Johnson. I stopped there to get some more information about the guys up on top. There wasn't much information. They didn't tell me about the second flag. It couldn't have been deliberate. That was about eleven o'clock.

And then he [Campbell] appeared with Bill Genaust. They were in the 5th Division. They were division photographers.

I mentioned the flag. I don't know whether they knew at the time, or whether I was giving them fresh information. But I do know I mentioned it to them and said, "I understand that there's a flag up there and I want to go up." Then I said to them, "Let's go up. You fellows have rifles. You could protect me." You know, I kind of smirked about it.

So then we started going up the hill. We didn't stick together. We didn't go up shoulder-to-shoulder. We were often 50 to 100 feet apart; then we'd come back together, depending on what the terrain was like where we walked. Others came up to us or we encountered some others. By the time I got to the top, scattered over an area of say 50 square yards there probably were about 50, 60 people up there, with more coming along.[10]

One of the men Rosenthal encountered on his trek up Suribachi was Technical Sergeant Louis R. Lowery, the photographer for *Leatherneck* magazine. Lowery was limping down the mountain after a 40-foot tumble over the lip of the crater to avoid a well-aimed Japanese grenade. His camera was smashed, but his film of the first flag raising at the summit of Suribachi was fortunately undamaged. When he met Rosenthal, Sergeant William H. Genaust, and Private First Class Robert A. Campbell, the threesome were, according to Rosenthal's recollection, about one-third of the way up the mountain. At that time Lowery and Rosenthal were not acquainted, although Lowery knew Rosenthal's two Marine companions, motion picture photographer Genaust and still photographer Campbell.

"Rosenthal stopped me as I was heading toward the ship with my film," Lowery recalled.

"Rosenthal asked if I thought there was any use in his going up there. I told him I thought there were good shots to be had because you could see almost the whole beach, with a panorama of the ships and equipment below.

"He thanked me, and then kept on going."[11]

Rosenthal recalled their brief encounter:

We hesitated for a minute, and Lowery was talking to the guys he knew. I don't know even to this day whether I precisely could quote him, but I know the sense of it: "I was already up there and I've already got pictures. You guys are late." We knew we were late [for the flag raising].

"It's a hell of a view up there." These things came in short phrases. I knew then that it meant that from up there I could see the shore with those ships unloading. I'd have the vantage point that the Japanese had when we were landing.

I didn't have any thought that there would be a second flag raising. Didn't know it until I got to the top.

It was not until I got to a rise near the top (at this moment I was 100 yards away) that over the brow I could see the [first] flag up there. And walking another 50 feet, then this pole emerges, that long pole with this little flag against the sky. Even now as I talk about it I get kind of a jolt. I stopped. Our flag. And then I went on. When I got closer,

I saw these guys working on a pole and I asked them what they were doing. I remember distinctly saying, "Hey, what's doing, fellows?" Just like that: the newspaperman coming in on the scene of the crime.[12]

Later, Rosenthal learned that Private First Class Rene A. Gagnon, a runner from the 2nd Battalion's Company E, had carried a second, larger flag up with a fresh radio battery for First Lieutenant Harold George Schrier's patrol. It was this flag, still in its triangular fold, that a group of men kneeling on the ground were trying to attach to a pipe.

They were having a little difficulty with getting a rope to tie on it. They wound and rewound the light rope line to fasten the flag's upper and lower left side to the staff so that it would not slip down.

The intent was a noble one, expressing the idea that "once our flag is up there, our flag is always up there. It's never going to be a moment that the American flag is not there. So, if they're going to take one down, we're not going to have a hiatus. We're going to raise another one."

It wasn't announced. It was something that we had to assume. Schrier wasn't talking to us. He was talking to the men who had the flag in their hands. I had to presume from the way that the men, when I first encountered them working on this flag, said that they were going to replace it, that they were going to do it simultaneously.

This is something I forgot. In my brief tour, my initial brief tour [around the summit], I asked if the guys who raised this [first] flag were around. It was my intention to get those first guys up there, to get a picture of them and their hometown names. "This is the squad that raised that first flag." Although I was not thinking in terms of first flag or second flag then. I asked, and I was given vague answers: "I don't know where they are." "Oh, one of them is around here somewhere." I did make an effort. I remember now, I made an effort to get them.

I positioned myself to get a flag going up. And my caption for the picture was "A flag going up on Suribachi." I had no idea, no reason for even dreaming that there was going to be a comparison or a discussion about which flag went up first.

So we started taking positions. I had to estimate how far back to go to get the whole picture, knowing the pole was about 18 or 20 feet long. Would I back up to make sure I could get a longitudinal? To make sure I got it, I started back downhill. To raise myself a little bit I found some old sandbags and a couple of rocks, and I pushed them together. There was a whole Japanese command post up there that had been destroyed by shellfire, by either aerial bombardment or naval bombardment. Anyway, I pushed those into position. I got up, and I figured that would be about it.

Genaust came across in front of me, going to the side a little--about arm's length--saying as he did so, "I'm not in your way, Joe?" I turned and said, "No, Bill." By being polite to each other we almost damned near missed it.

"There it goes, Bill!" I caught it out of the corner of my eye. Bill swung his movie camera up. I swung my camera up. Steady. Just time enough. Got to get it. It's on its way. Then it all came together. The wind caught the flag and passed it over the figures. Perfect! Otherwise, with inertia it would drag behind. No composition. Just noontime. The lighting was sculpture-type lighting. The men are straining because that is not a wooden flag pole. That is an iron pipe that had been left there for either drainage or a water system, I don't know what. The pipe probably weighed 150 pounds. It took all of those guys. And it needed that guy down in front to hold it into the ground. And the last figure, which is the Indian, throwing up his hands. All of those elements.[13]

In 1955 Rosenthal wrote:

I can best sum up what I feel after 10 years by saying that of all the elements that went into the making of this picture, the part I played was the least important. To get that flag up there, America's fighting men had to die on that island and on other islands and off the shores and in the air. What difference does it make who took the picture? I took it, but the Marines took Iwo Jima.[14]

Unaware that at age 33 he already had created his own defining moment, Rosenthal went about methodically completing his self-assigned work at the crest of Suribachi: looking for other photo opportunities in the activities of Marines securing the summit. The AP photographer was not alone in his work. There were other men with cameras present, plying their trade that day.

Pride of place had already gone to *Leatherneck*'s Lowery, who, earlier that morning, had documented the 3rd Platoon's raising of the first flag. Lowery's descent of the mountain intersected with Rosenthal's ascent. For a moment Lowery, Rosenthal, and Rosenthal's two companions, Campbell and Genaust (both given the Suribachi assignment by their 5th Division photo officer, Warrant Officer Norman T. Hatch), met and exchanged a few words.

At the base of the volcano, Rosenthal had snapped a picture of a gun emplacement and then passed his Speed Graphic to Genaust, who photographed Rosenthal posed with Campbell, his friend from the *San Francisco Chronicle*. These were the second and third pictures taken by Rosenthal's Speed Graphic that day, the first having been Rosenthal's shipboard photo of Smith and

Forrestal.[15] Genaust also took footage of the gun emplacement with his Bell and Howell movie camera, using Kodacolor film with an ASA of only 10 (as opposed to an American Standards Association film speed of 200 or more used today). The Marines had only recently (in 1944) begun to use color film in their movie cameras.[16]

As the three men trudged up Suribachi's steep slope, they occasionally encountered Marines clearing Japanese caves with demolition charges. Rosenthal captured one of these explosions in the day's fourth shot on his Speed Graphic. Genaust also got detonation scenes on movie film.[17] None of the three photographers was racing to the top of Suribachi to catch a flag raising, as evidenced by their leisurely progress, with various digressions, up the mountainside.

Arriving finally at the top about noon (according to Rosenthal), they could see a small American flag snapping in a stiff wind on top of its tall pole. Genaust trained his movie camera on the little flag, capturing in its frantic motion the ferocity of Suribachi's wind, a wind that made it a good day for flags to fly--and to be photographed.[18]

Also at the summit to photograph the flags were two other photographers-- men whose presence has not been acknowledged by serious attention for nearly fifty years: Private First Class George Burns, staff still photographer for the Army magazine, *Yank,* and Sergeant Louis R. Burmeister, a 20-year-old photographer from the 5th Division's 28th Regiment.   Of these two photographers little has been known, and their work has not been acknowledged in any of the general accounts of the Suribachi flag raisings.[19]

Here is Burmeister's account (given shortly before his death in November 1993) of how he got to the top of Suribachi:

I was assigned to the 28th Regiment. Free to go just about any place I wanted to go. I climbed out of my foxhole in the morning and, of course, I had my breakfast and got ready for the day. Then I found out somebody said something about going up the mountain, that there was a crew that went up there. I grabbed my camera and I said "I'm going." I didn't ask permission or talk to anybody. I just left.

That was early in the morning. It must have been 8:00 in the morning or something like that. Close to it.

I tailed right along with them [Schrier's patrol]. Scared stiff, I tell you. We didn't know what we were going to get into. There were land mines all over the place. Japs were under the ground most of the time, and every time you went past a little hole you thought you were staring at a gun because there were Japs dug in so deeply.

They had big cannons on railroad tracks that they could roll out and fire and then roll back in again. It was sort of hard to knock them out. And, of course, they had all kinds of mazes, of underground caverns and tunnels.[20]

After the tension of the climb, Burmeister was met by the fury of the wind at Suribachi's summit.

> What a windy place! It was so windy. Your pants when the wind blew through sounded like flapping. You know how a flag will flap in the breeze? You could hardly talk to anybody, it was so noisy from the wind.
>
> When we got up to the top I said very little to anybody, because, first of all, it was so windy. And being the photographer, that kept me from horning in on anything that was going on. I just wanted to observe. I stayed in the background. All professional photographers will do that.[21]

And there was a bumper crop of professional photographers poised at the mountaintop that day. All five chronicled here--Rosenthal, Campbell, Genaust, Burns, and Burmeister--set themselves to record the raising of a second flag, which was about to replace the first.

Rosenthal elected not to take a photograph of the first flag or to attempt to catch the moment when that flag, on its way down, passed the second flag, on its way up: "The wheels in my head went spinning around and I simply rejected the idea as competing action."[22] Positioning himself with the best possible perspective was crucial for Rosenthal. There would be no retakes, no second chances.[23] While touring the area around the group of men engaged in tying the second flag to its staff, Rosenthal, Genaust, and Burns posed under the first flag for a photo taken by Campbell.[24]

Selecting a site some 35 feet from where the flag would be raised, Rosenthal constructed his small platform of rubble and sandbags just inside the crater's rim. He silently debated the merits of a vertical versus a horizontal composition for his shot of the imminent flag raising.[25] His ultimate choice will come as a surprise to many: the original uncropped photograph is clearly a horizontal composition; the print was cropped to produce a vertical composition.

Genaust opted to record the second flag raising from the same perspective Rosenthal had chosen, but he delayed getting into position until almost too late. Crossing in front of Rosenthal, Genaust came perilously close to blocking Rosenthal's shot and missing his own. In the nick of time, Genaust stopped "about three feet from my right," according to Rosenthal.[26]

Genaust's motion picture footage is quite revealing, capturing (as still photography could not) the flow of action throughout the flag-raising sequence. His film first catches the six men standing to position the flagpole for its upward sweep. The upward thrust begins. One frame shows the six men, the staff, and the flag at virtually the same fraction of a second Rosenthal immortalized in his still shot. Almost immediately the flagpole is erect. Then the Genaust film follows a group of Marines carrying rocks from the site of the first flagpole over to buttress the base of the newly raised flagpole.[27]

In that moment of the flagpole's upward sweep, Rosenthal could take just one shot, since each photograph made on a bulky Speed Graphic camera required three steps: cocking the shutter, pulling the tab, and releasing the shutter.[28] Genaust's film presents solid evidence that the second flag raising was not a Hollywood-style production featuring AP photographer Joe Rosenthal as director, the 28th Marines as the cast, and Iwo's Suribachi as the movie set. Rosenthal has always appreciated the fact that Genaust's film documents the uninterrupted upward sweep of the flagpole, exonerating the AP photographer from any accusation that he "posed" his picture.[29]

Far over to the right of Rosenthal and Genaust, Campbell selected his own vantage point. Poised just slightly down inside the crater, he hoped to capture the moment when both flags simultaneously crossed in midair, the juxtaposition Rosenthal had decided against. As it turned out, Rosenthal was well served by Campbell's decision to photograph both flags, since Campbell's photograph helped establish that the second flag raising was a one-time operation, and not the contrived result of a series of retakes.[30] Campbell's photo also settles the question of whether the same piece of Japanese pipe was used for both flagstaffs. Obviously it was not.[31]

Burmeister also corroborated Rosenthal's story:

> The picture [of the flag raising] was not posed. If it was posed we would have probably had their faces toward us. You notice in the picture nobody's facing us. We had to take it in a hurry, because it would all be over with if you delayed anything. But because of the wind and because of the noise there wasn't much conversation. A lot of people think it was a posed picture.[32]

Burmeister said that at the top of Suribachi he took about twenty shots with his 4 X 5 Speed Graphic, including one at about the same time that Rosenthal took his flag-raising photograph. "I took a picture of Rosenthal taking a picture. And then I stepped right in and took the same picture. Just about the same. He was a little short guy, so he had to pile up some rocks. I was taller, so I just was able to stand on my tiptoes and get the same shot."[33]

When Burmeister came down the mountain, he followed the usual procedure, giving his film to a runner. After returning to the States later that spring, he saw Rosenthal's then-famous flag-raising picture. But Burmeister saw none of his own pictures developed or printed. He told his father, however: "I was there, too, and took photos." His father replied: "Why didn't *you* get credit?"[34]

This was a question Burmeister pondered for thirty-five years until, in 1980, an inquiry was made to the Pentagon on his behalf. At that point, a half-dozen of his photographs were unearthed, the only ones Burmeister would ever see.[35] Included in the photos received from Washington was a picture of the first flag at the top of its tall pole, and a picture of a Navy chaplain, Lieutenant (jg) USNR Father Charles F. Suver, S.J., officiating at a Roman Catholic Mass celebrated up on Suribachi. Burmeister recalled the Mass taking place sometime after the second flag raising.[36]

Another overlooked photographer, George Burns of *Yank* magazine, also took pictures of the first and the second flags. Thirteen years later, in 1958, Burns gave an account of that day:

> It's hard to realize that just 13 years ago I sat down on the blasted peak of Mt. Suribachi, Iwo Jima's dead volcano, pulled out a rumpled notebook and jotted:
> "D-plus-4 . . . Today at 10:25 a.m., the first American flag flew over Mt. Suribachi. Of course, they are still fighting on the north end of the island, and I will go up there tomorrow."[37]

His article in the *New York Mirror Magazine* continued: "And there were five of us shooting pictures--Joe, myself, Pvt. Bob Campbell, whose camera wasn't ready when the flag went up, Marine Sgt. Bill Genaust, who was taking movies, and another service photographer whose name I have never learned."[38] That anonymous service photographer was, in all probability, Burmeister, who continued to remain invisible to the American public for so many years.

Another well-documented moment on top of Suribachi occurred shortly after the second flag had been duly raised and photographed. Having snapped what he hoped was a good picture of the flag going up, Rosenthal took two other pictures as backup for his action shot. His second photo was of the now-vertical flagpole, steadied by three Marines. He considered this composition perhaps too static. He tried a third picture of the flag, this one involving a group of Marines he helped coax into congregating in front of the flagpole, joking with the unwilling men and promising them that this would be "an historic photo." Genaust stood to Rosenthal's left, filming the group; Burns stood to Genaust's left to take his still shots. Campbell, off to the right and slightly below the other photographers, caught Rosenthal (and Genaust's camera arm) in his version of the Marines waving helmets and guns at the photographers. This admittedly posed picture completed Rosenthal's film pack. He loaded a new pack and took a second shot of the Marines, who were still cheering obligingly. This composition was nicknamed his "gung-ho shot."[39] Shortly after the group posed in front of the flag, a wide-angle shot of the crater's rim caught more Marines engaged in mopping-up operations. This photograph was taken by an anonymous Coast Guard photographer recently arrived on the scene. His photo offers the most comprehensive view of the terrain in the vicinity of the flag.[40]

Rosenthal and Burns themselves became the subjects of another picture, posed under the flag and taken by Campbell on Rosenthal's smaller Rolleiflex camera.[41]   Then Campbell reverted to his own camera for a quiet, almost elegiac picture of a lone Marine guarding the newly raised flag.   By a happy coincidence, visible down below at the landing beach was LST 779, the ship that had provided a second flag for Suribachi.

NOTES

1. "I wanted to get in. They wanted to keep me out. I did have patriotic motives. I thought of my parents, who came here at the turn of the century. This is what America did for me. It became almost obsessive to me. I wanted to do something more than take pictures of people at home. I wanted to be able to use what I had" (Rosenthal interview with the authors, October 28, 1993).

2. Rosenthal interview with the authors, November 5, 1992; *Current Biography*, June 1945, 49-50, passim.

3. Rosenthal and Heinz, "The Picture That Will Live Forever," *Collier's*, February 18, 1955, 62.

4. Ibid., 63.

5. Ibid., 64.

6. Rosenthal interview with the authors, November 5, 1992.

7. W. C. Heinz, "The Unforgettable Image of Iwo Jima," *50 Plus*, February 1985, 59.

8. Rosenthal interviews with the authors, November 5, 1992, and April 7, 1993.

9. Rosenthal interview with the authors, April 7, 1993.

10. Rosenthal interviews with the authors, November 5, 1992, and October 28, 1993. This account by Rosenthal differs somewhat from that of Bernard C. Nalty in his pamphlet, *The United States Marines on Iwo Jima*, 1962, 1967, and 1970 editions, distributed by the Historical Division, USMC. Nalty directly connected Rosenthal's climb up Suribachi with the ascent of Marines carrying the larger flag: "As this second and larger (96 by 56 inches) flag was being carried up the slopes of Suribachi, Associated Press photographer Joe Rosenthal noticed it and instantly started in close pursuit." Nalty also credited the four-man patrol led by Strank as carrying "this set of colors up Suribachi's slopes" (Nalty, 5). An article by Benis Frank contained a similar error. Rosenthal did *not*, as Frank stated, accompany a "second patrol" which "took this flag up to Suribachi's top." Rosenthal arrived after that second flag was already being attached to its improvised staff. Nor had Rosenthal, "like the other photographers on the island, sent his films out to the command vessel off shore." See Benis Frank, "Does Book on Iwo Jima Memorial Bash a Marine Icon?" *Fortitudine*, Vol. 21, No. 3, Winter 1991-1992, 10.

11. Tom Bartlett, "The Flag Raisings on Iwo Jima," *Leatherneck*, February 1985, Vol. 68, No. 2, 20.

12. Rosenthal interview with the authors, November 5, 1992.

13. Ibid.

14. *Collier's*, February 18, 1955, 67.

15. Rosenthal interview with the authors, November 22, 1993. Rosenthal explained that his photo of the gun emplacement was ruined in the processing lab on Guam, evidence that the path from photo to finished print was mined with hazards, hazards that his flag-raising photo, taken three shots later, escaped.

16. Genaust film, National Archives; Weinberger interview with the authors, December 8, 1993. Harrold Weinberger was in the G-2 photo section for the 4th Division on Iwo Jima.

Genaust used a Bell and Howell Autoload for his flag-raising sequence (Hatch interview with the authors, January 14, 1994).

17. Rosenthal interview with the authors, November 22, 1993; Genaust film, National Archives.

18. Genaust film, National Archives.

19. A brief article by Burns appeared in the *New York Mirror Magazine*, March 16, 1958. Articles on Burmeister appeared in the *Medina* (Ohio) *Sun Sentinel*, April 3, 1980, the *Medina County Gazette*, February 25, 1991, and *Northern Light*, November 1992. Burmeister also received mention in an article by Tom Bartlett in *Leatherneck*, February 1991. Until their inclusion in this book, for all intents and purposes, both men have been unheralded by the national press or by historians of the Iwo experience.

20. Burmeister interview with the authors, January 21, 1993.

21. Ibid.

22. Rosenthal, as quoted in *Los Angeles Times*, March 3, 1983.

23. Rosenthal interview with the authors, November 5, 1992.

24. The National Archives attributes this photo to Campbell; Marling and Wetenhall identify Campbell as one of the men *in* the photo with Rosenthal and Genaust (*Iwo Jima*, 66).

25. Rosenthal interview with the authors, November 5, 1992; *Collier's*, February 18, 1955, 62, 65.

26. *Collier's*, February 18, 1955, 65.

27. Genaust film, National Archives.

28. Hatch interview with the authors, December 28, 1992. Rosenthal took his flag-raising photograph with his Speed Graphic, set between f/8 and f/11 at 1/400th of a second. He was using an Agfa Ansco-Superpan Press filmpack (Rosenthal interview with the authors, July 14, 1994).

29. Rosenthal interview with the authors, November 5, 1992. It is difficult to explain why, in the face of all this evidence, allegations continue to be made about the fraudulence of Rosenthal's photograph; for example, see Dan van der Vat, *The Pacific Campaign* (New York: Simon and Schuster, 1991). See Appendix B.

30. Rosenthal acknowledges his appreciation of Campbell's photograph. Rosenthal interview with the authors, November 5, 1992.

31. Both Lindberg and Marshall at one time thought the same pipe was used as a flagstaff for both flags (Lindberg to Mrs. Evelley ["Mrs. Hansen"], letter dated January 27, 1947; *Fortitudine*, Vol. 9, No. 2, Fall 1979, 4-5).

32. Burmeister interviews with the authors, January 15 and 21, 1993.

33. Burmeister interview with the authors, January 21, 1993.

34. Burmeister interviews with the authors, January 15 and 21, 1993.

35. Dennis Seeds to Albee, letter dated May 10, 1993.

36. Burmeister and Hatch estimated the time of the second flag raising as being about 2 o'clock (Burmeister interview with the authors, January 21, 1993; Hatch interview with the authors, January 9, 1994). Rosenthal remembered the time differently: "I was sure that I took the picture just about 12 o'clock" (Rosenthal interview with the authors, October 28, 1993).

37. *New York Mirror Magazine*, March 16, 1958. Burns made the natural assumption that of the two flag raisings, the first would be the one with sufficient historic significance to warrant mentioning.

38. Ibid. Rosenthal took issue with two passages in the Burns article, one that claimed that the Rosenthal picture "was not spontaneous" and that the men who raised the flag "were urged to do so for a group of photographers"; and the other, that "few realize that this picture depicts the second flag raising."

Rosenthal wrote Burns:

You state the second flag-raising picture was not spontaneous and that it was set up at the urging of photographers. Can you specify the photographers who made such a request? And of whom they made the request?

You say that "few realize that this picture depicts the second flag-raising." Is this in spite of the AP dispatches at the time; story on Blue network at the time as well as newspaper interviews; two-page illustrated article in *Life* March 26, 1945; numerous references in news clippings and on the air year after year; articles in magazines with circulations like *Readers' Digest, True, Collier's* in 1955? All of which related repeatedly the facts of first and second flag-raisings (Rosenthal to Burns, letter dated November 3, 1961).

Burns replied with an apology, admitting that he was mistaken in claiming the picture was not spontaneous (Burns to Rosenthal, letter dated November 13, 1961, courtesy of Mr. Rosenthal).

39. Rosenthal interview with the authors, November 5, 1992.

40. The National Archives identifies the photographer as a member of the Coast Guard. The authors have been unable to obtain further identification of this photographer on Suribachi.

41. Rosenthal interview with the authors, October 28, 1993.

Henry and Gertrude Hansen. Sgt. Henry O. Hansen, one of four Hansen sons in uniform, is seen here with his sister, Gertrude. Henry impressed a close family friend as being typical of the kind of men the Marine Corps chose during World War II: rugged, full of grit, and determined to stick with whatever they started to do. Courtesy of the Hansen family.

THE BOSTON HERALD

LATE CITY EDITION

VOL. CLXXXXVIII, NO. 56 — BOSTON, SUNDAY, FEBRUARY 25, 1945—SIXTY-TWO PAGES — TEN CENTS

YANKS RIP 5 MI. ON COLOGNE PLAIN

South Half of Iwo Won in Bloody Drive

World Peace Plan Takes Form Slowly

Problem of Reshaping European Map Not Solved Despite Conferences

By BILL CUNNINGHAM

NAVY FLIERS BLAST TOKYO

FLEET AIDS MARINES IN ISLAND FIGHT

Maze of Caves, Mines, Hot Rocket Fire Fail To Hold up Devildogs

GUAM Sunday, Feb 25. AP

30 Towns, Hordes Of Nazis Captured In Air-Land Punch

PARIS, Sunday, Feb. 25 (AP)

Thousands of Vehicles, Trains Destroyed

Veterans' Pleas to Harvard Disclose Dynamite in GI Bill

By LAWRENCE DAME

Suffolk Downs Still Gold Mine For Anyone with Funds to Buy It

By W. E. PLAYFAIR

PUTTING IT THERE TO STAY—Marines of the 28th Regiment, Fifth Division, plant the American flag atop Suribachi, Iwo Jima volcano and highest point on the island, in battle still raging to control enemy's front doorstep.

NEW CURFEW PENALTIES SET

Violators Face Loss Of Workers, Rations

WASHINGTON 24. AP

Reds Near Heart Of Burning Breslau

LONDON Sunday Feb 25 AP

PREMIER OF EGYPT SLAIN

Shot at Session After Reading War Decree

CAIRO Feb 24 (AP)

NINTH GATHERS SPEED

LAST OF JAP FANATICS SLAUGHTERED IN MANILA

MANILA Sunday Feb 25 AP

80 Appeal Job Shifting WMC Order

Airport Flood Bars Flights On N. Y. Run

Draft of Men 30-33 Speeded by Order

Only Those 'Necessary' to Work In Essential Industry Exempt

WASHINGTON Feb 24 (AP)

Locke Ober's Place In Boston

BY LUCIUS BEEBE

Locke-Ober Cafe
3 and 4 WINTER PLACE, BOSTON

BANQUET and DINING ROOMS

HOTEL KENMORE

First Appearance of Rosenthal's Flag-raising Photograph. Americans saw the instantly famous photograph as a wirephoto appearing February 25, 1945, on Sunday's front pages. From the start the press made no mention that the photograph was of a *second* flag raising on the embattled island. Published with permission of the *Boston Herald*.

Lowery Photograph of the First Flag Raising. *Life* magazine in its March 26, 1945 issue was the first to publish this Lowery photograph and to identify this flag as the *first* flag raised. *Life* did not identify the men pictured, but the Hansen family quickly recognized the standing figure (on left) grasping the flagpole as Henry Hansen. (Michels is in the foreground; behind him left to right are Thomas, Schrier, and Lindberg.) Courtesy of Doris Lowery. Photograph provided by the Hansen family.

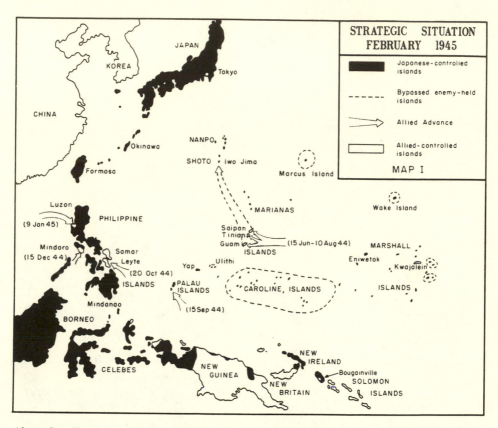

Above: Iwo Jima's Strategic Location. The small island in relation to the comprehensive plan for the invasion of Japan. Marine Corps Historical Center.
On opposite page: Iwo Jima's Landing Plan for the Invasion. The landing plan for the amphibious assault on Iwo Jima is illustrated. The landing stage at Green Beach for the 2nd Battalion, 28th Regiment, 5th Division is shown on the far left. Marine Corps Historical Center.

KITANO POINT

KANGOKU ROCK

OKITA

362-B

O NISHI

AIRFIELD NO. 3
(UNDER CONSTRUCTION)

ORANGE 1   O-2

362-A

ORANGE 2

MOTOYAMA O

362-C

KAMA ROCK

WHITE 1

AIRFIELD NO. 2

WHITE 2 O-1

382

TACHIIWA POINT   O-2

BROWN 1

O MINAMI

5 X
X
X A

BROWN 2

X X   QUARRY
X

PURPLE

AIRFIELD NO. 1

O-1
EAST BOAT BASIN

23 ≡ 25

BLUE 2

26 25

23 23

BLUE 1 (1/25 and 3/25 landed abreast)

25 25

YELLOW 2

28 ≡ 27

27 27

23 23

YELLOW 1

27 27

RED 2
FUTATSU ROCK

MOUNT SURIBACHI

28 28

27 27

RED 1

28 28

GREEN

TOBIISHI POINT

LANDING PLAN

1000   500   0   1000

YARDS

MAP III

Top: Marines Land on Iwo Jima. Marines from the 5th Division are positioned on Iwo's deadly landing beach in the shadow of Suribachi on D-Day, February 19, 1945. Campbell photo. National Archives.
Bottom: Marines Advance on Suribachi. Material evidence of the fire power expended on the volcano's capture is illustrated here. Burmeister photo. National Archives.

Top: Suribachi. The extinct crater's rim was the primary objective of the 28th Regiment's 2nd Battalion on the morning of D+4, February 23, 1945. Navy photo. National Archives. *Bottom*: First Patrol on Suribachi. The first reconnaissance patrol was sent up Suribachi early on the morning of February 23 by the 2nd Battalion's F company. Left to right: Watson, White, Mercer. Standing: Charlo. Burns took this shot on the volcano later in the day. Photograph provided by Sherman Watson.

Above: Third Platoon Assaults Suribachi. Two Marines in the foreground climb Suribachi with the added burden of 72 pounds of flame-throwing equipment. The men ahead of them are in single file, veering off to the right, and climbing the mountain in a zigzag fashion. Lowery photo. Photograph provided by Doris Lowery.

On opposite page: Preparing to Raise the First Flag. Men of the 3rd Platoon tie the first flag to a piece of Japanese pipe near the crest of Suribachi. Left to right: Schrier, Thomas, Hansen, and Lindberg. Lowery photo. Photograph provided by the Hansen family.

First Flag on Suribachi. The first American flag flies over Japanese home territory in this photo by a previously unheralded 5th Division combat photographer, Louis Burmeister. Photograph provided by Louis Burmeister.

Secretary of the Navy Forrestal and Lieutenant General Smith. Rosenthal, soaking wet from an accidental plunge into the Pacific, took this photo of Forrestal (left) and Smith (right) early on the morning of D+4. In the background is Suribachi where Rosenthal would soon make photographic history. Published with permission of AP/Wide World Photos.

Three Photographers at the First Flag. Genaust, Rosenthal, and Burns (left to right) pose beneath the first flag for this shot by Campbell. Slightly behind the three photographers (and out of view) Marines are preparing to raise a second flag. National Archives.

The Two Flags of Suribachi. The small first flag is lowered simultaneously with the raising of the larger second flag in this action shot by Campbell. Campbell's photograph helps to refute the recurrent erroneous charge that Rosenthal staged this second flag raising. National Archives.

Rarely Seen Uncropped Version of the Rosenthal Flag-raising Photograph. The photograph in a cropped vertical version made Rosenthal famous. As he prepared to take the shot, he debated the merits of horizontal versus vertical composition. This uncropped print, made directly from the original Rosenthal negative, reveals that he decided on horizontal composition. Published with permission of AP/Wide World Photos.

Genaust Motion Picture Sequence of the Second Flag Raising. From these six selected Genaust movie frames it is possible to pinpoint the moment in the upward sweep of the pole when Rosenthal took his epic photograph. The Genaust film captures one uninterrupted upward motion of the flagpole, and it documents the fact that Rosenthal's photo was not posed. National Archives.

Above: Rosenthal Taking his "Gung-ho" Photograph. Campbell photographed his companions, Genaust (extreme left, holding his Bell and Howell movie camera) and Rosenthal (standing on a sandbag as he did when he took his famous flag-raising shot) as both men took the "gung-ho" shot. This photograph, taken after the second flag raising, *was* posed. National Archives.
On opposite page.
Top: Rosenthal's "Gung-ho" Photograph. Rosenthal's version of the "gung-ho" pose. Published with permission of AP/Wide World Photos.
Bottom: Burns's "Gung-ho" Photograph. Burns, a combat photographer for *Yank* magazine, took a version of the "gung-ho" pose. Photograph provided by Joe Rosenthal.

Terrain Surrounding the Second Flag. Standing down inside the crater's rim, an unidentified Coast Guard photographer took this unique and revealing shot that captures the men and the terrain in the vicinity of the second flag shortly after the "gung-ho" pose. The third figure standing fully to the right of the pole and along the horizon is Rosenthal. National Archives.

On Guard at the Summit. With the second flag raising accomplished and guy lines attached, Campbell took this shot of a lone Marine guarding the flag and observing the beach activity far below. The second flag was commandeered from LST 779, the ship positioned on the landing beach nearest to the mountain. National Archives.

Rosenthal and Burns under the Second Flag. In the only known photograph of Rosenthal with the flag that he immortalized, Campbell (using Rosenthal's Rolleiflex camera) caught the AP photographer in conversation with *Yank* photographer, Burns. Courtesy of Joe Rosenthal.

Top: Celebrating Mass on Suribachi. Combat photographer Burmeister remained at Suribachi's windy summit after the second flag raising and took this photograph of Father Suver celebrating mass. Photograph provided by Louis Burmeister.
Bottom: The Cost of Iwo Jima. By the time the flags were raised, Marine casualties had already reached a horrific total. Near the landing beach, bodies awaiting burial are sprayed with disinfectant. Kiely photo. Courtesy of Arthur Kiely.

Above: Recognition for a First Flag Raiser. Thomas, a member of the platoon that raised the first flag on Suribachi, is congratulated by General Smith aboard the flagship *Eldorado*. On the left is Marine combat correspondent Beech; Beech would later accompany the surviving raisers of the second flag on the nationwide Mighty Seventh bond tour. Kiely photo. Courtesy of Arthur Kiely. *On opposite page*: Marine Corps Identifies the Rosenthal Flag Raisers. Recognition of the men who raised the second flag was only beginning in April 1945 when their public identification appeared nationwide. (The identification of Hayes and Sousley in the flag-raising photograph was reversed.) Published with permission of AP/Wide World Photos. Clipping provided by the Hansen family.

Pfc. Franklin R. Sousley
(Dead)

Pfc. Ira H. Hayes

Sgt. Michael Strank (Dead)

PhM2C John H. Bradley (Wounded)

Pfc. Rene A. Gagnon

Sgt. Henry O. Hansen (Dead)

Sousley   Hayes   Strank   Bradley   Gagnon   Hansen

Await Homecoming of Iwo Jima Hero

PAULINE HARNOIS, FIANCEE, LEFT, AND MRS. IRENE GAGNON, MOTHER
Thrilled Over Homecoming of Sole Survivor of Mt. Suribachi Flag Raising
(Associated Press Photo)

FLAG RAISING PICTURE ON WAR LOAN POSTER

Top: Apple Pie, Mom, and High School Sweetheart. The enterprising press posed the family of homecoming flag-raiser Gagnon. Published with permission of AP/Wide World Photos. Clipping provided by the Hansen family.
Bottom: The Mighty Seventh. Admiring the Seventh War Loan poster, whose design was based on the acclaimed flag-raising photograph, are Denig, Rosenthal, Gamble, and Vandegrift (left to right). Published with permission of AP/Wide World Photos. Clipping provided by the Hansen family.

Top: Ira Hayes, Reluctant Hero, Returns Home. Hayes poses for the first of many publicity photos immediately after his April 1945 return to the States. Doyle photo. Marine Corps Historical Center.

Bottom: Survivors of the Second Flag Raising. Reunited for the first time since Iwo Jima, the three surviving flag raisers in Rosenthal's photograph pose with Gamble. Left to right: Gagnon, Gamble, Bradley, and Hayes. Doyle photo. Marine Corps Historical Center.

MOTION PICTURE INDUSTRY'S AID TO WAR BOND DRIVE

Top: Mighty Seventh Comes to Boston. The *Boston Sunday Globe* on May 13, 1945 announced the Seventh War Loan bond tour's arrival in Henry Hansen's home town. Reprinted courtesy of the *Boston Globe*.

Bottom: Bond Tour's Official Launching in New York. The three Gold Star Mothers meet the three survivors who helped their sons raise the second flag on Iwo Jima. (Madeline Evelley is on the far left.) Each of the six received a $1,000 war bond and wide publicity. Raisers of the first flag and their families went unrecognized. Clipping provided by the Hansen family.

TATTERED IWO FLAG OVER HUB

Historic Relic Hauled to Peak of State House to Mark Start of 7th War Loan Drive

FLAG AND MEN WHO MADE HISTORY

Rosenthal's Flag on Tour. In Boston the three flag-raising heroes pose for the press holding the flag made famous by the Rosenthal photograph. Front-page headlines and photographs such as this epitomized the heroic myth of Suribachi. Clipping provided by the Hansen family.

On opposite page: Hayes Identifies his Comrades. The Rosenthal photograph was numbered for identification by Hayes in December 1946 and forwarded to the USMC Investigation Board. 1. Sousley 2. Gagnon 3. Strank 4. Bradley 5. Block 6. Hayes. Marine Corps Historical Center. *Above*: Hayes Identifies the "Gung-ho" Marines. Key figures in the flag-raising investigation were identified by Hayes in December 1946. Hayes himself appeared at the extreme left bottom of Rosenthal's "gung-ho" photograph as the helmeted figure represented by the top half of the head. Block is the only missing member of Strank's four-man patrol. Marine Corps Historical Center.

Mother Offers Proof Hansen Helped Raise Flag on Iwo

PICTURE TAKEN BEFORE FLAG-RAISING—While the Marines who raised the flag on Iwo Jima had their backs to the camera, this photo shows three of them face-to. The man in the center, his family agrees, is Sgt Hansen of Somerville. Caption on the picture, taken Feb. 23, 1945, reads: "Preparing to raise flag atop Mt. Suribachi."

(AP Wire Photo)

PRINT OF ORIGINAL, signed by photographer Rosenthal and his Marine buddies, strengthens Mrs. Hansen's claim.

CAPTAIN SAYS HANSEN DID—This letter from Sgt Hansen's company commander to his mother affirms the Somerville Marine's part in the Iwo flag-raising.

Rosenthal's Photograph in the News Again. The press was quick to report Hansen's 1947 demotion from the ranks of Rosenthal's flag raisers. (The larger photograph is one of only two Lowery flag-raising photographs released in 1945, here mistakenly attributed to AP. The arrow incorrectly points to Thomas; Hansen is the third figure from the left, with front of the helmet showing.) Published with permission of AP/Wide World Photos. Article reprinted courtesy of the *Boston Globe*. Clipping provided by the Hansen family.

Top: First Flag on Display. The first flag on Suribachi flew approximately two hours. Today it remains on display in near mint condition at the Marine Corps Historical Center in Washington as a companion to its more famous counterpart. Author's photo.

Bottom: Second Flag, Front and Center. Tattered by the winds of Iwo Jima, the second, larger flag raised on Suribachi is displayed in the Marine Corps Historical Center gallery behind a small sculpture based on Rosenthal's photograph. Author's photo.

Joe Rosenthal, D-Day + 50 Years. Rosenthal at his San Francisco apartment today. Long may he wave! Author's photo.

Chapter 6

A Volcanic Eruption

For 1/400 of a second, Joe Rosenthal made time stand still at Suribachi's summit. But the men whose images he captured there were soon swept on by the swift current of events to their quite separate destinies: some to injury and evacuation; some to death just days later in the bloody action north of Suribachi; some to a victorious departure from Iwo Jima a long month later on March 26, 1945; and some, including Rosenthal himself, to face the clouds of glory (and of controversy) gathering on the American horizon.

When Rosenthal, Private First Class Robert R. Campbell, and Sergeant William H. Genaust left the summit of Suribachi shortly after noon on February 23, they missed one last photo opportunity. This time it was the young photographer assigned to the 28th Regiment who recorded the event: a Mass celebrated by Lieutenant (jg) USNR Father Charles F. Suver, S.J. According to James E. Fisk, who assisted Suver in the service, the chaplain had announced on D-Day as the two men stood on the landing beach and looked at the formidable heights of Suribachi: "Fisk, I'm going to say Mass up there the day we take it." When Suver fulfilled his vow, Fisk was there beside him. "It is my firm belief," he wrote, "that it was the most solemn Mass ever said anywhere."[1]

Sergeant Louis R. Burmeister recorded the unique occasion and in his account of the event, resolved the long confusion as to whether this Mass was celebrated before or after the second flag raising: "I took the photos of the Catholic Mass that we held *after* we raised the second flag."[2]

Unaware of what they were missing, Rosenthal and his two companions trudged back down the mountain. Rosenthal recalls their return:

Halfway down the hill again, Bob Campbell and I took shots of each other. At that point we were out of the line of fire, so we could play at this sort of thing. These were shots for our own albums later, if we did get back.[3]

Campbell would survive the deadly Iwo Jima campaign, return to California, and share many years with Rosenthal at the *San Francisco Chronicle*. Genaust would not be so fortunate. He was killed on March 3 in the northern offensive.

Early on that February afternoon Rosenthal's attention was focused on the task of getting his day's film out to the command ship. And getting some lunch.

> I was getting a little bit hungry and I walked over to the command post. I bummed a little package of K-Rations. For some reason I looked at my watch. And it was a few minutes after one o'clock.
>
> And I do remember that this day--because I thought I had enough film to get on its way--this day I didn't wait until late in the afternoon before going back to the command ship. I generally had tried to get back to the command ship around five o'clock. This day I'm pretty sure I was on the command ship by 2:30.[4]

Rosenthal's practice was never to send his film to the command ship via runner, as most photographers did. He followed the routine of personally delivering his undeveloped film to the *Eldorado*. He had learned not to depend on others to get his film off the chaotic beach and out to the seaplane that made daily flights to Guam from the fleet off Iwo Jima. There on Guam Murray Befeler, the picture pool coordinator, had the film developed, and then made his selection of prints to wirephoto back to the States.[5]

Arriving aboard the *Eldorado* with his film, Rosenthal was asked by some of the correspondents whether he'd gotten a picture of the flag raised on Suribachi. Rosenthal replied: "The picture I got is the second flag to go up."[6] It was a question whose answer would prove far more significant than the photographer could ever have imagined.

One of the assembled correspondents, Hamilton Faron of the Associated Press, sent in a dispatch explaining that Platoon Sergeant Ernest I. Thomas, Jr., had planted the flag on Suribachi. "The small flag," Faron added, "was supplanted soon by a larger one."[7] Faron's story was the basis for an article in the Sunday, February 25, edition of the *New York Times*. It was this article which first informed the American public that two flags had been raised on Suribachi. In light of subsequent charges surrounding the disclosure of the number of flags raised, it is interesting that the original source for this first report was apparently Rosenthal himself.

After sending his film off to Guam, Rosenthal spent the night of February 23 aboard the *Eldorado*. During the Iwo Jima campaign, neither he nor most of the other photographers knew how their pictures actually turned out until long after their film was developed on Guam. Days, even weeks could pass between the time a picture was taken and its print was seen by the photographer who took it. So when Rosenthal went back in to shore the next morning, back to the work of capturing for an American public the horror and heroism that constituted daily life on Iwo Jima, he had no suspicion that in a matter of hours one of his photographs would be emblazoned across the nation's Sunday editions.

Then late one day he returned to the command ship to be greeted by an unexpected message. "I went back out to the command ship a couple days later with another batch of photos. There the AP man had a radio message from the Boston/New York office which said: 'Congratulations on fine flag-raising photo.' And that was the first time. I had not seen the picture. I did not know."[8] Rosenthal suspected that the congratulatory message referred either to his flag-raising photo or to his "gung-ho" shot. But not having seen either, he was in the dark.

So was everybody else on the island. News of a photograph that had caught the attention of the nation was radioed from the States to Iwo Jima. But without seeing the actual image, no one, including Rosenthal himself, could fathom what all the commotion was about.

Among the most curious was a man with a professional interest in matters photographic: Warrant Officer Norman T. Hatch, the 5th Division's chief photo officer on Iwo Jima. So one day when Rosenthal was at the 5th Division's command post, Hatch quizzed the unassuming AP photographer about his recent celebrity.

> I said to him one time when he was up at the CP: "Joe, what in the name of God did you take that's causing all this fuss?" He told me: "Norm, I really don't know. The place, the time and everything happened so fast, I just didn't know that I got a good picture." But when I asked him what he thought it was [that was causing all the public reaction], he said, "Well, I guess probably it was a shot of the guys all around the flagpole that I took after the flag was up." I said, "Joe, that couldn't be. We've done that a hundred times in the Pacific and nobody would have raised that much fuss."[9]

In a *Collier's* article, written with Bill Heinz in 1955, Rosenthal stated: "Millions of Americans saw this picture five or six days before I did, and when I first heard about it I had no idea what picture was meant."[10] Rosenthal's uncertainty persisted until he left Iwo Jima on March 2, arriving on Guam two days later.[11]

Guam was not only the headquarters of Admiral Nimitz, but it was also press headquarters for the correspondents and photographers covering the Pacific campaign. And there at press headquarters Rosenthal saw his flag-raising photo for the first time. The picture pool coordinator, Murray Befeler, did the honors. Rosenthal described the occasion:

> He gave me an 11 by 14 print of it. Then there were comments, and

somebody came up with a picture of the gung-ho picture. I remember talking to him and remember being asked if I posed it, and I said, "Yes, yes, I had to work on them, as a matter of fact, to get up there because they were all tired and dirty and they were still aware that there were caves around and there were occasional pistol and gunshots into the cave openings. Occasionally a grenade would go off. From inside the caves you'd hear shots, and then silence."[12]

In 1992 the authors asked Rosenthal whether on Guam he immediately recognized the merit of his flag-raising photograph. With characteristic wry humor, he replied: "Who am I to differ with all these other experts?"[13]

On Guam "the experts" of the press corps would certainly have agreed that Rosenthal had taken an outstanding photograph at the summit of Suribachi. Where differences arose was in the matter of just how Rosenthal had achieved his photographic triumph. Very quickly the lines were drawn. There were those who believed Rosenthal had capitalized on his good luck in arriving at the right place at the right time, combining luck with skill to produce a memorable picture. Then there were those who believed Rosenthal had posed the flag raisers, staged the event, and, in effect, produced a photograph that was an example of clever theater, not raw reality. In brief, this camp believed Rosenthal had faked a flag raising.

The story of how these two diametrically opposed interpretations of Rosenthal's photograph clashed in the American press is a narrative steeped in irony, coincidence, and missed opportunity. It is also an object lesson in the proliferating damage that occurs when the honest differences between honest men are not resolved.

One of the "experts" on Guam was First Lieutenant John S. Bodkin, an AP photo editor on military leave to the Navy. Bodkin was stationed on Guam as photo editor at headquarters when Rosenthal's undeveloped film containing his flag-raising shot had arrived with the daily film shipment from Iwo Jima. Bodkin later estimated that the flag-raising photo was developed and radiophotoed to the States at about 10:00 P.M. Guam time or 7:00 A.M. New York time, Saturday, February 24. His own reaction on first seeing the photograph was: "Here is the one for all time."[14]

Bodkin had occasion to defend this photograph shortly after first admiring it. He described two incidents, typical of the criticisms buzzing around Rosenthal's photo like a swarm of wasps around a ripe peach.

About three days after the picture was radiophotoed, a Marine officer stopped me and accused Joe Rosenthal of stealing film made by a Marine photographer and shipping it in as his own. I asked the Marine one question, "What make of film was your Marine photographer using?" "Eastman," he replied. "The same as all the other services are using."

"Rosenthal's flag-raising shot is on Ansco film, which is the film being used by the Still Picture Pool, just to avoid accusations such as this," I said. The confrontation ended.

A couple of days later, Geoffrey Tebbutts, correspondent for the *Melbourne Herald*, flagged me down while I was driving a jeep from headquarters to Agana.

"Too bad Joe Rosenthal's flag-raising picture was a fake," Tebbutts said. We were bowling right along at a good clip. I jammed on the brakes, almost sending the Australian through the windshield.

"Geoff, Joe is an AP photographer, and in civilian life I am an AP photo editor. One thing we do not do is fake pictures or stories. If you think his picture is a fake, you can get out right now and walk to Agana." He smiled and said, "I guess you're right about that."[15]

Rosenthal himself arrived on Guam on March 4, more than a week after his film was delivered. In the midst of his new celebrity as the man who had taken the most talked-about photograph of World War II, he was asked to write a piece about how he got to the top of Suribachi to take the picture. His story, dated March 7, 1945, appeared the following day in the *San Francisco Chronicle*. In his brief (400-word) account, he described his arrival at Suribachi's summit.

As the trail became steeper, our panting progress slowed to a few yards at a time. I began to wonder and hope that this was worth the effort when suddenly over the brow of the topmost ridge we could spy men working with the flagpole they had so laboriously brought up about three-quarters of an hour ahead of us.

I came up and stood by a few minutes until they were ready to swing the flag-bearing pole into position.[16]

It did not occur to Rosenthal that for the purposes of this short article, he ought to comment on the fact that his photograph captured the raising of a second, larger flag approximately two hours after an earlier flag raising. He had already acknowledged, on the very day he took the photograph, that two flags had been raised on Suribachi and that he had photographed the second one. Unaware of omissions in press reports back in the States, he assumed the record had been set straight.

Oblivious to the possibility of a misinterpretation, he did not again recount the flag-raising sequence in full detail. In light of the controversy soon to erupt with all the violence of the Suribachi volcano in its heyday, Rosenthal ruefully reflected that he would have many occasions to wish he had drawn the distinction between the two flag raisings in that first article: "I think, yes, in retrospect it was an omission that I did not repeat this knowledge, but I simply figured it was already known. It was well-known, and I did not give it a thought."[17]

Four days before Rosenthal left Guam, one of the chief players in the flag-raising photograph controversy arrived at Apra Harbor from Iwo Jima on March 11. It was Time/Life correspondent Robert Sherrod.[18] In terse, telegraphic style, the outlines of the position taken by Sherrod (and soon by his editors) on the subject of Rosenthal's famous photograph emerge from the pages of one of the small spiral notebooks Sherrod carried into combat.

Mar. 12
AP Joe Rosenthal's picture of
Suribachi flag raising--so famous
he's going back [to the States] for
lecture tour--was fake.
Was taken second day--rehearsal.
But what a picture! Were the
4 men killed (2) or wounded (2)?
[Sherrod assumed Rosenthal's picture
was of only 4, not 6, flag raisers.][19]

Mar. 13
        Photographer, S/Sgt Louis
Lowery of Leatherneck, was in--he
took pictures of raising flag on
Suribachi.
        Joe Rosenthal's historic
picture was grand photographically
but, in a fashion, at least,
historically phony--like Washington
crossing the Delaware.[20]

Mar. 14
        0300 Last night (tonight) I
wrote 1100 words on slightly phony
picture of flag raising on Suribachi--
printed 1st page TIME Mar. 5.
Real flag raising had taken place
several hours earlier.[21]

The meeting between Sherrod and Lowery on March 13 would have lasting consequences for Rosenthal, who, unaware of trouble brewing, was busy attending briefings on the next Marine invasion he planned to cover. Okinawa was the island designated for a massive amphibious landing, an objective as yet kept secret. Rosenthal already had filed for permission to accompany the Marines' 6th Division when his photo chief, Befeler, received a radio message for Rosenthal from the AP office in New York. As Rosenthal recalled:

> Murray Befeler was there and he handed me this communication. He said: "They want you to arrange for transportation to New York." We looked at each other and I said: "Well, apparently the flag picture is catching on." We were already getting clippings and stuff like that and knew that it made a stir. I said to Murray (whose position there was like my superior): "Well, I would like to make the initial phase of Okinawa since I am all free. Frankly, I am getting kind of tired anyway, but I would like to make at least the opening phase, the first couple of days, and then go back to New York." He relayed that information. A message came back that this was not a request. Arrange for transportation as soon as possible. So I left Guam. I believe it was on the 15th of March. The Ides of March.[22]

With Rosenthal's departure from Guam, the possibility that he might have talked with Sherrod or Lowery and cleared up their misperceptions of his role in the second flag raising was lost. Just how significant a loss this was took less than twenty-four hours to manifest itself.

En route from Guam to San Francisco, Rosenthal stopped in Honolulu on March 16, still happily oblivious to the storm soon to come crashing down on his head. Nearly fifty years later, Rosenthal reconstructed the events that occurred after his plane landed in Honolulu:

> I was greeted by the bureau chief of AP. He had a message from New York saying "'*Time* Views the News,' a radio program in New York, says: 'The already heralded photograph of the flag raising on top of Mt. Suribachi is historically a phony. The photographer, being late for the first flag raising could not resist re-staging it.' Will you comment?"
>
> So I sat down and I said: "If the correspondent means that the picture that I took is not the first flag to be flown from Mt. Suribachi, he is correct. I did not select this spot for the second flag. I did not select the men for the picture. I did not in any way signal for it to happen, but I was aware that it was going to happen."[23]

Rosenthal recognized that he was called upon to answer highly serious charges, allegations that challenged his personal and professional integrity. The journey home to a just reward for work well done was fast deteriorating into a situation in which he felt he was being called on the carpet by his employers at AP for conduct unbecoming a combat photographer. With more than a little trepidation, he prepared to leave Honolulu for the last leg of his trip.

I left [Hawaii] in the evening. I got into San Francisco Bay on this sea
plane, which took about fourteen hours. All the time I did not know
whether I was in the doghouse or not. I was anxious to have it straight,
and I had precisely said that anything that could be involved in it [the
picture], I did not control. They have also used the very words "in no
way staged it." But at the same time, I was not talking to those who
would be judging it. I was simply uncomfortable, sleeping part of the
time, not all of the time. These things happen. It is up to me to tell the
story, tell it accurately, tell it as it is. I arrived at the naval base where
the sea plane came in, loaded with injured, just crammed. I got off and
was greeted by the commander of the base. I was greeted by the guy
from the AP office here [San Francisco]. He greeted me fondly. It was
St. Patrick's Day, the 17th of March. He said, "Don't worry about a
thing."[24]

Relieved, Rosenthal reported to the chief of AP's San Francisco bureau, their
main office on the West Coast. "Don't worry about a thing," the bureau chief
said, echoing his assistant's earlier message. "I have got the word back from
New York." Summarily dismissing the problem, he asked Rosenthal what he
wanted to do. The anxious, weary photographer asked if he could have two or
three days in San Francisco to see his friends before leaving for New York.[25]

Rosenthal's request was granted. But his few days in San Francisco brought
little in the way of peace and tranquility. "When I arrived in San Francisco,"
he reported, "I found that I was now a celebrity. I, who had never been asked
for an autograph in my life, was now being asked to sign dozens of these
pictures."[26]

Immediately, the press descended on him. His hometown paper, the *San
Francisco Chronicle,* led the pack. The day following his return, the
Chronicle's front page carried his picture autographing copies of his famous
photograph, accompanied by an interview taken a "few minutes" after his
plane's arrival. Billed with the lead, "The Photographic Historian of Iwo Jima
Tells How He Got That Shot of Suribachi," the interview quoted Rosenthal on
how his famous photograph had been made: "When I got to the brow of the
hill, I saw a small flag on a short pole which they were taking down and they
were about to put up a large flag on a tall pole."[27] Rosenthal clearly stated that
his photograph was of a *second* flag raising.

The photograph was news and so was the photographer. When Rosenthal
reached New York, he was greeted by the demand for yet another interview.
With typical modesty, he responded that catching the memorable moment on
Suribachi was just "one of those things. It was like shooting a football game,"
he explained. "You don't know what you have."[28]

After his celebrity welcome, Rosenthal was closeted with his employers at
AP's New York office. They were far from critical. In fact, they asked him

how he wanted them to respond to the erroneous story reported in the radio broadcast, "*Time* Views the News."[29] As Rosenthal described the situation, Kent Cooper, president of AP, invited the young photographer into his own office:

"Joe, we are solidly behind you, and we want to know what you would like us to do."

"I would like to have an apology from Time/Life and a correction," I said. They put it on a platter. It was an addition to their next [radio] program. I got a fabulous offer for the picture from a reputable organization in Hollywood. I went back to Kent Cooper and asked if there could be some kind of arrangement for a permanent interest. He asked: "What did you have in mind?"

I said that I knew there were entrepreneurs who wanted to capitalize on this, and that I would say somewhere in the area of a 5 or 10% interest in the continuing value.

He said, "If you don't mind, Joe, wait outside. It will be a matter of a few minutes while I discuss this with my advisors."

In about 15 minutes he brought me in and said: "The problem you've brought up is one we've given a lot of thought ourselves. Now we've refined it and want to put it to you for your own reaction. What we would like to do is to turn over to the Navy Relief Fund all profits from this photo."

So here I was on the other side of the table. I was saying: "I think that's wonderful." In my mind were, on wings, loads of cash floating away. And at the same time I understood that they [AP] were assuming the copyright was theirs. They would control the use of the photo and limit it more or less to a patriotic theme. I was more interested in that.

My relationship with AP was good even though I left them for another job. I was treated wonderfully by Associated Press in so many ways. I can't say: "They did me wrong; I might have been a millionaire." What kind of millionaire would I have made anyhow?[30]

It has taken decades to unravel the story of just how the false allegations that Rosenthal "faked" his flag-raising photograph came to be broadcast on the radio program, "*Time* Views the News." Rosenthal himself thought the misunderstandings began on Guam when he first walked into press headquarters and gave an affirmative response to the question as to whether he had posed his "gung-ho" photograph of Marines assembled at the second flagpole on top of Suribachi. Rosenthal believed his remark had been overheard by one of the correspondents on Guam and that this correspondent incorrectly assumed the remark referred to the earlier photograph taken of the six men raising the flag.[31]

Rosenthal suspected that this correspondent was Time/Life's Robert Sherrod. He knew Sherrod had gone ashore on Iwo with the Marines on D-Day, covered the campaign for over two weeks, and then returned to Guam while Rosenthal was there in March.[32]

Sherrod was indeed the correspondent who filed the story broadcast by "*Time Views the News.*" This much of Rosenthal's presumption was correct. Where his reconstruction of the chain of events went astray was in the matter of Sherrod's source for his story. Sherrod had not been at press headquarters the day Rosenthal first saw his Iwo Jima photographs and first responded to the question about whether one had been posed. Sherrod did not arrive on Guam until March 11, a week after that day when Rosenthal discussed his photographs at press headquarters. On March 15, Rosenthal left Guam for Honolulu and San Francisco. But in the interim another Iwo Jima photographer had appeared on the scene in Guam, a man destined to play a key role in the flag photo controversy. Sherrod's notebook entry for March 13 indicated that the photographer who had accompanied the 3rd Platoon up Suribachi and photographed the first flag raising at the summit had come by to see him with a sensational story about two flags and their photographs.

Nearly forty years later Sherrod described Lowery's visit in an article in the Marine publication, *Fortitudine.*

> He was more than lukewarm under the collar, calling the Rosenthal, "grand photographically but, in a fashion, historically phony, like Washington crossing the Delaware." What Lowery was sore about was the failure to credit him with photographing the first, or "real" flag raising. The quality of the photographs was for him a secondary issue.[33]

In a 1992 interview with the authors, Sherrod was even more explicit about Lowery's demeanor that day on Guam:

> Lowery was very bitter about his photograph not being used because it showed the *first* flag raising, while Joe's showed the later event. It was Lowery who led me into the error on the Rosenthal photo. I should have been more careful. I accepted the version of a man who was boiling mad.
>
> I got it from Lowery. He said it was posed. It wasn't the original flag raising. So I accepted it. He was very bitter about it.[34]

Sherrod's notebook entry referring to his visit from Lowery was dated March 13. The day before, an entry dated March 12 stated: "AP Joe Rosenthal's picture of Suribachi flag raising--so famous he's going back for lecture tour--was fake. Was taken second day--rehearsal."[35]

It is unclear whether this information, recorded the day after Sherrod arrived on Guam, was also attributable to Lowery. Sherrod's notebook does not give his source for the judgment that Rosenthal's photo was "fake." All of Sherrod's later statements indicate that his authority for believing Rosenthal posed his picture was Lowery. There is corroborative testimony to the fact that even before Lowery left Iwo Jima for Guam he was angry about the attention given Rosenthal's flag-raising photograph and the lack of attention accorded to Lowery's own photos of the first flag raising. When the news reached Iwo Jima about the national sensation caused by the Rosenthal picture, Lowery sought out his friend at the 5th Division command post, the chief photo officer, Norman Hatch. In a 1992 interview with the authors, Hatch reconstructed his meeting with Lowery and offered an explanation for Lowery's discontent:

Nobody knew anything about Lou's photography of the first flag except Lou. All right, now the reason for this dispute in my mind is this: I talked to Lou many times about it. Lou was, in the truest sense of the word, pissed off. Why? The system was set up in the public relations side of this business for this operation [Iwo Jima] that we received almost immediately current radio reports about what was going on on the island.

The first reports about this fantastic flag-raising picture came over the radio [the news clippings came later], and everybody heard it and everybody talked about it. Well, anyway, because of the radio broadcast and this fantastic, this big flag-raising deal, Lou became concerned, because naturally he had risked his life to get up there along with Schrier's platoon.

At that time (and this doesn't necessarily speak too well of the Marine Corps in a sense), to help the correspondents who couldn't get to where all the action was, a lot of times the information officers would have the stories the CC's [combat correspondents] had written unattributed to these guys, so they [the civilian correspondents] could use them, you know. And Lou was positive in this case that in deference to a press type his material had been held up, without any knowledge that this was an absolute fact.

Now mind you, none of us had ever seen the picture as yet. All we had heard were the radio reports. Lowery felt he was being put upon because of press relations as much as anything else: that his material had probably been held back because Rosenthal was the press guy. He wouldn't have blamed anyone individually.

What I was saying earlier happened with the writing correspondents, not the photographers. Most times the photography went right on through without ever being touched by human hands, in a sense.

So Lou's claim really had no merit whatsoever. But he was so angry that he was not being recognized. This was a big thing, the biggest battle we'd had in the Pacific.[36]

Before leaving Iwo, Lowery and Hatch finally saw a news clipping of the famous Rosenthal photograph. Hatch recalled the scene: "It came back before I left Iwo. So when we saw what it was, I think I said to Lou at that time, 'Lou, you couldn't beat that no matter what you tried to do.' And he said, 'No, that's for sure. That's one hell of a good picture.'"[37] From the moment Lowery saw the famous image, he never disputed its qualities as a photograph. But he did continue to question what it was credited as depicting.

More fuel was added to Lowery's discontent once he reached Guam, where copies of *Time, Newsweek,* and other publications featuring the Rosenthal photo were available. Everything in print made the assumption that Rosenthal had caught the first flag raising on Iwo Jima.

Lowery knew it was *he,* not Rosenthal, who had made the risky climb up Suribachi with the 3rd Platoon, *he* who had taken photographs of the first flag raising when Rosenthal was nowhere in sight. Lowery knew that when he left the summit of Suribachi, the first flag was already flying. He also knew that he had passed Rosenthal climbing the volcano after that flag was raised. So it was not illogical of Lowery to conclude that the Rosenthal flag raising was posed. Why else would a second flag have been raised? To add insult to injury, here it was weeks later and still nothing had been seen of Lowery's coverage of the *first* flag raising. Where the hell were *his* photographs?

Certainly Lowery's anger, though ill founded, was completely understandable. It was also understandable that he would pay a visit to Sherrod on Guam to complain about the injustice being perpetrated by the press. How else could the truth become known?

When Lowery talked to Sherrod, his complaint no longer focused on the preference he assumed Rosenthal's photo had received in its transmission back to the States. What was most galling to the *Leatherneck* photographer was the question of the authenticity of Rosenthal's picture. Lowery's story seemed plausible to Sherrod. Before him was a *Leatherneck* photographer who had actually been present at the first flag raising, telling him that Rosenthal was nowhere in sight at that time and stating flatly that Rosenthal's flag raising was posed. Rendering Lowery's account still more plausible was the quality of the Rosenthal photo itself. The photograph seemed too good to be true. Anything that perfect *had* to have been posed.[38]

The same day, after Lowery took his leave of the Time/Life correspondent, Sherrod filed his story on the "slightly phony picture of flag raising on Suribachi."[39]

One of the many ironies of the flag-raising controversy is that had Sherrod checked Lowery's allegations with Rosenthal, who was at that time still on Guam, the story of the photo being faked could have been nipped in the bud. But Sherrod had heard earlier that Rosenthal was "so famous he's going back for lecture tour."[40]   So Sherrod was under the erroneous impression that Rosenthal had left Guam as of March 13.   "Rosenthal was on a plane back to the States.   So I sent this [the cable to Time, Inc.] in."[41]   Actually, Sherrod had had some 48 hours in which he might have contacted Rosenthal before the photographer left Guam.

When Sherrod's cable arrived at the offices of Time, Inc., in New York, it must have generated considerable editorial interest.   The famous Rosenthal photograph was *not* taken of the first flag raising.   It had been staged.   Here was a sensational scoop.   But *Time* and *Life,* being weekly publications, could not respond quickly.   Radio, however, could.   As it happened, Time, Inc., had an afternoon radio program, "*Time* Views the News," which aired on New York's WJZ.   On March 14, the program broadcast a version of Sherrod's March 13 cable alleging that "Rosenthal climbed Suribachi after the flag had already been planted. . . .   Like most photographers [he] could not resist re-posing his characters in historic fashion.   He posed them and snapped the scene."[42]   New York's AP office heard about this broadcast and demanded a transcript.

This much transpired without Rosenthal's knowledge.   En route from Guam, he was ignorant of *Time*'s charge of fraudulence until his plane landed in Honolulu.   From there he sent his categorical denial of the accusations to AP headquarters in New York.   AP "sent a photo editor across Rockefeller Plaza to the Time-Life Building."[43]   The AP editor threatened: "If you print that [the story that Rosenthal's photo was posed], we'll sue for a million dollars."[44]   Prudently, *Time* cabled Sherrod on Guam for clarification of his story.

Sherrod recorded the events of March 17 with these entries in his notebook:

Mar. 17
rec'd cable from Welch:
"for Press--clarify--did Rosenthal
pose picture of a genuine flagraising?"
    Capt. Miller called me in & said
"You ought to know this--
Capt. Steichen doesn't
think that picture was posed. He's got
a Marine movie of the same scene. . . ."
Steichen said: "A flag
raising is a ceremony--not a
battle scene." I agree. He also
said he wouldn't consider the
picture posed--& he thought
it was a great picture. I
agreed but said it depended on
what was meant by 'posed.'
    Marine Photographer Lowery

gave me a copy of the grinning,
waving Marines grouped around the
flag from Feb. 28 issue Akron Beacon
Journal. I said: "That one
<u>was</u> 'posed.'"[45]

In light of his renown as a world-class photographer, Captain Edward Steichen's defense of Rosenthal in the debate with Sherrod over what constituted a "posed" picture is particularly interesting, as is the distinction he drew between a battle scene and a ceremony, such as the Suribachi flag raising.[46] But neither the American public nor Sherrod's editors at Time/Life were engaged in such aesthetic niceties. At this point all *Life* magazine wanted was to confirm that it had a scoop. And to illustrate the exposé of Rosenthal's photograph as a fraudulent misrepresentation of the first American flag raising on Suribachi, *Life* wanted the *authentic* photos of that first flag raising taken by Sherrod's informant. Knowing Lowery to be a photographer for *Leatherneck* magazine, *Life* approached *Leatherneck* for prints of Lowery's Suribachi photographs.

Leatherneck proved strangely unaccommodating, and *Life*'s editor apparently informed Sherrod of the rebuff. An exasperated Sherrod commented in his notebook:

<u>Mar. 16</u>
This Rosenthal mess! Life
now can't get pix [Lowery pictures of
first flag raising] from LEATHERNECK
--but running my story as report.[47]

Life, the nation's leading picture magazine, was not prepared to take no for an answer from the editors of *Leatherneck*. Pressure would be brought to bear to obtain the Lowery photographs.

As for Lowery himself, he labored under a double disadvantage. Rosenthal's flag-raising photo was heralded far and wide as *the* picture of the first flag raised over Iwo Jima. To counter Rosenthal's claim to fame, Lowery had exactly nothing. It was now well over two weeks since Rosenthal's pictures had appeared in the American press, and still there was no sign of *any* of Lowery's numerous shots of the assault on Suribachi and the *authentic* first flag raising. Where were his pictures? Why had they failed to see the light of day?

Woven into this complex web of emotions and events--Lowery's frustration, Sherrod's cable, *Time*'s radio broadcast, Rosenthal's denial, and *Life*'s pursuit of Lowery's missing photographs--was a new strand: the role of the Marine Corps in what might be called the battle of the press. The scene, which had already shifted from Iwo Jima to Guam to Honolulu to San Francisco to New

York, would now shift again--this time to Marine Corps Headquarters in Washington, D.C., and the office of the commandant of the Marine Corps, Major General Alexander Archer Vandegrift. March 16, 1945, found a rather unlikely meeting in progress, with Vandegrift serving as host to *Time*'s Alan Bibble and AP's Alan J. Gould. These gentlemen represented the feuding parties in what was coming to be known as the flag-raising controversy, a controversy to which it was thought the Marine Corps might provide some resolution.

In one of those synchronicities so disapproved of in art but so prevalent in life, at the very hour when matters were coming to a head in Vandegrift's office, across the Potomac River at Washington's National Airport, a young warrant officer from the 5th Marine Division's photography unit on Iwo Jima was arriving with the latest batch of film shot by his Marine combat photographers. Vandegrift ordered Lieutenant Colonel Edward R. Hagenah from the Division of Public Information to meet the plane and escort the warrant officer back to Vandegrift's office without delay.

Deplaning, the last thing Norman Hatch expected (or wanted) was a command performance at Marine Corps Headquarters.

My flight from Iwo was practically, for those days, nonstop. Of course, it wasn't; we had to refuel. I stopped at Guam and changed planes and, still carrying all the film, went to Pearl. When I got on the plane I was extremely tired because now I had been traveling for about 2-1/2 to 3 days and was still in my combat gear, and I really hadn't had a shower or anything and felt pretty rough.

We came into San Francisco and then I could get a shower and a clean shirt, but I was still wearing my combat fatigues because I didn't have a green uniform. So that's when I came into Washington National from San Francisco. When I got off the plane, there was Lieutenant Colonel Hagenah, whom I had known from earlier days. So I was totally surprised and I said, "Colonel, what are you doing here?" Since when did I rate an official greeting? Because I'm only a warrant officer at this stage of the game.

Then he said, "Well, I've got a little mission for you."

I said, "What's that?"

He said, "You're going to go see the commandant."

I said, "Not like this I am. No way, I've been traveling for 4-1/2 days and it just isn't going to be."

He said, "No, it *is* going to be, because there are people waiting in his office right now and you're the only answer to his questions."

I said, "What are the questions?" And I'm beginning to get worried now. What the hell do I know that somebody else doesn't know?

He said, "It's about the flag raising."

I said, "What about it? There were two flag raisings. There's nothing unusual about that. The first one was a small one, you know," and I went through the litany on that.

He said, "That's not the problem. There's a misconception in the country as to whether or not AP took the first flag raising."[48]

Reluctantly, Hatch got in Hagenah's waiting car where he learned more on the drive to Marine Headquarters. There was a controversy over the flag raising, Hagenah explained, "occasioned by the fact that Bob Sherrod of *Time* magazine had written an article which he sent to *Time*."[49]

AP climbed the ceiling. I haven't gotten into what the story content was yet, but apparently it [Sherrod's article] was causing enough confusion that AP felt that they should visit with the commandant and *Time* to get it squared away. That's what that was all about. And I guess some way or another they'd gotten wind of the fact that I was coming.

The word probably went out: "Did anybody hear from the 5th Division?" So the G1 section came up with the fact that this one warrant officer was flying in. God help it if it had been any other warrant officer. Some engineer or whatever who wouldn't have had any knowledge.

But I had what was known as the D2 journal with me. Now, this is the intelligence officer's minute by minute discussion of what happens during the campaign. It's a diary that's pretty much used by everyone when they're doing an after-action report to determine who, what, when, and where.[50]

Arriving at headquarters, Hatch was ushered into Vandegrift's office.

The three of them were sitting there in the commandant's office and Hagenah brought me in and introduced me. I knew the *Time* man [Bibble] because I had received my training at "The March of Time," and this fellow was the bureau rep for *Time* magazine in Washington.

The commandant said, "We have a small problem here and it concerns the flag raising." He gave me his version of what had been going on, which was basically that we put up two flags.

I said, "Well, that's very simple. I can pull the D2 journal and I can give you the times of these things happening and the reasoning behind them."

This stems from the fact that the intelligence section, when they got ready to put the second flag up, Lieutenant Colonel George Roll, who was our D2 intelligence officer, came to me and said, "Norm, the General [Keller Rockey] has decided that that flag is not large enough up there for the rest of the island to see. He wants to put up an official flag which will be much larger. This will also give the ships at sea an opportunity to see that we own part of the island now."

Now, the problem as I discerned from the conversation in the commandant's office was that AP was not saying that theirs was the first flag raising, but they also were not knocking it down. They were just letting it ride.

It was finally decided then and there that AP would indicate whenever the subject came up that they did not take the first flag raising, and would identify the photo as being the second flag raising. It wasn't anything that anybody would make them do: like to put a caption "This is not the first flag raising," or anything like that.[51]

Hatch's extemporaneous report clarified the events surrounding the second flag raising for the benefit of all present in Vandegrift's office. But the commandant himself had an agenda item for this meeting. Once again, Hatch was able to come to the aid of the Corps.

I knew that Bill Genaust had gotten the flag raising on movie film even though I hadn't seen it. I played a big role in this one, because the commandant turned to AP and said, "You know we'd like to use that photograph. It's going to be wonderful publicity for us and it would be a great thing to use."

And AP says, "Well, that's no problem at all. We'll be very glad to let you use it. In fact, we'll even give you dupe negatives, and the fee is only going to be $1.00 a print."

Dead silence. Vandegrift turned to me and said, "What do you think of that?"

I said, "I don't think we have to do that because we can put it out in color."

He said, "What do you mean?"

And I said, "We have footage by Bill Genaust. In it he has the flag raising in 16mm film. There is always one frame that is sharp. We can make color 8 by 10s from that."

Once again there was kind of a dead silence and Vandegrift looks back over to AP.

AP says, "Well, we'll be glad to give you the use of Rosenthal's photo. Just credit AP."

That was the end of that little discussion. I guess we spent probably an hour in the commandant's office.[52]

It was an hour Hatch would long remember as "a hell of a situation for a poor little warrant officer who was 24 years old."[53]

Hatch's bluff enabled Vandegrift to obtain what the Marine Corps greatly desired: free and unlimited use of the Rosenthal photo. *Life's* hope to procure the Lowery flag-raising photo also appears to have been fulfilled that day. Although there is no written evidence that Bibble broached the subject with Vandegrift, there is every reason to suspect that he did. *Life,* previously thwarted by *Leatherneck* in its attempt to obtain the Lowery photos, went to press a few days later and published the Lowery flag-raising photograph, property of the United States Marine Corps. *Life's* March 26 issue also quoted at length from a "dispatch sent to *Leatherneck* by a Marine correspondent" describing the two flag raisings.[54] Use of this dispatch must also have come courtesy of Vandegrift. The riddle posed in Chapter 1 as to how *Life* obtained the Lowery photograph and "scooped the national press" now appears to be solved.

Thanks initially to Sherrod, and now (presumably) to Vandegrift, Time/Life had its scoop--complete with a photograph of the *first* flag raising. It should be noted that *Life's* March 26 story was greatly toned down from Sherrod's initial March 13 cable and the version broadcast by "*Time* Views the News." Hatch's reading of the D2 journal in the presence of *Time's* representative must have had its impact. While correctly stating that Rosenthal's "dramatic picture" was of a "second flag raised on the peak," *Life's* article took care to cast no aspersions on the genuineness of this second flag raising or its commemorative photograph.[55] For it was also thanks to Sherrod that Time, Inc., had been threatened with a serious lawsuit by AP. On the very day of *Life's* March 26 issue, Rosenthal flew into New York. There he generously opted not to press legal charges, in return for an apology from *Time.*

Later, Sherrod would learn of his near-calamitous error and be mightily relieved that his March 13 cable had not appeared in print: "After I learned how wrong I had been I blessed my good luck that neither magazine [*Time* nor *Life*] had exposed my ignorance. I had got away with something and possibly avoided a lawsuit." Sherrod stated that he was unaware until the 1960s, however, that his March 13 cable had been the basis for a broadcast by "*Time* Views the News."[56]

Sherrod did not get off completely unscathed. While still on Guam, he made this notebook entry:

> Mar. 20
> Personally I think honesty--
> knowing honesty--in journalism
> will always pay off eventually.
> Therefore, I'm not particularly
> interested in popularity, if it
> means sacrifice of honesty. And
> I don't mind the reaction to the

> Rosenthal picture story--I only
> told the truth.

> July 28, 86   Well, not so fast--
> [Forty-one years later, Sherrod added this 1986 notation at the
> bottom of the page, with an arrow pointing toward the word "truth."][57]

It can be assumed that Sherrod was catching some sort of flack, either from his editors back in the States at Time/Life or from his fellow members of the press on Guam, some of whom apparently took the position that Sherrod should have checked Lowery's story with Rosenthal before adopting the position that Rosenthal's photograph was a fake.[58]

In retrospect, the March 16 meeting in Vandegrift's office could be viewed as a catharsis. Rosenthal's reputation was cleared. *Time* was informed of the circumstances surrounding the second flag raising and was made aware of the folly in further pursuing Sherrod's allegations that Rosenthal's photograph was a fake. And since *Time* was not pursuing the staged flag-raising story, the way was cleared for AP to abandon its threat of a lawsuit. Vandegrift, keenly aware that the Rosenthal photograph would be "wonderful publicity for us and . . . a great thing to use," had secured AP's consent to publish the photo freely. And Time/Life, earlier thwarted by *Leatherneck,* had apparently received Vandegrift's blessing to publish the Lowery photo of the first flag raising.

The facts were now known by all the interested parties: Rosenthal's photograph was clearly of a second flag raising, an event representing a legitimate Marine Corps-ordered and Marine Corps-executed exercise, not a staged event orchestrated by a civilian photographer. And here the flag-raising controversy should have been laid to rest.

One of the byproducts of the meeting at Vandegrift's office was that Lowery was at last recognized as having photographed the first flag raising. *Life* published his flag-raising picture in the March 26 issue. Lowery had every reason to expect further recognition and the publication of his entire series of flag-raising photos in *Leatherneck*'s forthcoming edition.

But when the April 1 issue of *Leatherneck* appeared there was no mention of Lowery or the two flag raisings, much less any Lowery photographs of the first flag raising. Instead, dominating the magazine's back cover was a full-page reproduction of the Rosenthal flag-raising photo. The Corps was already benefiting from the arrangement Vandegrift had negotiated with AP.[59] The balance of Lowery's flag-raising photos did not appear in *Leatherneck* or, for that matter, anywhere else. It was as though Lowery's photographs of the first flag raising, and all the men responsible for erecting that flag, had disappeared into the volcano's crater.

The likely author of this disappearing act could be presumed to be that party with the most to gain from eliminating any awkward evidence that the Rosenthal photograph, currently reflecting glory on the Marine Corps, represented a second flag raising of no strategic or historic significance whatsoever. For by March 16 when Vandegrift was presiding over his meeting with Bibble and Gould, the American public had already embraced Rosenthal's photograph as *the* picture of *the* first flag raised over Japanese home territory.

So when Hatch read aloud from his D2 journal to the gentlemen of the press assembled in Vandegrift's office, his confirmation that there had been two flag raisings on Suribachi and that Rosenthal had missed the first one could not have been precisely music to Vandegrift's ears. The Marine Corps was apparently faced with the major inconvenience of having one flag too many, or at least of having the right photograph of the wrong flag.

Vandegrift's thorny problem would be solved if, by some act of legerdemain, the first flag raising (including all flag raisers, Marine combat photographer, and photographs) could be made to disappear. It was a ripe moment for a bit of skillful damage control. If Lowery's photographs were withheld from publication by *Leatherneck,* and also not released to the civilian press or other military periodicals for publication, it might be possible to count on the American public's notoriously short attention span to forget there had ever been a flag other than Rosenthal's.

Lowery would be in no position to demand that his photographs of that first flag raising be published. He was a Marine first and a photographer second. He was, in short, still very much under orders.[60] And so were the men who had raised the first flag: whoever and wherever they were, living or dead, they were still Marines. If told to keep quiet about their flag-raising experiences, it could be assumed that they would.

All that need be done was to let the dominoes fall as they apparently were already tilting. The national press and the general public had long since confused and conflated the two flag raisings into one glorious moment of American victory, so history might well conveniently be replaced by legend.

This is, of course, a hypothesis. Vandegrift did not leave a written record of his strategy for dealing with the issue of the two flag raisings. The topic is not treated in his memoirs; and there is no mention of the matter in his letters or personal papers for this period.

There does remain, however, a smoking gun in the form of two documents: two Marine Corps internal memoranda filed away in the National Archives. One memorandum, dated two years after Vandegrift's March 16, 1945, meeting, was from R. A. Campbell, editor/publisher of *Leatherneck* magazine, to Brigadier General William E. Riley, the Marine Corps director of public information. The topic for consideration was:

Subject: First Iwo Jima Flag Raising
                    Photographs, publication of.
     1.   It is requested that photographs of the subject named event, now in

the custody of THE LEATHERNECK magazine, be released for publication in THE LEATHERNECK.[61]

The second memorandum, also dated March 6, 1947, was from Riley to "Commandant, USMC," and contained Riley's recommendations. Of these interesting matters, more will be said in due course.

There appeared to be only one break in Vandegrift's defensive line, a line necessitated by the indiscretion of one of his own Marine photographers. Time/Life knew (thanks to Sherrod) that Rosenthal and his photographs did not have the field entirely to themselves. Sherrod had alerted his editors to the existence of some photographs Lowery had taken of an earlier flag raising on Suribachi. *Life* had approached *Leatherneck* for access to these photographs; but, as of Sherrod's notebook entry dated March 16 (the day of the summit conference in Vandegrift's office), *Life* was knocking on a locked door.

Why was one of Lowery's closely guarded photographs released to *Life*? Was it on orders from Vandegrift? If so, he would seem to have been shooting himself in the foot, assuming that he had an interest in downplaying publicity relating to the inconvenient fact that the acclaimed Rosenthal picture did not represent the first flag raised on Suribachi.

Deprived of the kind of documentation historians swear by, we are reduced to offering this hypothesis: that Time/Life's Alan Bibble managed to convey to Vandegrift that, with or without his blessing and with or without a Lowery photograph, *Life* intended to run a story on the two flag raisings. After all, *Life* had Sherrod's story to rely on. By cooperating (and allowing *Life* to have its scoop), the Marine Corps could perhaps hope to have the double dose of flag raisings dealt with more generously than might otherwise be expected.

One thing is certain: *Life* magazine's story about the two flag raisings, on the newsstands a week after the meeting in Vandegrift's office, was a mild-mannered piece of journalism, a far cry from any hatchet-job on Rosenthal or the Marine Corps. After that one publication *Life* seemed to lose interest in pursuing the story.

Certainly, *Leatherneck* magazine did not rush into print with flag photos by Lowery. The *Leatherneck* issue for April 15, 1945, published some photographs Lowery had shot at the summit of Suribachi, but *none* of the focus of Lowery's photographic mission: the first flag raising.[62]

Security at Corps Headquarters remained tight. Vandegrift's ban on publication of Lowery's flag photos seems to have extended to another Corps photographer and to other Marine Corps publications. *The U.S. Marines on Iwo Jima*, published later in 1945 and written by Marine combat correspondents and public relations officers returned from Iwo Jima, contained a full-page reproduction of Rosenthal's flag-raising photo but not a single Lowery picture of the first flag.[63]

At this point, Lowery might well have wondered why he had risked his hide (and broken his camera) to photograph the first flag raised over Japanese home territory. For the lack of recognition accorded his pictures, however, he had more to blame than the favoritism accorded the civilian press, or the alleged slow-boat transportation of military film versus the deluxe treatment of civilian film. His enemy, in all probability, was his own commandant, who also may have been responsible for the disappearance of Louis Burmeister's series of flag-raising photographs.[64]

Vandegrift's decision to suppress the Lowery photographs marks a crossroads in the saga of the two flag raisings.[65] From the very first day when Rosenthal's photograph hit the front pages, there existed a public misimpression that this photograph depicted the first American flag being heroically raised under the most strenuous combat conditions. This misimpression was purely unplanned and unplotted, an accident of timing, coincidence, and careless reporting. There is no foundation here for a conspiracy theory that would blame the Marine Corps, AP, or Rosenthal for originating this national case of mistaken identity.

Conspiracy theories are not always the best perspective from which to make historical judgments. Too often it is happenstance, honest mistakes, or something that was once called human frailty that direct--or misdirect--the course of human events. Such was the case in the early days of the flag-raising story.

Then sometime around that date so resonant with warning for men in positions of power, the Ides of March, a choice was made. The dominoes tilting toward national acceptance of the one-flag, one-photograph concept of events on Suribachi were given a nudge. The existing evidence points to the commandant of the Marine Corps as the responsible party.

The failure to correct a misimpression, or the decision to suppress evidence that might call into question a prevailing misimpression, probably falls more in the category of a sin of omission than a sin of commission. So it might be well to restate the domino metaphor and say that Vandegrift, seeing the dominoes beginning to tumble, withheld support. He was doing little more than AP, which had agreed to refrain from billing Rosenthal's picture as representing the first flag raising, but which felt no compulsion to take out full-page ads announcing that Rosenthal had missed the first flag but caught the second.

In mid-March Vandegrift's decision to give aid and comfort to the heroic myth by suppressing publication of Lowery's photographs of the first flag raising might have seemed to him a minor matter. But his action would soon snowball into an avalanche. Rosenthal's picture was on its way to becoming a national icon, and the men he photographed at Suribachi's summit were moving out of history and into legend.

NOTES

1. James E. Fisk, "Mass on a Volcano," *The Catholic World*, Vol. 168, January 1949, 315, 316.

2. Burmeister interview with the authors, January 21, 1993. Rosenthal said he wished he had known to stay for Father Suver's Mass (Rosenthal is a Roman Catholic). He believed the Mass had to have occurred *after* the second flag raising, not (as reported in some accounts) *between* the times of the two flag raisings. "It couldn't have happened while I was there. And it was highly unlikely that such a group would have been up on top *before* I got there" (Rosenthal interviews with the authors, November 5, 1992, October 28, 1993, and November 22, 1993).

3. Rosenthal interviews with the authors, November 5, 1992 and October 28, 1993.

4. Rosenthal interview with the authors, October 28, 1993.

5. Rosenthal interview with the authors, November 5, 1992.

6. Ibid.

7. Hamilton Faron dispatch, courtesy of Mr. Rosenthal.

8. Rosenthal interview with the authors, November 5, 1992.

9. Hatch interview with the authors, December 28, 1992.

10. *Collier's*, February 18, 1955, 65.

11. Rosenthal, with *Newsweek* correspondent Hipple, left Iwo Jima by ship on D + 11. They spent one night on Tinian, then flew to Guam. In a recent interview Rosenthal clarified his earlier statement: "That, I think, is just a little off the mark. I did have an idea when I first heard about it. I did not know whether I had caught the flag raising at the precise fraction of a second. 'I did not know' is not the same thing as 'I thought it was something else'" (Rosenthal interview with the authors, November 5, 1992).

12. Rosenthal interview with the authors, November 5, 1992.

13. Ibid.

14. John S. Bodkin, *Photo Credits, Editor & Publisher*, March 22, 1980.

15. Ibid. Rosenthal described the way civilian film from the war zone was handled on Guam:

> Lt. Bodkin's assignment as a photo editor at CINCPAC was to "edit" and disseminate the photos that originated from military photographers, and to cooperate with the Civilian Still Photo Pool Coordinator who was Murray Befeler.
>
> The Civilian Still Photo Pool was staffed by photographers in the employ of AP, International News Photos, Acme Newspictures and Time-Life.
>
> It was Befeler's judgment and expertise that expedited our photos to the U.S.
>
> All film was funnelled from the battle area to the Navy's magnificently staffed photo lab on Guam, where the censors and the editors and expediters gathered. The censors quickly scanned negatives and captions and passed most of it.
>
> The process permitted Befeler to be close in with the select group to very quickly see what was coming through. Civilian Befeler then rated the quality and established priority selections. It was part of his job to request special transmission by radio of top photos of his selection. These were radioed from

Guam to San Francisco. Then all originals caught the first available plane. (Rosenthal to Albee, letter dated December 16, 1993).

16. *San Francisco Chronicle*, March 8, 1945.

17. Rosenthal interview with the authors, November 5, 1992.

18. Sherrod Notebook 7, 20.

19. Ibid., 26.

20. Ibid., 27.

21. Ibid., 32.

22. Rosenthal interview with the authors, November 5, 1992.

23. Ibid.

24. Ibid.

25. Ibid.

26. *Collier's*, February 18, 1955, 66.

27. *San Francisco Chronicle*, March 18, 1945.

28. *Portland Press Herald*, March 27, 1945.

29. Rosenthal interview with the authors, November 5, 1992.

30. Rosenthal interviews with the authors, November 5, 1992, and October 28, 1993. Rosenthal, in deciding how to respond to the "*Time* Views the News" broadcast, also felt he needed to weigh the matter of AP's relationship to Time/Life. He recalls his keen awareness that Time/Life was "probably a million-dollar-a-year client of Associated Press."

31. *Collier's*, February 18, 1955, 66.

32. Rosenthal interview with the authors, November 5, 1992.

33. *Fortitudine*, Vol. 10, No. 3, Winter 1980-1981, 8.

34. Sherrod interview with the authors, July 20, 1992.

35. Sherrod Notebook 7, 26.

36. Hatch interview with the authors, December 28, 1992.

37. Ibid.

38. Sherrod interview with the authors, July 20, 1992; Sherrod, *On to Westward*, 304.

39. Sherrod Notebook 7, 32. It seems likely that when Lowery talked to Sherrod on Guam he was not aware that two of his photographs of the first flag raising had appeared in the March 9 issue of *Yank*. These were the only Lowery photographs of the flag-raising sequence to be published in 1945.

40. Ibid., 26.

41. Sherrod interview with the authors, July 20, 1992.

42. Sherrod, *On to Westward*, 305.

43. Ibid.

44. Sherrod interview with the authors, July 20, 1992.

45. Sherrod Notebook 7, 55-57.

46. Robert Sherrod, in an article published in *Fortitudine,* expanded on his debate with Edward Steichen on Guam:

> Edward Steichen, the illustrious photographer, pleaded with me not to reveal that Rosenthal's photograph wasn't the real first one; for the greater glory of the Marine Corps it was better unsaid, he said.
>
> I admired Captain Steichen, USNR. . . . But I had to disagree with him: I said the truth about the flag hoistings would come out eventually, and it was

better now than later. I filed the story (Robert Sherrod, "Another View of the Iwo Flag Raisings," *Fortitudine*, Vol. 10, No. 3, Winter 1980-1981, 9-10).

47. Sherrod Notebook 7, 53.
48. Hatch interview with the authors, December 28, 1992.
49. Ibid.
50. Ibid.
51. Ibid.
52. Ibid.
53. Ibid.
54. *Life*, March 26, 1945, 18.
55. Ibid., 17-18.
56. Sherrod, *On to Westward*, 304-305.
57. Sherrod Notebook 7, 69.
58. In 1992 Rosenthal gave the authors this footnote to Sherrod's Guam notebook:

I saw Murray Befeler in San Francisco years afterwards, and he was describing to me how things were going at press headquarters in Guam. He said, "Joe, you can't imagine how everybody jumped on Sherrod. We told him: 'You were here when Joe was here, and you never said a word to him.'" He [Befeler] said, "Even if he wouldn't believe you, he should have asked you" (Rosenthal interview with the authors, November 5, 1992).

59. *Leatherneck* (Pacific edition), April 1, 1945.
60. Even after he was mustered out of the service in the summer of 1945, Lowery continued to work for the Marine Corps as the civilian photo director of *Leatherneck* until he retired in 1982 (Doris Lowery interview with the authors, July 19, 1992).
61. R. A. Campbell, editor/publisher of *Leatherneck*, to director, Division of Public Information, memorandum dated March 6, 1947, unsigned carbon copy, National Archives.
62. *Leatherneck* (Pacific edition), April 15, 1945.
63. Henri et al., *The U.S. Marines on Iwo Jima*, 72.
64. Since Burmeister photographed *both* flags, his pictures (like Lowery's) provided inconvenient evidence of two flag raisings. Thanks to the article in *Life*, it was public knowledge that Lowery had been up on Suribachi on February 23. But Burmeister's presence there had been given no publicity in the States. Vandegrift, deciding to suppress Lowery's photographs, could easily have extended the policy to include Burmeister's.

There is evidence that earlier on Guam there were those who thought Lowery's film should be destroyed rather than forwarded to Vandegrift's office. William P. McCahill, officer-in-charge, Public Relations Section, office of the commander in chief, Pacific, discussed (in a series of oral history interviews at the USMC Historical Center in 1982) the arrival of Lowery's film on Guam about a week after Rosenthal's film had been received.

A couple of packs of film came in from Lou Lowery of *Leatherneck*, which were the original flag-raising shots. Some of the more cautious Navy people at CinCPac, Guam, suggested I really ought to destroy those films, and I said, "No, that wouldn't be right. I'll send them under separate cover to Gen Denig, and

let him make the decision as to what to do about them." Because, of course, by
then, the President and the whole country were so enamored of the Iwo flag-
raising film that to have anybody even suggest that it was a phony would not
have been very smart, so it was quite a while later before that whole series of
Lowery's films were [*sic*] released (Colonel William P. McCahill, Oral History
Transcript, History and Museums Division, USMC, Washington, D.C., 1989,
54).

65. There have been innumerable unsubstantiated claims that the Marine Corps
suppressed the Lowery photographs. Previously, however, the charge of suppression has
not been buttressed with credible documentation.

Chapter 7

Heroes on Parade

A news media event of the first magnitude was set in motion by President Franklin D. Roosevelt's order to bring home the men Joe Rosenthal had photographed raising the American flag on Iwo Jima. The flag raisers were to add the luster of heroism to fundraising efforts in the forthcoming Seventh War Loan drive. Roosevelt had decided to send in the Marines.

The order, issued in late March, was one of the last by the wartime president, who died in office three weeks later. It proved to be a decision with long-term consequences for Major General Alexander A. Vandegrift, the Corps, and the heroic myth of the Suribachi flag raising. Close on the heels of Vandegrift's own decision to suppress Technical Sergeant Louis R. Lowery's photographs of the first flag raising came Vandegrift's call from his commander in chief to consult about the return of the men in Rosenthal's photograph of the second flag raising. In all probability, Roosevelt was unaware that two American flags had been raised on Iwo Jima on February 23. Like most of his fellow Americans, the president had seen only one memorable photograph of one victorious flag raising. He wanted the cast of characters from that dramatic event brought home to a hero's welcome.[1]

Abruptly, Vandegrift was faced with the unexpected consequences of his making the Rosenthal photograph the sole, official representation of the Iwo Jima flag raising: the men in Rosenthal's photo automatically would become the official heroes of Suribachi. Thanks to a presidential order, he would soon have more than a set of inanimate photographs to deploy. He would be dealing with a group of live Marines to be presented to the American public as the men who raised the one and only flag on Iwo Jima. Vandegrift, the Marine Corps, and the government of the United States were becoming parties to the perpetuation of the heroic myth of Suribachi.

Roosevelt, in his project to enhance the public appeal of the Mighty Seventh bond tour with the presence of a few live heroes fresh from combat on Iwo Jima, could not have imagined the difficulties involved in carrying out his order to locate and deliver the men in Rosenthal's photograph.[2] But obtaining an official identification of these flag raisers and arranging their transfer to Washington for a public relations assignment would prove severely taxing to the ingenuity of the Corps.

On March 30, 1945, a telegram marked "Confidential" was wired by Marine Corps Headquarters to the Pacific:

TRANSFER IMMEDIATELY TO US BY AIR . . . 6 ENLISTED MEN AND/OR OFFICERS WHO ACTUALLY APPEAR IN ROSENTHAL PHOTOGRAPH OF FLAG RAISING AT MOUNT SURIBACHI. . . . ADVISE ESTIMATED TIME ARRIVAL US. MARPAC DIRECTED BY COPY THIS DISPATCH TO TRANSFER PERSONNEL CONCERNED MARCORPS IMMEDIATELY UPON ARRIVAL US.[3]

A presidential order is often more easily delivered than carried out. Even before Roosevelt's prodding, the Marine Corps Division of Public Information was attempting to name the unknown heroes in Rosenthal's photograph. Requesting the names of the flag raisers from Rosenthal's employers at Associated Press had proven to be a dead end. Rosenthal had been unable to get a left-to-right after taking his flag-raising shot. AP had no answers. The Marine Corps would have to rely on its own resources.[4]

There were other complications. By the time the March 30 telegram from Headquarters was received, the Suribachi flag raisings were buried in five weeks of past history. The Iwo Jima campaign was officially over. The 5th Division's all-too-few surviving troops had departed Iwo's inhospitable sands and were at sea, bound for Hawaii.

Weeks earlier, however, while the battle on Iwo Jima still waxed hot, combat correspondents had requested names and even personal interviews with the men who raised the flag in Rosenthal's picture. And for a very brief time there was a flurry of both press and military public information interest in the *first* flag raising. This interest was short-lived, however, confined to that two-day span between the February 23 flag raisings and the February 25 publication of Rosenthal's picture.

Shortly after the first flag raising, Platoon Sergeant Ernest I. "Boots" Thomas, Jr., was identified and ordered out to Vice Admiral Richmond Kelly Turner's flagship. There he was hailed as the "Marine who led his men up the bitter slopes of Mount Suribachi and planted the American colors at the summit."[5]

Arriving at the *Eldorado* "with the stubble and dirt of battle still on him," as Marine Corps combat correspondent Technical Sergeant Keyes Beech reported, Thomas met with Turner and Lieutenant General Holland M. Smith. With "the praises of the high-ranking officers still ringing in his ears," the young battle-worn Marine was then interviewed in a broadcast radioed directly to the United States.[6]

Beech's report elaborated on the Thomas interview:

> It was during this interview Thomas insisted that others should be sharing in the credit.
>
> "I didn't do it all by myself," he protested. "Those fellows who were with me ought to be out here, too."
>
> But it was Thomas who, when his platoon leader was hit, took over and led the Marines to the peak where the colors were raised. The story he told about the valiant fight was all about others, rarely about himself.[7]

A brief article appeared on page 28 of the Sunday *New York Times* on February 25, the same day Rosenthal's flag-raising photo appeared on the *Times'* front page. This story, based on press accounts from the *Eldorado*, identified Thomas as "the Marine who raised the United States flag atop Mount Suribachi," despite Thomas's protests that others should be sharing the credit. This short piece also mentioned that a larger flag was soon raised.[8] A not-too-careful reading of the *Times* story on page 28 could, however, lead to the false assumption that Thomas was a flag raiser in the Rosenthal photograph on page one.

After his moment of recognition aboard the *Eldorado*, Thomas returned to the island, to his platoon mates, and to the battle that would claim his life. In any event, his flag raising had not been immortalized by the Rosenthal photo, so neither he nor any others who participated only in the first flag raising would be sought out again by the spotlight of celebrity. For the men in the Rosenthal photograph it would be an entirely different story.

Although Rosenthal's photograph was published in the United States on February 25, it took some time for the photograph to make its way back to Iwo Jima. Eventually, the photo arrived in the form of news clippings from the States. But most of the Marines engaged in the daily struggle for survival had little time to expend on flag raisings, flag raisers, or even a dramatic photograph that might be front-page news in the States, but that was of minimal concern on the lethal island called Iwo Jima.

The little island, however, was inhabited by more than fighting men. Iwo also housed a press colony whose mission was to keep news from the battlefront before the American public. Almost as soon as Rosenthal's photo arrived, civilian and military reporters on the island were hard at work, hoping to dig out the story behind the picture. Dave E. Severance, former commander of Company E, recalled those first tremors of press interest:

> If I remember correctly it was 2-3 weeks later [after the flag raisings] before there were rumblings about a picture, and questions asked as to

who was in the picture. I must confess, I shared little interest in the
subject at the time . . . we were fighting for survival, covering an area
meant for a normal company, but manned by two small 20-25 man
platoons commanded by corporals or sergeants. Naming flag raisers was
a subject far from my mind. I probably made some inquiries, but many
of the men who had been on the patrol were gone, and George Schrier
had taken over Dog Company, 2nd Battalion after he came off the
mountain. Most of the questions probably went to him.[9]

One of those reporters seeking out First Lieutenant Harold George Schrier
was Beech, the correspondent who had interviewed Thomas aboard ship a couple
of weeks earlier.

. . . when newspaper clippings of the picture reached Iwo Jima, I went
to 1st Lt. Harold G. Schrier, who led the first patrol to reach the top of
Suribachi, in an effort to identify the men. With the help of Schrier and
PFC Rene A. Gagnon I identified five men, left to right, as follows:
PFC Franklin Sousley, Sgt. Michael Strank, Hospital Corpsman John H.
Bradley, PFC Gagnon and Sgt. Henry O. Hansen. It was not until my
return to Marine Corps headquarters at the conclusion of the campaign
that I learned there were six rather than five men in the picture.[10]

According to Beech, Schrier and Private First Class Rene A. Gagnon had helped
him to make these five preliminary identifications some time before President
Roosevelt's order was issued.[11]

Once the flag raisers were identified, reporters naturally sought interviews.
Severance found himself confronted with numerous requests.

Strank and Hansen had been killed by that time. Reporters were
clamoring to interview the remaining men. Gagnon . . . [was] not in the
front lines at that time, and [was] available to talk to them. Sousley was
in a very critical area where it was dangerous for a man to leave his
foxhole, and I would not expose him to that danger just to talk to
reporters. Several days later he was killed.[12]

"No one," added Severance, "seemed to be interested in the names of the men
who raised the first flag."[13]

On the day the battle for Iwo Jima was finally won, March 26, 1945,
Severance and the surviving fifty men of Company E left Iwo's shores. After
a visit to the island's raw new cemetery, where Hansen, Thomas, and too many
other men of the 5th Division were buried, Company E marched to the island's
west coast and boarded the *Winged Arrow*.[14] Safely at sea, they could look
back at the island's unforgettable profile, where Suribachi, casting its long

shadow, brooded over a ravaged landscape.

It was at sea that the March 30 telegram from Marine Headquarters was received, the telegram relaying the presidential order that the six Rosenthal flag raisers return to Washington immediately. The six, however, were no longer a unit. Hansen, Strank, and Sousley lay buried in the 5th Division cemetery. Pharmacist's Mate Second Class John H. Bradley, the Navy corpsman, had been wounded and evacuated during the campaign. The fifth man, Gagnon, was on board the *Winged Arrow* proceeding toward Hawaii. And the sixth man had not yet admitted to being one of the heroes of Suribachi.[15]

On Iwo the search for the Rosenthal flag raisers had ended with the identification of five men, since the newspaper clippings failed to reveal that there was actually a sixth man in the photo. The lack of clarity in news photo reproductions provided ideal cover for the man seeking to conceal his participation in Rosenthal's photograph.

Private First Class Ira H. Hayes, a full-blooded Pima Indian from Bapchule, Arizona, was that sixth man. He was aboard the *Winged Arrow* with Gagnon when the order arrived to send *six* flag raisers home. Severance placed First Sergeant John A. Daskalakis in charge of locating the flag raisers. At this point, however, Gagnon was the only known flag raiser on board. Daskalakis found Gagnon with no difficulty, but Hayes did not step forward to volunteer. "Hayes, Pima Indian that he is, didn't open his mouth. He didn't admit it to me." So having instructed Gagnon that he was to return stateside immediately, Daskalakis thought his task was completed.[16]

Gagnon knew better. He sought out Hayes, who told him not to disclose the name of the missing flag raiser. Hayes was adamant in not wanting to return home, to the point that he threatened Gagnon "with bodily harm" if Gagnon revealed that Hayes was one of the men in the picture.[17]

Gagnon kept Hayes's secret and left the *Winged Arrow* unaccompanied by his fellow flag raiser on April 3. The ship was then anchored in Eniwetok's commodious lagoon, where it had stopped over, en route to Hawaii.[18]

Ninety-six hours after leaving his fellow Marines aboard ship in mid-Pacific, Gagnon was standing in Marine Headquarters in Washington, D.C. The staff at Headquarters had cast a wide net for six Marines but had drawn in only one lone private. Making do with what he had, the public information officer began his interrogation. Lieutenant Colonel Edward R. Hagenah reported the proceedings:

On Saturday, 7 April 1945, Private First Class RENE A. GAGNON reported in to Headquarters. . . . I [gave] him an enlarged print of the Rosenthal picture. He said he had seen the picture before but that it had been a newspaper clipping and not very clear as to detail. . . . I then asked Gagnon to name the others. He did so slowly, calling the names of Strank, Bradley, Sousely [*sic*] and Hansen. He pointed out that he had been sent up Mt. Suribachi with a new battery for a "walkie-talkie" and had given a hand when the new flag was ready to be put in place on the "long piece of Jap pipe." He added he knew all the men well and that Bradley was "a Corpsman."[19]

Gagnon reported that three of the men, Hansen, Strank, and Sousley, had been killed. He also told Hagenah that Bradley had been wounded in the leg.[20] This much Gagnon had already rehearsed earlier when questioned by Beech and Schrier on Iwo. From careful study of the Rosenthal photo, Hagenah and other staff members in the Office of Public Information had long since determined that there were six figures raising the flag. Gagnon named only five, the number that previously had satisfied Schrier and Beech. Hagenah was not to be so easily satisfied. Standing in front of the enlargement of the Rosenthal print, pencil in hand, Hagenah continued his questioning.

I asked him to give me the names again, only this time to jot them down. I handed him a pencil and piece of scrap paper. He wrote: Strank, Bradley, Sousely [*sic*] and Hansen. At my suggestion he then added his own, a total of five. It was then I asked him for the name of the sixth man, pointing out with a pencil the six figures. Gagnon studied the photograph closely for several minutes finally admitting that there were six in the picture. I again asked for the name of the sixth man but Gagnon only stared down at the picture. Finally, after further questioning, he said that he knew the sixth man but could not name him. I asked why? After some further hesitation Gagnon said that he had promised not to give his name as the man did not want to be identified.[21]

That a Marine would not want to admit to being one of the famous Iwo Jima flag raisers was almost beyond belief. Hagenah kept his composure and continued to probe for the name of the sixth man.

Gagnon was visibly upset and realizing that he was fresh from combat, nervous and under a strain, I reasoned slowly and deliberately with him, insisting however that he would have to name the other man due to the many factors connected with the picture, especially his return stateside under orders. Sometime later Gagnon very reluctantly said that the sixth man was "an Indian" and that he was known as "the Chief"; his name was Hayes, Private First Class IRA H. HAYES, Company "E," Second Battalion, Twenty-eighth Regiment, Fifth Marine Division.[22]

The jig was up. Hayes's days of anonymity were over. A dispatch ordering Hayes's immediate return was sent on April 9 to Commanding General, 5th

Marine Division. The 28th Marines were still at sea, three days out of Hilo, Hawaii.[23] On board ship destiny caught up with Hayes. A message arrived via high transfer line from the command ship to *Winged Arrow*. This time the request named a name, and Hayes, who hoped he had successfully eluded identification, was nailed.[24]

Daskalakis, confronting Hayes, asked: "Why the hell didn't you tell me that you were in the photograph?" The now-cornered Marine replied, "Oh, I don't know." Astonished and exasperated, Daskalakis exclaimed: "I don't know *why* you didn't tell me."[25]

Once in Hawaii, Hayes, in an agitated state, reported to Captain Fred E. Haynes, an operations officer in the 28th Regiment. Haynes, determined to sort the matter out, checked with "a couple of the commanders, including Dave Severance." These officers concluded that, willing or not, Hayes was the man in the Rosenthal photo.[26]

Identifying Hayes and convincing him to leave his unit and return to the States for duty were two different matters, however. First Lieutenant John Keith Wells, the former leader of Company E's 3rd Platoon, was recovering from his extensive wounds at a hospital in Pearl Harbor. He gave this account of Hayes's stubborn refusal to cooperate with the Corps' attempt to dress him up as a hero and send him to the States to be paraded around the country.

Ira Hayes would not come back to the States on the bond tour. This was unbelievable. The United States government asked him to, and he told them no. The Marine Corps asked him to, and he told them no. The colonel and the captain and everybody--and he said no. And finally he agreed that he would, providing they carried him to the hospital to see me at Pearl Harbor.

They brought him--an entourage! Can you believe: a colonel and a captain and all the Marine Corps news people, including the old boy that draws "Gizmo" and "Eight ball" in *Leatherneck*. They all came in. I thought, "Man, he's in trouble. There's no way I can get him out of that."

So I told him we were getting ready for Tokyo. There was already the estimate out that we were going to have a million casualties when we hit Japan. I told him, "Why don't you go on back and see your MADRE and PADRE, and if you don't like what's going on, come on back and we'll get ready for the Big Show." He and I had been in the paratroops together in the same outfit. I'd known him for years. We all knew one another. We were like family.

But the point is, naturally, he thinks he's a fraud [because Hayes had not participated in the *first,* the *real* flag raising]. That's what Hayes thought. In their eyes--Hayes, those Indians, they don't look at things like we do. Gray areas? There *is* no gray area. Everything was black or white. So in Hayes' mind, he wasn't in *the* flag raising.[27]

Nevertheless, with the encouragement of his former officer, Hayes submitted to the one incontrovertible truth of military life: that orders were orders, and that *he* was under orders from his commander in chief. On April 15 Hayes was on a plane to the States, and on April 19 he reported to Marine Headquarters in Washington, D.C.[28]

Ten days earlier, when the order had gone out for Hayes's return, Hagenah had also notified the Bureau of Medicine and Surgery that Bradley had been a participant in the Iwo Jima flag raising. The Bureau promptly requested that Bradley "be included in any honors to be accorded Gagnon and Hayes." Bradley's return to Bethesda Naval Hospital was immediately authorized.[29]

Bradley had ministered to one of the other flag raisers, Hansen, at the time of Hansen's death. Bradley himself had led a charmed life on Iwo Jima, moving about the island to tend dozens of the wounded and dying, unscathed in the midst of carnage. Then on March 12, 1945, his luck ran out. With both legs severely injured, the corpsman became a patient in the competent care of his own medical unit.[30]

Taken to the 2nd Battalion's aid station, "where the medical officer in charge of his own detachment . . . fixed him up," Bradley was then sent to the field hospital, where some shell fragments were removed from his legs. The next morning he was on a plane to Guam, from which point he was shipped to the U.S. Naval Hospital in Aiea Heights, Hawaii, to be reunited with injured men of the 5th Division.[31]

Bradley's treatment up to this point was what would have been given to any wounded veteran of the Iwo Jima campaign. But with his identification as one of the flag raisers, his status immediately changed and, as he said, "things happened fast." He was authorized to travel to Bethesda Naval Hospital, arriving in Washington, D.C., to be met at National Airport by Hagenah.[32]

The three surviving flag raisers from Rosenthal's photograph were now all back in the United States and under Hagenah's care. It was time for them to go to work in their new role as ceremonial figures in the Seventh War Loan bond drive. Gagnon was recalled to Washington from a visit home to New Hampshire. Hayes now met Gagnon for the first time since his betrayal. Hagenah reported the scene of their confrontation in the office of the director of the Division of Public Information, Brigadier General Robert L. Denig: "Hayes was sullen at first, although I learned later that he 'forgave' Gagnon for revealing his identity."[33]

The three men got their first major dose of national recognition that day at Marine Headquarters, where they "were photographed as a group and individually, there being a heavy demand for press pictures of them."[34] Gagnon had already enjoyed some preliminary celebrity when his name appeared in a brief AP story datelined Pearl Harbor on April 7. In this story Gagnon was incorrectly identified as "the only Marine in Associated Press Photographer Joe Rosenthal's famous Mt. Suribachi flag raising picture to survive the battle."[35]

The following day the error was corrected in a release written by Marine correspondent Beech, who had also just returned stateside. On April 9 an AP story based on the Beech release accompanied Rosenthal's photo with five of the flag raisers identified for the first time by name--courtesy of Gagnon. The stark caption under the figure at the flagpole's base read: "Sgt. Henry O. Hansen (Dead)."[36] The article disclosed that three of the six men in the photograph had died in "later bloody fighting on Iwo Jima." In addition to Hansen, there were Strank and a Marine whose name would not be disclosed until his next of kin could be notified. This unnamed Marine was Sousley.[37]

Boston area news reporters immediately located Hansen's family in their Somerville home. His sister and his mother were besieged with calls for interviews. Their private grief became a public affair. Rosenthal's photograph of six anonymous figures raising a flag had fascinated the country for weeks. The public appetite for details about the personal lives of the flag raisers was one the press had no need to whet, only to satisfy. At last the story of Suribachi could be fleshed out with photographs and interviews with the families of the dead Marines, and with firsthand accounts gleaned from those flag raisers who had survived the Iwo Jima campaign.

"Somerville Man in Iwo Picture," proudly proclaimed one local headline. "Iwo Jima Flag Raising Hero Killed by Japs," read another. Interviewed for the accompanying story, a grieving Mrs. Evelley described how she had been notified on March 27 of her son's death. She showed reporters where the service publication, *Yank,* had listed him as one of the flag raisers "among the epochal fighting men whose gesture made photographic as well as military history." Hansen's photograph in battle dress uniform, the family's prized possession, was lent to some of the stories: "His to do . . . and die," Hansen's picture was captioned in yet another paper, which credited him as representing "the foremost figure in the historic picture of flag raising on Iwo Jima."[38]

The story of Hansen's participation in the Rosenthal flag-raising picture soon expanded well beyond New England. Newspapers across the country were carrying personal pictures of the six flag raisers to enhance the Rosenthal photograph, which, to the frustration of reporters, had revealed none of the men's faces.

A composite photo of the six flag raisers was run in an AP story on April 22 above a typical heroic caption: "The valiant six who raised the flag on Iwo are here identified." The accompanying article's headline editorialized: "Six Men Who Raised Flag on Iwo Symbolize Melting Pot That Has Made America Strong," a theme much played upon and a continuous source of pride to the Marine Corps.

The six men who planted the flag atop Mount Suribachi on Iwo Jima are symbolic of the melting pot that is America and her fighting forces. Among the six were a full blooded Pima Indian, the son of an immigrant Czech coal miner, and a Kentucky farm boy.

They ranged in age from 19 to 25; they had been in service from 18 months to six years. Their temperament varied from "one of the nicest, quietest boys in town," according to a local policeman, to "a daredevil who wanted action," according to his mother.

All had been eager to enlist, and one outslicked induction doctors to do it. Three of them died on Iwo and another was wounded--an index to the terrific cost of that bleak Pacific island.

But unknown to them, all were to become famous due to "a historic photograph in which," Admiral Nimitz wrote to AP Photographer Joe Rosenthal, "you caught a moment in the lives of six of our valorous marines . . . which will live forever in the minds of their countrymen."[39]

Mrs. Evelley was quoted as describing her son, the man at the base of the pole, as the "daredevil who wanted action."[40]

For Hansen's mother interviews were the order of the day. She may have termed him a daredevil at the time when he first joined the Marines in June 1938, but in another interview she reported that her son had changed from adventurous adolescent to serious adult by the last time she saw him in early 1944.

"Over a year ago he last came home," said his mother today. "He had just come back from Bougainville, where he was a marine paratrooper.

"He was very serious, no longer a boy. He told me he dreaded going back, but he felt he must. He said after the war he was going to hibernate to New Hampshire for a while, and then marry Marjorie Rice of New York City. He was looking forward to a civilian job, for he'd been a marine since he was 18--after his graduation from Somerville High.

"See," said his mother, "see the photograph--that's my son, with his left hand gripped around the flag's staff. Henry put the American flag on Iwo Jima."[41]

Meanwhile, Gagnon also was receiving his share of publicity. In him the press early on had one flag raiser who was hale, hearty, and home in the States. Once having identified his five comrades in the Rosenthal photo, Gagnon was granted a brief leave to return home to New Hampshire. The press tracked him all along the way. In fact, they even beat him to his own front door. The story of the hero's return made for perfect press: Gagnon, as his portrait in news accounts revealed, was movie-star handsome; and he had a photogenic girl friend and an apple-pie mother waiting to welcome him home from the wars.

On the eve of his arrival, reporters caught his mother and fiancée (both of whom, by happy coincidence, worked together in a local war plant) at the family's house in Manchester. There in the down-home kitchen the press found a classic photo opportunity: Pauline Harnois, Gagnon's attractive fiancée, and his mother, Mrs. Irene Gagnon, standing by the old family stove preparing the returning hero's first home-cooked meal. Both women were interviewed about the impending return of their Marine. According to the news article, Gagnon had written his mother: "When you see the newsreel in the movies about putting the flag on the mountain, that was where I was." The article continued:

> But long before Mrs. Gagnon had received this letter from her son, Miss Harnois had seen the picture, and with feminine intuition had recognized one of the Marines as her sweetheart. Penciling a circle around the head, she sent the picture to Gagnon at his Pacific base with the message: "I'm sure this must be you."[42]

Miss Harnois's intuition had been extraordinary, given the limited view of Gagnon in Rosenthal's photograph. Innumerable other sweethearts and parents had also thought they recognized a loved one in the famous picture. To be officially identified as one of the six flag raisers was roughly equivalent to winning a national lottery.

The next day newspapers reported Gagnon's "surprise" visit home: "Mrs. Irene Gagnon, 43, got the surprise of her life when she came home from church and found her son waiting for her. Shortly afterwards they hurried off to Hookset and 'popped in' on his 19-year-old sweetheart Miss Pauline Harnois."[43] Newspapers carried photographs of the "Marine hero of Mt. Suribachi flag-raising," seated between his mother and fiancée, eating his favorite home-cooked dish.[44]

As to any hard news, any substantive information about the famous flag raising, Gagnon was not at liberty to speak. "The Marine is under strict orders not to give an interview on his Iwo Jima experiences," the local paper explained.[45] The press was stonewalled by the Marine Corps concerning Gagnon's flag-raising activities. The only details available about Gagnon's exploits on Suribachi were those in the official Marine release prepared by Beech. That bare-bones statement quoted Gagnon briefly:

> "It was a big flag and looked swell. For a flagpole we had to use a piece of Jap pipe. After the flag went up and while we were standing there our lieutenant said to hurry up, because there was plenty of work to do.
> "There was, too," said Gagnon, "because there were still Japs around the place."[46]

The Beech release identified the lieutenant as Schrier, "who led a patrol to the top of Suribachi on the morning of February 23." "It was Schrier, Platoon Sgt. Ernest I. Thomas, Jr., of Tallahassee, Fla., and Hansen who raised the first and smaller flag on Suribachi," Beech's release revealed. The local article also concluded with the news that the famous picture in which the Manchester Marine figured was "actually of the second Iwo Jima flag raising."[47] Clearly, there was an initial disclosure that an earlier flag raising had preceded the one Rosenthal photographed. But such clarifications were soon forgotten in the hectic days to come.

For Gagnon, his mother, and his fiancée these were heady times. Interviews and guest appearances crowded their calendar. The city of Manchester planned to "stage a big homecoming welcome to the Manchester boy."[48] But the parade in Gagnon's honor was abruptly canceled at the news of Roosevelt's death on April 12, 1945. After a brief period of mourning, the nation got back to business, the business of conducting and financing a war. Gagnon and the other surviving flag raisers were destined to play a prominent role in that part of the war effort currently being organized on the homefront.

For Hansen, however, the war had already ended. The same week that Gagnon was being lionized in Manchester, the Hansen family was preparing for a pre-burial Mass on April 14 at St. Ann's Church in Somerville. The interview calls of an inquisitive press continued to mingle with calls and letters of condolence. Officials, friends, even strangers wrote. Angier L. Goodwin, congressman from Massachusetts' 8th District, sent his "very deep sympathy for the loss of your son," and Senator Leverett Saltonstall expressed his "heartfelt sorrow for your loss."[49]

Particularly touching, and perhaps most meaningful to Hansen's mother, were the letters from her son's commanding officers on Iwo Jima. Company E's commander, Severance, spoke of Hansen's courage and his role in the second flag raising:

Henry's loss will be long remembered by you and his comrades with whom he served, and survived. The picture of the flag raising on Mount Suribachi is a living Memorial to Henry since he was one of the six men who raised that flag. I realize that mere words cannot ease your grief nor your loss of Henry. Words are so futile in these circumstances. I sincerely hope that this letter has been of some comfort to you.[50]

Severance made no mention of Hansen's participation in the *first* flag raising on Suribachi. It was Hansen's platoon leader, Wells, who wrote of Hansen's "standing by the first flag raised on Iwo Jima." Focusing on Hansen's activities in *his* platoon, Wells chose not to refer to Hansen's role in the second flag raising.[51]

These letters helped meet the need, common to bereaved parents, to know the details of how a son has died in battle. Particularly comforting to a Catholic family was the letter from a Roman Catholic chaplain attached to the 28th Marines, who assured Mrs. Evelley "that Henry had the opportunity to receive the Sacraments before he died."[52] Richard Cushing, archbishop of Boston, also wrote Hansen's mother a condolence letter that would occupy a place of honor in the family's collection of memorabilia.[53] Finally, there were the pictures of Hansen's grave in the 5th Marine Division cemetery at the foot of Suribachi, sent to the Hansen family along with a copy of Major General Keller E. Rockey's address delivered at the cemetery's dedication.[54]

Once press accounts had identified Hansen as being in the Rosenthal photograph, his family also began to receive letters from people they had never met, people eager to express their sympathy to at least one of the families bereaved by the terrible casualties that were the price paid for Iwo Jima. Some sent news clippings along with their letters. One clipping from the March 11 issue of the *Chicago Sunday Tribune* displayed the Rosenthal gung-ho photograph: the shot of sixteen disheveled Marines, waving and cheering in front of a wind-swept flag. Smiling out from the crowd was the clearly identifiable face of Henry Hansen.[55]

All this correspondence was intended to comfort the Hansen family. The letters and clippings were carefully preserved in a white box of memorabilia, along with two letters that undoubtedly caused a stab of grief. These were Mrs. Evelley's last letters to her son, returned unopened with the instructions: "USMC Reports Undeliverable. Return to Sender."[56]

While Hansen's mother and sister were preoccupied with matters relating to his death, the surviving flag raisers found themselves swept up in a new campaign. Their mere presence in Rosenthal's flag-raising photograph had transformed their lives. Early on the morning of April 20 in the nation's capital, Hagenah escorted Gagnon, Hayes, and Bradley (stumping along on his crutches) to meet Theodore R. Gamble, director of the War Savings Division at the Treasury Department. In Gamble's office "a huge press conference had been arranged," and the three men were "questioned in great detail and at length."[57]

Next the group was taken to meet Secretary of the Treasury Henry Morgenthau, Jr., who in turn escorted them to the White House to meet the country's new chief of state, Harry S Truman.[58] Morgenthau presented Truman with the first copy off the press of the Seventh War Loan poster, based on Rosenthal's famous photograph. The poster's caption, "Now All Together," was to be the motto of the War Loan drive scheduled to begin in three weeks.

The White House ceremony, a preview of the bond drive, was clearly an opportunity for wide publicity. The press was present in force. Newspapers the next day carried stories and photographs of Truman and Morgenthau, flanked by the three uniformed heroes: Gagnon, pointing to himself in the poster, Bradley, supported by his crutches, and Hayes looking on.[59]

The flag-raising heroes had initially hoped to be received by Roosevelt. Bradley later explained, "President Roosevelt was instrumental in getting us back." "We sure wanted to meet him. It was a disappointment to us that he had died."[60] Yet meeting Truman proved to be a great thrill. "The little guy was as cheerful as anybody I've ever met," Hayes exclaimed. "He was always smiling and made me feel right at home." Bradley was similarly impressed. "I was very nervous before going in to meet the commander in chief of our armed forces. But after I got in, I felt no different than going into an office in my own home town to meet a local business man."[61]

This milestone day was only a precursor to the parade of personal appearances soon to become a way of life for these newly minted war heroes. Holding their first joint press conference, the trio told reporters "how they hoisted the Stars and Stripes into place on a 'very heavy' piece of Japanese pipe." Following the White House visit, they were ushered off to the United States Senate where they were accorded the unusual honor of a five-minute Senate recess so they could be brought onto the Senate floor. As they appeared, the senators rose and applauded, with spectators in the gallery joining in. Finally, the senators filed by the three young heroes to shake their hands.[62]

Hagenah subsequently reported the afternoon's events, which included a private luncheon hosted by Speaker of the House Sam Rayburn. "Later they joined the Congressional party attending the opening ball game at Griffith Stadium where, standing as a trio at home-plate, they were accorded a tremendous welcome by 35,000 fans."[63]

In all that was said and done, there was no reported mention of the fact that the flag these three survivors had raised was not the first flag raised on Suribachi.[64]

Hayes, Gagnon, and Bradley were assigned to the Treasury Department for the duration of the bond tour. They were to be accompanied on the tour by correspondent Keyes Beech, who knew many men of the 28th Marines. Marine Headquarters had ordered Beech and four other correspondents home to write a "popular-priced book," *The U.S. Marines on Iwo Jima*. Now, at the Treasury Department's request, he would join the three flag raisers to act as their guide, adviser, and NCO in charge.[65]

The bond tour, long in preparation, was scheduled to begin on May 15 in New York City. From there it would proceed through major U.S. cities from coast to coast, ending in the nation's capital on July 4. Gagnon, Hayes, and Bradley were to make the entire circuit as the tour's featured attractions. The Treasury Department was pulling out all the stops in its effort to raise the maximum number of dollars. Preparations throughout the country were extensive, intense, and varied. A 55-foot replica of the scene in Rosenthal's flag-raising photograph would be erected in Times Square. A 103-foot ship's model, resembling the superstructure of an Essex class aircraft carrier, was being built in Rockefeller Center. *The Fighting Lady* would remain at the plaza as the hub for bond appeal activities.[66]

On the morning of May 9, as the nation was still recovering from VE-Day celebrations, three uniformed men stood prepared once again to raise the very flag they had raised on Suribachi. Now the scene was Capitol Hill. A Marine Corps band played the National Anthem. Numerous dignitaries stood by while a crowd of thousands watched the heroes of Iwo Jima pull a halyard to raise their tattered flag over the Capitol Building.[67]

Among those present were Forrestal, Vandegrift, Morgenthau (whose Treasury Department had arranged the ceremony), Rayburn, and assorted senators and congressmen. Vandegrift informed the spectators that the three flag raisers present were the only survivors of the six flag raisers Rosenthal had photographed. The others, he explained, had been killed by mortar shells. Forrestal, "who was on Iwo Jima, said he could never again see a Marine without a feeling of reverence." Rayburn focused attention on the well-worn flag itself, reminding the audience that "this flag was a symbol of determination to accept nothing less than unconditional surrender from the Japanese."[68]

So it was that the famous flag (in reality the *second* one raised on Suribachi), "tattered along its outer edge from the Pacific winds that whipped it as it waved on Mount Suribachi," came to fly over the nation's capital. Brought back from Iwo Jima by Colonel Harry B. Liversedge, commanding officer of the 28th Marines, the flag was inaccurately being touted as "the original flag that was raised by Marines on Suribachi." It would be "lowered at sundown as retreat is sounded in the many nearby military posts." Vandegrift announced that from Washington the flag would travel ceremoniously from coast to coast with the Seventh War Loan tour, and that at the tour's conclusion the treasured standard would be placed in the Marine Corps museum in Quantico.[69]

Inevitably, Mrs. Evelley was swept up in the wave of preparations for the bond drive. As mother of one of the deceased Marines pictured on the Seventh War Loan poster, she was invited by the Treasury Department to come to New York and help launch the drive. Her presence was requested to dedicate the country's fundraising effort "to your son Henry, who gave everything he possessed, that, among other American ideals, Old Glory might be planted squarely between the eyes of a fanatical and cruel Japanese enemy."[70] The press conveyed this latest development in the flag-raising story under the laconic headline: "Iwo Hero's Ma Aids Bond Push." An accompanying news photograph pictured her and her daughter, who held the March 26 issue of *Life* magazine and pointed to her brother supporting the flagpole in the Lowery photo of the first flag raising.[71]

With the other two Gold Star Mothers, Mrs. Evelley would stand on platforms, shake countless hands, submit to hordes of photographers and reporters, and receive a $1,000 War Bond, not because her son had participated in the first flag raising, but because he had participated in a subsequent flag raising photographed by Rosenthal. It was this photograph that transformed the lives of Hansen's family. Without the photograph, Hansen would have remained merely one of the 5,931 Marines who died in a costly campaign to capture an obscure island that few, if any, citizens in Somerville, Massachusetts, had ever heard of in the years preceding 1945.

If the flag raising on Suribachi was a defining event for the Hansen family, it was becoming a career for Gagnon, Bradley, and Hayes. On Friday, May 11, New York City was host to two ceremonies in support of the War Loan campaign. Three days earlier Nazi Germany had surrendered unconditionally. There was ample reason for celebration as thousands gathered to launch the campaign for America's final foray against the last remaining foe. Ceremonies in Times Square and on Wall Street were replete with unveilings and speeches by Vandegrift and by the ever-oratorical Mayor Fiorello La Guardia. Alluding to the flag, Vandegrift asserted that the "faith, toil and invincible determination of all real Americans advanced the Stars and Stripes to Iwo Jima." The three survivors unveiled an overpowering 50-foot statue of the flag raising. Then, once again, the "two Marines and the sailor hoisted the same weather-beaten flag on the statue's flag pole that they had planted on Iwo."[72]

The three men appeared later at a Wall Street ceremony where again Vandegrift spoke. By day's end, the strain was beginning to show on the new heroes. A correspondent reported that the flag raisers "looked a bit harried and confessed that appearing for the Seventh War Loan Drive 'is not as much fun as it would seem.'"[73] Yet the three men had barely hit their public relations trail. Within the next forty-eight hours they and their battle-weary flag were due in two different directions: Philadelphia and Boston.

The flag-raising trio arrived at Boston's South Station the following Sunday afternoon, May 13, to be greeted by Miss Harnois, Gagnon's fiancée, and by the omnivorous press corps. The next day's news coverage featured a picture of all three heroes clasping hands with Miss Harnois in a pose reminiscent of the three Musketeers.[74]

Planned to the minute, their itinerary was a crowded one. Advance stories announced that the three flag raisers were to be joined in a program rich in prominent politicians, movie stars, and military brass. Sunday's feature event, the "Parade of the Purple Hearts," would be reviewed by Governor Maurice Tobin at the State House and by Mayor John E. Kerrigan at City Hall. The Hollywood guests, like the three Iwo Jima heroes, were to be in the parade itself. Film stars included Jane Wyman, "whose actor husband, Ronald Reagan, is in the Army Air Corps," and Cesar Romero, a petty officer in the Coast Guard.[75]

"Parade, Stars, Exercises Open 7th War Loan Today," proclaimed the headlines of one typical front-page story.[76] Pictures and cartoons abounded in the Sunday papers.[77] Pressed into service shortly after their arrival at South

Station, the flag raisers were installed in the parade's lead jeep, and the cavalcade advanced. The crowd's enthusiastic response was duly reported by the press: "All along the route, even before a police radio car announced who was 'in the car behind me' the thousands of spectators who lined the streets of Boston several deep knew that here were the heroic flag-raisers." "Ain't that something," exclaimed "Chief" Hayes. "I didn't think the people would know us." Gagnon, of course, had a "hometown" advantage: the "dark-haired, slender youth hailed scores of friends from Manchester with obvious delight as he rode along the route of the parade in a jeep with the other two survivors."[78]

Marching up Beacon Hill to the State House, "the parade halted for a ceremony that will have a place in Massachusetts history":

> The Marines had with them the very flag they raised on the top of the mount, carried it with them to the flagpole in front of the State House, and while the band played the national anthem the three survivors of Suribachi raised it to the top, and lowered it again.
>
> Then they released it from the flag shrouds and carried it back with them to the jeep. The flag is now in their custody and they are charged with the duty of guarding it. It must always be in their possession. It was an impressive and moving ceremony.[79]

The flag's condition and the reverent care accorded it were noted by the press: "There are bullet holes in this flag, and it is handled as tenderly as the ancient battle flags in the State House hall of flags. Although it was flown only for a minute or so during the State House ceremony, the thousands who stood in silence among the fighting forces standing at attention got a terrific kick out of seeing the identical flag that cheered the Marines on to victory at Iwo Jima."[80] Photographers snapped the three raisers in all manner of poses with "the historic colors": holding the flag, admiring the flag, raising the flag. Rosenthal's photograph had not only made six men into public heroes; it had also transformed an ordinary flag into a national relic.[81]

Hayes, Gagnon, and Bradley were barely back in the jeep with their "victory flag" when dark clouds unleashed a deluge on the parade and its 200,000 spectators. At the concluding ceremonies on Boston Common everyone was soaked--raisers, stars, politicians, and spectators. Tobin introduced "all three heroes" to the crowd. Discounting the weather, the water-logged men grinned and agreed, "This is the easiest thing we have done yet."[82]

Hayes "glowed with pride" as Tobin introduced him as "the only man here who can claim to be a real American." The handsome Marine replied, "I'm an Indian and I'm damn proud of it." Bradley, in his once-crisp Navy uniform, spoke to the day's purpose: "It was a little thing we did. Everyone can do as much if they will spend everything they can spare to buy bonds." "We put the flag up on Iwo, but the quicker you put up for War Bonds the quicker we'll put up the flag on Tokyo."[83]

Hy Hurwitz, a former Marine combat correspondent now reporting for the *Boston Globe,* had covered the activities of the three flag raisers from an enviable position beside them in the lead jeep during the Parade of the Purple Hearts. Hurwitz even managed to coax some details about the ascent up Suribachi from the reluctant hero, Hayes.

> The pole on which the historic flag was raised was a piece of rusted Jap pipeline. Hayes and another Marine were ordered out to find something on which to tie the flag. "We looked for five minutes," said the Chief, "when we spotted a piece of Jap pipeline. It was the only thing available and while we didn't want anything Japanese attached to our flag, we wanted to hoist the flag to let the Japs know that we were up there for keeps."
>
> It wasn't until Hayes and three other Marines were halfway up Mt. Suribachi that the men knew what they were going up to do. Sgt. Mike Strank, who was later killed, was in charge of the group. He had something sticking out inside his dungaree shirt. "Halfway up," said Hayes, "he told us what we were going to do. We really went right up there then."
>
> The men knew the significance of the flag-raising. They knew it would arouse the ire of the Japs who were still around the top of the mountain. But the flag had to go up, regardless of consequences.[84]

Hayes apparently did not disclose to Hurwitz (or if he did Hurwitz did not choose to report it) one significant detail: that his group raised the *second* flag at the summit. Clearly, Hayes *did* refuse the title of hero, however. "How can I feel like a hero," he added, "when only five men in my platoon of 45 survived, when only 27 men in my company of 250 managed to escape death or injury."[85] There were undeniable signs that the young Marine felt remorse, if not guilt, that he had survived to be heralded a hero while so many of his comrades never left Iwo Jima alive.

Bradley, for his part, stressed that credit for the flag raising should be shared. He admonished reporters: "Tell the fellows that it took everyone on that island and the men in the ships offshore to get the flag up on Suribachi."[86]

All three of the flag raisers were young men barely in their twenties. None was the product of a sophisticated background. They virtually had been plucked from the battlefront and plunked down on the homefront, moved at lightning speed from a foxhole to the White House, from the company of corporals to the company of generals. This absence of a transition period, and the problems it presented, caught the attention of reporter Hurwitz. The three men, he commented, "are trying to acclimate themselves to civilization after some hazardous escapades on Iwo Jima."[87]

From the Mighty Seventh's very beginning, there was evidence in news stories that spotlights and fanfare were not home territory for the three flag raisers. Hayes confided to Hurwitz in Boston that he had not wanted to return to the United States in the first place. Hurwitz seized on the story, reporting under the headline, "Hayes, Iwo Jima Hero, Wants to Return to Battle."

> He didn't want to come back.
>
> No, not with the memory of his many buddies killed and wounded on Iwo Jima and with plenty of war against the enemy Japs still ahead of us.
>
> But Pfc Ira Hayes, one of the three remaining members of the 5th Marine Division which hoisted the historic flag on Mt. Suribachi last Feb. 23, was ordered back to the States so he could help boost sales in the Seventh War Bond drive.
>
> A full-blooded Pima Indian from Arizona, Hayes feels more at home with a BAR (Browning automatic) or a tommy gun in his hand than he does before a microphone or the huge throngs which have been greeting the heroic survivors during their country-wide tour.[88]

Despite being ill at ease with their new celebrity status, the three survivors appreciated the tour's importance, Hurwitz reported. "The flag-raising survivors will be on tour until July 4. The importance of their public appearances has been duly impressed upon them. Even 'The Chief' realizes the value of raising the War Bond quota. 'But I'll be very happy when I can get back to my outfit,' he said on departing."[89]

Hurwitz tracked the trio up to their departure for New York, when he filed his last story about the flag raisers and their deceased comrade, Hansen.

> The three flag-raisers left Boston yesterday for New York. They met with one disappointment here. They had hoped to meet the mother of Sgt. Henry O. Hansen of Somerville, one of the original flag-raisers. But ironically, Mrs. Hansen [Mrs. Evelley] left Boston for New York before the survivors arrived for a War Bond tour.
>
> Bradley was only five feet from Hansen when the Somerville Marine was killed. He took Hansen's wrist watch and he was looking forward to presenting it to his buddy's mother.[90]

So it was in New York on Tuesday, May 15, that Mrs. Evelley first met the corpsman who had tried to save her son's life. She had traveled to New York to participate in the official launching ceremonies for the national bond tour. The setting, a noon-hour rally in front of the Sub-Treasury Building on Wall Street, was hardly appropriate to the personal dimension of her encounter with Bradley. On a platform high above an audience of 10,000 observers, Mrs. Evelley, Mrs. Charles Strank, and Sousley's mother, Mrs. J. Hensley Price, met the three young men who had survived to come back home to their families.

The weather, so unpatriotic in Boston, favored the New York opening. The sun broke through at 11:45 A.M., just as the Manhattan Beach Coast Guard band began its bombardment of the nation's financial capital with martial airs. At noon "the crowd's murmuring hushed" as "three motherly women," the Gold Star mothers, were escorted to the platform. The mothers wore dark orchids; "their faces and their eyes showed bewilderment and awe at their reception and at their surroundings." There was a sudden silence as heads were bared in the sun and "the throngs came to attention for the National Anthem."[91]

Emil Schram, New York Stock Exchange president, stepped to the microphone to announce that "Symbolically, we are dedicating our greatest War Bond effort to that illustrious group who raised Old Glory on Iwo Jima." Schram told the crowd that three members of this "brave group are with us today" and, as he waved at the three survivors who stood stiffly at attention, the crowd applauded. The other three, he added, "have made the supreme sacrifice." Then as he introduced the three survivors the "cheers and echoes welled again," and the band struck up "Anchors Aweigh."[92]

Silence again fell on the street below. Then the drums rolled as Bradley, Gagnon, and Hayes presented the three Gold Star mothers "the actual flag which their sons helped to raise" on Iwo Jima. The three survivors yet again raised their tattered flag from Iwo Jima. As Old Glory rose slowly on its staff, nine Coast Guard trumpets played "To the Colors." When "the drum roll ended and the trumpets' notes faded the silence was deeper." The silence finally "gave way to fresh waves of cheering" as Schram, exhibiting a true sense of place, presented the mothers of the "Iwo martyrs" and the three survivors each a $1,000 Series E War Bond. The ceremony then appropriately concluded with the "Marine Hymn." The Mighty Seventh, as it was called, had officially begun.[93]

Mrs. Evelley had spoken earlier of how difficult it would be to meet the other men who were in the flag raising with her son, how "the grief in her heart" would be renewed. An AP dispatch attempted to do justice to the moment: "Three Gold Star mothers met three marines today and the touch of their fingertips called up memories that caused onlookers to fall silent and avert their eyes. . . . Few words were spoken by either group. Each seemed to understand what was in the others' hearts."[94] The occasion moved the usually impassive Hayes to reveal his feelings to his family. "Yesterday in NY," he wrote, "we met the mothers of the 3 dead Marines who were with us, and believe me, we all cried."[95]

Following the ceremony the guests of honor were treated to lunch and a tour of the Stock Exchange. "Awed by the reception the Big Town" had given them, the three mothers "sat in the Stock Exchange and reminisced briefly about their boys." The press reported the scene: "They just sat and sort of reminded themselves about the pride that was theirs." Mrs. Strank termed her son "a good boy, a good boy. He enlisted Oct. 6, 1939. Couldn't stay out." Before making the New York trip, Hansen's mother had said: "I wish only that the 42 other marines who went up Suribachi could get some of this glory." Mrs. Price recalled that when her son left their Kentucky farm, he told her: "Mom, I want to do something that will make you real proud of me." She added: "I don't think he could have done any greater thing than to help raise that flag on Iwo." One reporter, reflecting the prevailing national attitude, quickly responded: "No, ma'am, no one could."[96]

The flag raiser for whom Mrs. Evelley felt the greatest kinship was Bradley, the corpsman who had been Hansen's best friend in their unit. He had been with Hansen when he was shot and had attempted to save his life. Here in New York, Bradley was at last able to return to Hansen's mother the watch he had taken from his friend's wrist on Iwo Jima.[97]

Bradley found time to make a date that evening with Gertrude Hansen and with Hansen's fiancée, Marjorie Rice, a resident of New York. Hansen's best friend, his kid sister, and his fiancée shared a special bond, and their evening together kindled a friendship. "Gertrude," Bradley later wrote, "I'll never forget that evening in New York with you and Marge. I hope you enjoyed it half as much as I did."[98]

At last the Mighty Seventh was launched, focusing attention and heaping praise on the six flag raisers and their now-famous standard. Embarked on a trek across the country, the three survivors proved to be the central attractions in the War Bond tour that headed westward to Chicago, with whistle-stops in Rochester and Cleveland.

At each city news reporters and photographers swarmed to interview the three men Rosenthal's photo had turned into overnight celebrities. Gagnon, Hayes, and Bradley were virtually strip-searched for every detail of their family backgrounds, military experiences, exploits against the Japanese on Iwo Jima, and, perhaps most painfully, their recollections of the famous flag raising. In truth, the three survivors were caught in a tangled web not of their own weaving.

Hayes, as a full-blooded Pima Indian, was just the sort of exotic character the press loved to serve up to its receptive American public. As early as May 15 in New York, however, the Corps' public information officer, Hagenah, received his first inkling that there was trouble brewing with one of his star fund raisers. Hagenah later reported:

> On 15 May, during a routine telephone check on arrangements, Beech rather reluctantly advised me that "the Chief," as he called him, was "not happy," appeared "confused" and, when in these "moods," was troublesome. As Hayes was in an adjoining room, I requested to talk with him. He said he didn't "go for all the fuss being made over him" but assured me he would "do better."[99]

Hayes, at best a reluctant hero, was not a natural for the bond tour's limelight. Problems persisted, as Hagenah discovered when the tour reached Detroit on May 22. A swift decision was made at Marine Headquarters. Hayes was ordered to return to his unit in the Pacific for reasons not fully revealed to the national press. Hayes's bouts of drinking had apparently reached disruptive proportions.[100]

WASHINGTON < May 25 (AP)--An American Indian, one of the three survivors of the historic flag-raising on Iwo Jima, is being returned to overseas duty--at his own request.

He is marine Pfc. Ira H. "Chief" Hayes, 22, of Bapchule, Ariz.

Hayes, who already has served two tours of duty overseas, didn't want to leave his outfit, the 28th Regiment, in the first place. For that reason he was reluctant to acknowledge his role in the flag-raising when questioned in the field.[101]

Like a game of Ten Little Indians, the six original participants in the historic flag raising had been gradually reduced to one remaining pair: Gagnon and Bradley. Also missing from the spotlight and spangles of the bond tour was the man who had taken the defining photograph in the first place: Joe Rosenthal.[102]

Home from the wars, Rosenthal was installed at Associated Press headquarters in New York with his own desk, telephone, modest salary increase, and other luxuries not usually accorded to AP war photographers. In making national celebrities of Hayes, Gagnon, and Bradley, Rosenthal had inadvertently made one of himself. Accustomed to photographing the news from the vantage point of outside observer, he had to adjust to the unfamiliar role of newsmaker, the object of interest to the American people and the national press.

Everywhere he went, from San Francisco to New York, the unprepossessing young photographer was interviewed by reporters. No less a publication than the *New Yorker* magazine ran a story on him in its April 7, 1945, issue, detailing his conquest of New York:

We got hold of him at the New Weston the day after he arrived and he was already wobbling under the strain of the program the A.P. had laid out for him. He had been interviewed by the papers, dined with Kent Cooper, president of the A.P. (whom he'd never seen before), looked over the bond posters, arranged to broadcast on "We, the People," selected a series of his photographs for publication in *U.S. Camera,* lunched with the Dutch Treat Club and been fêted at Hamburger Mary's by several high ranking A.P. colleagues.[103]

The *New Yorker* article afforded Rosenthal a welcome opportunity to explain in the clearest possible terms that he had taken his photograph of the *second,* not the first, flag raising.

> Joe--nobody ever calls him Joseph--freely admitted that all the hoopla about the picture had come as a surprise to him. "I wasn't around when they raised the first flag on Iwo--the little one," he said. "My shot was taken about three-quarters of an hour later.". . . When Joe's picture was published, a commentator on the Blue Network said that the picture had been carefully posed by Joe. Later, he retracted the canard. "It wouldn't have been any disgrace at all," Joe told us, "to figure out a composition like that. But it just so happened I didn't. Good luck was with me, that's all--the wind rippling the flag right, the men in fine positions, and the day clear enough to bring everything into sharp focus."[104]

Despite the allegation that Rosenthal had "carefully posed" his picture, fellow members of his profession seemed to accept the photograph as authentic, and awards, congratulations, and plaudits showered down on the modest man from San Francisco.

Less than a week after his arrival in New York, he was awarded the Graflex diamond award as the year's outstanding press photographer. The award, it was explained, was both for his "outstanding devotion to duty in photographing the Pacific war in general, and more specifically, for your now famous picture of the flag raising on Mount Suribachi on Iwo Jima."[105]

He received one plaque from the New York Photographers Association and another plaque from the Catholic Institute of the Press at its first annual Communion breakfast at the Waldorf-Astoria. On this occasion, Brigadier General Carlos P. Romulo, United States commissioner of the Philippines, praised the flag-raising photograph as "the greatest picture of the war." For his part, Rosenthal turned the plaque over to the Associated Press.[106]

Sharing the front page on May 8, alongside the news of Germany's surrender, came the announcement that Rosenthal had received the prestigious Pulitzer Prize for news photography.[107] The Pulitzer awards were for 1944, and normally this 1945 photograph would not have been eligible. But the rule was suspended "for this distinguished example," the trustees of Columbia University announced.[108] The *New York Times* the next day declared "Joe Rosenthal's famous photograph of the flag raising on Iwo depicts one of the war's great moments," a "frozen flash of history" caught by his camera.[109]

U.S. Camera magazine gave a dinner in his honor, awarding him a $1,000 War Bond and a medallion for still picture achievement for his combat photographs of Iwo Jima's invasion.[110] The editors explained their selection in these terms:

> The Editors of *U.S. Camera* were guided in making their selection by the

conviction that the Iwo picture fully accomplished the ultimate purpose of photography, which is to make the viewer relive the events recorded. The Iwo picture caught the event so effectively that one who looks at it can virtually feel and hear the breeze which whips the flag. In a sense, in that moment, Rosenthal's camera recorded the soul of a nation.[111]

While Rosenthal and his photograph were receiving all variety of praise and honors, the photo was also being reproduced in unprecedented numbers. Its earlier choice as the official symbol for the Seventh War Loan drive had indicated a printing of 3.5 million copies of the poster alone, plus reproductions in thousands of newspapers and magazines to be seen by millions of readers.[112]

Reproductions of the photograph were being circulated in color, as well as in the original black and white. In April the *San Francisco Chronicle*'s front page offered a "beautiful color reproduction" of the photograph by "master craftsmen." "Worthy of a permanent place on the wall of home, school or office," the lithograph was offered to the public at cost, 25 cents.[113] Autographed copies of the photograph were in demand, autographed not just by Rosenthal, but by the flag raisers as well. Enlarged copies were circulated for autographs among high-ranking naval officers in the Pacific for presentation in Washington to Roosevelt and Forrestal.[114]

Rosenthal and his photo garnered yet another honor. From the start, the classic image had been proposed for a postage stamp. Now the proposal was made official: a three-cent stamp was to be issued on July 11, 1945. In honor of the Marines, the stamp's color would be green rather than the usual purple designated for three-cent denominations.[115] Hansen's image and that of his five comrades would now literally be seen across the nation. Their act would become a household word, a domesticated icon. Rosenthal's picture was well on its way to becoming the most reproduced photographic image in history.

To such an extraordinary welcome AP's highly improbable hero had come home. But Rosenthal, like the men he had photographed on Suribachi, had a limited appetite for celebrity. His style was to deflect the accolades heaped upon him, focusing the praise where he felt it was most deserved: on the ordinary rank-and-file fighting men of Iwo Jima. And at almost every juncture Rosenthal pointed out that his picture was taken on the occasion of the *second*, not the first, flag raising.

Not everyone was so punctiliously correct. The fact that another flag had been raised and photographed earlier that February morning was virtually ignored in the press, after *Life* magazine's "exposé" appeared in its March 26 issue.

In the heady spring of 1945, neither the American press nor the American public seemed in a mood to probe behind the scenes of the Mighty Seventh's dazzling production. As the bond tour moved magisterially onward, piling ceremony on top of ceremony, there was no mention of the first flag or of the men who raised it. Where were these other flag raisers? Had they, too, been killed on Iwo Jima with so many of their comrades? And where, for that matter, was the first flag itself--the very first American flag ever to fly over territory of the Japanese homeland? As far as the bond tour's programs were concerned, there were only *three* remaining flag raisers and *one* flag. News stories did not challenge the tour's official party line.

Nor was recognition given the Marine photographer who had climbed Suribachi with Schrier's 3rd Platoon that windy winter morning. It was as though Lou Lowery and his photographs had been submerged in some vast developing tank and kept suspended there in solution.

Of the five men later identified in Lowery's photograph published in *Life,* two, Hansen and Thomas, were to die in Suribachi's shadow. Three Marines in the photo, Schrier, Lindberg, and Michels, survived to leave the island.[116] But although the same number survived the first flag raising as survived the second, their destinies would trace markedly different trajectories.

As it happened, Hansen was to experience more acclaim dead than his platoon mates who had raised the first flag were accorded live. Hansen alone had joined the hallowed ranks of Rosenthal's Six. Public attention was showered on the Hansen family, not because Hansen had raised the *first* flag on Suribachi, but because he had been identified as one of the men in Rosenthal's photograph of the *second* flag. A dead participant in Rosenthal's flag raising had been deemed of greater publicity value than three live participants in Lowery's flag raising.

These three men in Lowery's photo were back in Hawaii, preparing for the proposed November invasion of Japan: the Big Show. While these survivors slept in barracks, dined on military rations, and drilled on the parade grounds of Camp Tarawa, the three survivors of the second flag raising slept in metropolitan hotels, dined at banquets with Hollywood stars, and rode in open cars along the parade route of the Mighty Seventh.

None of these disparate destinies had anything to do with the relative courage or competence of either trio of survivors. It was neither their valor nor the value of their contributions to the Iwo Jima campaign that distinguished one group of men from the other. None were more aware of this fact than Bradley, Gagnon, and Hayes. What set them apart from the first flag raisers was nothing more than a photograph. "But," as Robert Sherrod had admitted in his Guam diary, "what a picture!"[117]

By mid-May a point of no return had been reached concerning the matter of the two flag raisings. The conflict in the Pacific still raged. The invasion of Japan loomed on the horizon. Public support, in both money and manpower, had to be maintained for the war effort. It became almost a patriotic duty to bolster the heroic myth of Rosenthal's flag and its surviving flag raisers.

Everyone and everything connected with the famous photograph by now had taken on an aura of heightened significance. Even the flag in the photograph was hailed as "a symbol of determination to accept nothing less than unconditional surrender," as "the victory flag," "the historic colors," and, when inspiration failed, that old standby, "Old Glory." It was carried from city to city like some religious relic in a medieval pilgrimage. As the Mighty Seventh barnstormed across the country with one elaborate ceremony unfurling immediately after another, no attempt was made to reconcile the story of the heroes on parade with earlier stories of another flag raising.

Standing (figuratively) on the sidelines watching the parade go by were three of the men who had actually raised that first flag on Iwo Jima and the Marine photographer who had captured their brief moment of glory. It must have been a surreal experience for all concerned. Reality had been transformed into the heroic myth of Suribachi.

NOTES

1. Roosevelt's decision to bring the flag raisers home and to employ them for fundraising purposes came at the suggestion of Louis Ruppel, executive editor of the *Chicago Herald-American* (Ruppel to Roosevelt, telegram dated March 16, 1945, Investigation File, USMC Historical Center, hereafter referred to as Investigation File). Some documents in this file were in the form of copies or typed transcripts, not originals.

2. Roosevelt to Ruppel, telegram dated March 24, 1945, Investigation File.

3. Telegram, March 30, 1945, Investigation File.

4. Hagenah to Riley, memorandum dated September 24, 1946, Investigation File.

Later AP turned to the Marine Corps and Hagenah for information about the identity of the flag raisers, according to this account by Rosenthal:

I was not the one who identified the men in the flag-raising photo. My picture caption material was sent along with my film from Iwo Jima without a left to right. That's right, no names. It was after I, myself, had left Iwo Jima that the Marine Corps undertook to name names. This was in progress while I was back in New York a couple of weeks along; I asked AP for permission to visit my brother in Washington, and AP said okay and added they had been trying to get the identification out of MCHQ and would I inquire for it while down there. I did just that, and Col. Hagenah informed me that when they were ready to release it the Marine Corps would release it to everybody including the AP. I shrugged and reported the message to the Washington AP bureau chief. Subsequently, USMC distributed the identification to AP and others (Rosenthal to Severance, letter dated October 4, 1993, with copy to Albee).

5. Beech Press Release, March 1945, Investigation File.

6. Ibid. Severance believes Thomas may have been selected "because he was second in command of the patrol, and Schrier, having just taken over Dog Company, was probably too busy to go to the ship" (Severance to Wetenhall, letter dated July 24, 1989).

7. Beech Press Release, March 1945, Investigation File.

8. *New York Times*, February 25, 1945.

9. Severance to Wetenhall, letter dated July 24, 1989.

10. Beech Statement, November 15, 1946, Investigation File.

11. Severance reports that the Public Relations Department of the Corps also requested identification of the Rosenthal flag raisers during the Iwo campaign (Severance Statement, December 17, 1946, Investigation File).

12. Severance to Wetenhall, letter dated July 24, 1989.

13. Ibid. Equally devoid of interest was the "official" flag raising on March 14, 1945, during which the United States proclaimed sovereignty over the Volcano Islands (Smith and Finch, *Coral and Brass*, 274-275). On this occasion, the second flag on Suribachi was taken down.

14. Daskalakis interview with the authors, December 29, 1992.

15. Ibid.

16. Ibid.

17. Beech Statement, November 15, 1946, Investigation File. Beech adds that this threat was subsequently confirmed by Hayes's own statement.

18. Conner, *The Spearhead*, 125; Hagenah to Riley, memorandum dated September 24, 1946, Investigation File.

19. Hagenah to Riley, memorandum dated September 24, 1946, Investigation File.

20. Ibid.

21. Ibid.

22. Ibid.

23. Ibid.; Conner, *The Spearhead*, 125.

24. Daskalakis interview with the authors, December 29, 1992.

25. Ibid.

26. Haynes interview with the authors, December 29, 1992.

27. J. K. Wells interview with the authors, May 21, 1993.

28. Hagenah to Riley, memorandum dated September 24, 1946, Investigation File.

29. Ibid.

30. Bradley interview in unidentified magazine article, May 1945, Hansen MSS.

31. Bradley interview, May 1945, Hansen MSS; Daskalakis interview with the authors, December 29, 1992.

32. Bradley interview, May 1945, Hansen MSS; Hagenah to Riley, memorandum dated September 24, 1946, Investigation File.

33. Hagenah to Riley, memorandum dated September 24, 1946, Investigation File. Thanks to Hagenah's testimony, historians now have access to the story behind the headlines in the national press during April 1945.

34. Ibid.

35. *New York Times*, April 7, 1945.

36. *Boston Globe*, April 9, 1945; *The Union*, April 9, 1945.

37. *Boston Globe*, April 9, 1945.

38. Unidentified news articles, Hansen MSS.

39. *Milwaukee Journal*, April 22, 1945.

40. Ibid.

41. Unidentified news article, April, 1945, Hansen MSS.

42. Ibid.

43. *Portland Press Herald*, April 9, 1945.

44. *The Union*, April 9, 1945; unidentified news photo, Hansen MSS.

45. *The Union*, April 9, 1945.

46. Ibid.

47. Ibid.

48. Ibid.

49. Angier L. Goodwin to Mrs. Evelley, letter dated April 27, 1945, and Leverett Saltonstall to Mrs. Evelley, letter dated May 15, 1945, Hansen MSS.

50. Severance to Mrs. Evelley, letter dated May 1, 1945, Hansen MSS.

51. J. K. Wells to Mrs. Evelley, letter dated May 8, 1945, Hansen MSS.

52. Father Paul F. Bradley to Mrs. Evelley, letter dated April 25, 1945, Hansen MSS.

53. Archbishop Richard Cushing to Mrs. Evelley, letter dated May 1, 1945, Hansen MSS.

54. Address by Major General Keller E. Rockey, March 21, 1945, Hansen MSS.

55. *Chicago Sunday Tribune*, March 11, 1945, Hansen MSS. The photograph had been cropped; Rosenthal's original photo was of eighteen Marines.

56. Mrs. Evelley to Hansen, letters dated February 7, 1945, and February 28, 1945, Hansen MSS.

57. Hagenah to Riley, memorandum dated September 24, 1946, Investigation File.

58. David McCullough, *Truman*, (New York: Simon & Schuster, 1992), 368.

59. *Washington Post*, April 21, 1945; unidentified news photo, Hansen MSS.

60. *Boston Globe*, May 14, 1945.

61. Ibid.

62. *Washington Post*, April 21, 1945.

63. Hagenah to Riley, memorandum dated September 24, 1946, Investigation File.

64. This omission persisted in succeeding weeks. Although it is impossible to examine every account in every newspaper, a sampling of bond tour coverage by selected major metropolitan dailies has unearthed no story reporting that the men in Rosenthal's photograph had actually raised the second, not the first, flag.

More than thirty years after the Iwo Jima campaign, the Jacksonville *Times-Union* quoted Gagnon on the subject of the muzzling of the flag raisers by the Marine Corps:

> One of the men who raised the second flag on Iwo Jima said the Marine Corps covered up the first flag raising for public relations purposes.
>
> Rene Gagnon, a Marine private pictured second from the right in the immortal photo of the flag raising on Mount Suribachi, said in a telephone interview from his Manchester, N.H., home Thursday that the Corps hushed up the initial planting of the flag to use the second group of men and their photo to sell war bonds in the United States.
>
> "They didn't want the first flag raising to hurt the second flag raising," said Gagnon, now a travel agent. "They wanted to bring us (the second group of flag raisers) back to the country to help sell bonds" (Jacksonville *Times-Union*, March 10, 1978).

65. Hagenah to Riley, memorandum dated September 24, 1946, Investigation File.

66. *New York Times*, April 27 and May 4, 1945.

67. *The Union*, May 10, 1945.

68. Ibid.

69. *Washington Post*, May 9, 1945; *The Union*, May 10, 1945.

70. Unidentified news article, Hansen MSS.

71. Ibid.

72. *New York Times*, May 12, 1945.

73. Ibid.

74. Unidentified news photo, Hansen MSS.

75. *Boston Herald*, April 29, 1945, and May 9, 1945.

76. *Boston Sunday Globe*, May 13, 1945.

77. Ibid.; *Boston Sunday Herald*, May 13, 1945.

78. *Boston Daily Globe*, May 14, 1945; *Boston Post*, May 14, 1945.

79. *Boston Daily Globe*, May 14, 1945.

80. *Boston Post*, May 14, 1945.

81. Ibid; *Boston Herald*, May 14, 1945; *Boston Globe*, May 14, 1945.

82. Ibid.

83. *Boston Herald*, May 14, 1945; *Boston Post*, May 14, 1945.

84. *Boston Globe*, May 14, 1945.

85. Ibid.

86. Bradley interview in unidentified magazine article, May 1945, Hansen MSS.

87. *Boston Globe*, May 14, 1945.

88. Ibid., May 16, 1945.

89. Ibid.

90. Ibid.

91. *New York Times*, May 16, 1945; unidentified news photo, Hansen MSS.

92. *New York Times*, May 16, 1945.

93. Ibid.; unidentified news article, May 1945, Hansen MSS; *Program of Rally*, Hansen MSS.

94. Unidentified news article, Hansen MSS.

95. Huie, *Hero of Iwo Jima*, 39.

96. *New York Times*, May 16, 1945; three unidentified news clippings, Hansen MSS.

97. Unidentified news article, May 1945, Hansen MSS.

98. Bradley to Gertrude Hansen, letter dated July 14, 1945, Hansen MSS.

99. Hagenah to Riley, memorandum dated September 24, 1946, Investigation File.

100. Ibid. Ira Hayes had problems of alcohol abuse while still at Camp Pendleton prior to the Iwo Jima campaign, according to one of his regimental officers (Haynes interview with the authors, December 29, 1992). Marc Parrott, in his sympathetic account of Hayes's decline into alcoholism, agrees that the symptoms of addiction were manifested well before the 1945 bond tour, even predating Hayes's enlistment in the Corps. "But before Hayes enlisted, a commonplace but deadly strand had come into the pattern; early in '41, there was an arrest for drunkenness, first of dozens." See Marc Parrott, *Hazard: Marines on Mission* (Garden City, N.Y.: Doubleday and Co., 1962), 206. Although the official cause given for Hayes's untimely death on January 24, 1955, was exposure to winter weather conditions, a recent biography credits his death to a late-night drinking bout at an abandoned adobe hut outside Hayes's hometown of Bapchule, Arizona. See Hemingway, *Ira Hayes*, 158.

101. *New York Times*, May 25, 1945.

102. Rosenthal participated in preliminary bond tour ceremonies at New York's Waldorf-Astoria Hotel, where he gave a talk to the 200 representatives of the bond committee. En route home by train to San Francisco, he appeared at a similar event in Chicago (Rosenthal interview with the authors, March 4, 1994).

103. *The New Yorker*, April 7, 1945, 17-18.

104. Ibid., 18.

105. *Portland Press Herald*, April 2, 1945.

106. *Washington Post*, April 9, 1945.

107. *New York Times*, May 8, 1945.

108. *Washington Post*, May 8, 1945.

109. *New York Times*, May 9, 1945.

110. Ibid., June 6, 1945.

111. *Current Biography*, June 1945, 50.

112. *New York Times*, March 25, 1945.

113. *San Francisco Chronicle*, April 18, 1945.

114. Ibid., March 29, 1945.

115. *Boston Herald*, July 6, 1945.   The stamp "broke all previous records in cancellations of first day covers," according to the Office of the Postmaster General. Press releases indicated that 400,279 covers were sold (Isaac Gregg to Vandegrift, letter dated July 18, 1945, USMC Historical Center).

116. Lindberg had been injured and evacuated from Iwo Jima on March 1, 1945, when his right forearm was shattered by a Japanese bullet (*Minneapolis Star Tribune*, May 29, 1988).

117. Sherrod Notebook 7, 26.

Chapter 8

The Investigation

It was September 1946. World War II was a year-old memory. The Marine Corps never launched its invasion of Japan, the operation Ira Hayes and the men of the 28th Regiment had called the Big Show.[1] President Harry S Truman had given orders for a bigger show, orders to drop the atomic bomb on Hiroshima. The United States, for better or worse, had inaugurated a new era in world history.

But although peace had been declared, the Marine Corps was still engaged in battle. This time it was not against the Japanese; it was against the United States Army and the Air Force. And it was not the Halls of Montezuma or the Shores of Tripoli, but the marble halls of the United States Congress on the shores of the Potomac that was the new battlefield.

Just weeks after the formal Japanese surrender on September 2, 1945, Major General Alexander A. Vandegrift, commandant of the Marine Corps, waded into a campaign as arduous as an amphibious landing. The campaign concluded with the 1947 passage of the National Security Act, a complete reorganization of the United States military. It was only by skillful political maneuvering that the Marine Corps was able to maintain its identity as a separate branch of service, with its commandant answerable directly to the secretary of the Navy.

But in the autumn of 1946 the battle in Congress was still raging, and victory for the Marine Corps was far from sure. Vandegrift's memoirs for this period spelled out a litany of frustration. He spoke of his brother commanders in the Army and the Air Force, who "indulged in the most vicious infighting to gain their ends, a campaign that in turn claimed the major effort of the Navy and Marine Corps to preserve their integrity. I deeply resented the capital's atmosphere."[2] The commandant was stuck in the La Brea Tar Pit of Washington. The Marine Corps needed congressional support as it never had before. Its very life depended on it.

These conditions provided the setting for a drama that turned the spotlight of public awareness once again on the Iwo Jima flag raisers. The opening scene was played out on September 7, 1946. It took the form of a letter written by one of those very congressmen whose support Vandegrift was so vigorously soliciting on behalf of the Corps. Milton H. West, congressman from Brownsville, Texas, sent this brief communication to the commandant:

> Dear Sir:
>   Enclosed is self-explanatory correspondence received from Mr. E. F. Block of Weslaco, Texas, stating that his son, Corporal Harlan [*sic*] H. Block was one of the group in the famous flag raising on the peak of Suribachi, and urging that his son be given proper recognition.
>   I shall appreciate your giving Mr. Block's statement every consideration, and informing me of the action taken by your department.[3]

The first enclosure was a letter from Congressman West's constituent, E. F. Block:

> Dear Mr. West:
>   I am writing you concerning my son, Cpl. Harlon H. Block U.S.M.C. who was killed in action on Iwo Jima Mar 1 - 1945.
>   In studying the picture of the famous flag raising on the peak of Suribachi I was convinced that the Marine at the base was my son, and began writing to several Marines that I was acquainted with to inquire if my son was the one in the picture and have received assurance from them that it was, but could not get definite proof until I got in touch with Ira Hamilton Hays [*sic*] one of the survivors of the flag raising and I received a lengthy letter from him identifying and verifying that it was my son.[4]

The second enclosure was a letter written to E. F. Block's wife on July 12, 1946, by former Private First Class Ira H. Hayes. Hayes, who had returned to civilian life on the Pima Indian reservation at Gila River, Arizona, had apparently received a letter from Harlon Block's mother, asking for information relating to her son's role in the Rosenthal flag raising.[5] Hayes's reply was everything Block's bereaved parents could have hoped for, but one that boded ill for the family of Henry Hansen.

> Dear Mrs. Block:
>   I got your letter just recently and God knows how happy I was to get your letter.
>   I have prayed and waited for such a happening as this. I was kinda worried to make the first move.

I knew your son very well and was with him at the time he was killed. And you can well be proud of him for he died a good Marine and very outstanding on the battlefield. I'm writing this cause I know and was there and saw.

Harlan [*sic*] was in on this picture. But how they fouled up the picture, I don't know. I have Bradley to back me up on this and other score[s] of men in our old Company.

I was the last man to come back to the states for this 7th bond drive. I tried my darndest to stay overseas but couldn't. . . . And when I did arrive in Washington, D. C. I tried to set the thing right but some Colonel told me to not say another word as the two men were dead, meaning Harlan [*sic*] and Henson [*sic*]. And besides the public knew who was who in the picture at the time and didn't want no last minute commotion. Well all this error prompt[ed] me to go back to my old outfit after 2 wks. on the bond drive and still had a month and a half to go. And naturally by all means it did not seem right for such a brave Marine as your son, not get any national recognition.

. . . There may be a lots of accusations towards me for not letting this out any sooner, but I was just bidding for time in hearing from you. But now that you have done so I am happy. At last we can get this thing settled. You have Bradley and myself to back you up, in letting this error known.[6]

The commandant's office replied to Congressman West's letter on September 19, 1946, with a promise to institute "a thorough investigation."[7] The investigation began by pursuing Hayes's allegation that "some Colonel" had attempted to muzzle his objections to the reidentification of the sixth flag raiser. The colonel referred to was Colonel Edward R. Hagenah, who, in April 1945, had greeted Hayes when he returned from Iwo Jima. In light of Hayes's accusation, Brigadier General William E. Riley, the current director of the Corps' Division of Public Information, requested Hagenah to report on the circumstances surrounding the return of the three survivors, and their identification of the three flag raisers killed on Iwo Jima. Hagenah replied on September 24 with a detailed eight-page memorandum. It was Private First Class Rene A. Gagnon, he related, who first identified Sergeant Henry O. Hansen as the figure at the base of the flagpole. Hayes, upon his arrival, immediately "confirmed the names of those given earlier by Gagnon." Hagenah wrote that Hayes's claim now that the man at the pole's base was Block "came as a distinct shock." He concluded his memorandum by asserting that the undersigned "does wish to again state that in any or all of his many discussions with the survivors or of the event with others he does not recall hearing, reading or speaking the name of Harlan [*sic*] Block."[8]

Hagenah corroborated his recollections about Block by telephoning another surviving flag raiser, former Pharmacist's Mate Second Class John H. Bradley, at his Wisconsin home on September 22, 1946. Bradley "expressed surprise that Hayes should make any such statement." He reaffirmed his earlier identification of Hansen and agreed to send "a written statement to that effect."[9] He then complied with a notarized statement dated October 3, 1946.[10] A second affidavit soon arrived from yet another flag raiser, Gagnon.[11] Each man reaffirmed his 1945 identification of Hansen. A month later, on November 18, Riley forwarded these three documents (Hagenah's, Bradley's, and Gagnon's) to Vandegrift with his conclusions: "The records of this Headquarters indicate that Corporal Block was in no way connected with the subject flag raising." Riley recommended, however, in order that "the case may be closed and a decision made . . . a board of three officers be established to study the facts of the case."[12]

Accompanying Riley's memorandum was a complete recapitulation of the chain of events, with a list of all documents received. The final enclosure on Riley's list was labeled: "(L) Letter from the Honorable Milton H. West to the Commandant dtd 4 Nov 46." This second letter from West was missing from the USMC Investigation File when the file was examined by the authors in 1989.[13] What motivated the congressman to write a second time, and how that letter might have motivated Riley and Vandegrift to respond, remain matters for speculation.

On December 4, 1946, Vandegrift acted on the advice of Riley, his politically astute director of public information. Vandegrift sent a directive to Major General Pedro A. del Valle authorizing the creation of a three-member board to "determine who, in its opinion, were the participants in the Mount Suribachi Flag Raising as photographed by Mr. Joe ROSENTHAL of the Associated Press."[14]

Vandegrift selected officers who could be counted on to understand just how delicate the matter of reidentification of one of the famous six flag raisers was likely to be, officers aware that a request from a congressman was never to be taken lightly. The battle in Congress was not yet won, and, as Vandegrift said, "We needed every ear we could gain."[15]

On December 10, the investigation board's recorder, Lieutenant Colonel Allan Sutter, flew out to the USMC recruiting office in Phoenix, Arizona, to assist Hayes in the preparation of his affidavit.[16] Hayes swore that the figure at the pole's base was Block, offering two areas of evidence to support his position. First, he commented on apparent differences in clothing between that worn by the figure in the Rosenthal flag-raising photograph and that worn by Hansen in the Rosenthal "gung-ho" group photograph taken shortly thereafter. Hayes pointed out that in the "gung-ho" photograph Hansen was wearing a cloth patrol cap, crossed bandoleers, and parachute boots with trousers tucked in. None of these features, he said, were part of the dress of the figure at the pole's base in Rosenthal's flag-raising photo. Second, Hayes stated that he, Block,

Sergeant Michael Strank, and Private First Class Franklin R. Sousley were members of a four-man patrol "who went up Suribachi to raise the large flag." Hayes maintained that Bradley and Gagnon were already on the mountain when his four-man patrol arrived. He further stated that in April 1945 when he discussed "Block's presence with the other survivors, Gagnon and Bradley, they admitted it might have been Block to me, but were'nt [*sic*] sure."[17]

Research has proven that Hayes's affidavit was inaccurate in several respects, one being the nature of the orders given Strank's four-man patrol. Company E's commander, Captain Dave E. Severance, ordered Strank to assemble the patrol to lay telephone wire up the mountain, not to raise a flag. Quite clearly, on the testimony of both First Sergeant John A. Daskalakis and Second Lieutenant Albert T. Tuttle, it was Gagnon who took this second flag up the mountain. Gagnon himself later stated that he had taken this flag up Suribachi.[18]

Sutter returned to Washington with Hayes' affidavit, which he presented to a meeting of the investigation board on December 13. With Hayes's seriously flawed statement before them, the board apparently adopted the position that Block could be the man at the base of the pole. They decided that Bradley and Gagnon should be informed of Hayes's affidavit. Both men promptly were sent copies of the Rosenthal group photograph and Hayes's affidavit, along with a request to sign a second affidavit. They were instructed that a "prompt reply is necessary."[19]

While the board waited for these replies, a letter dated December 16 arrived from Severance, stating that he was unable to vouch for "the exact whereabouts" of Block at the time of the flag raising. In the last paragraph, he commented on Hayes's persistent identification of Hansen (not Block) as the sixth flag raiser, even when Hayes returned to the 5th Division camp in Hawaii in 1945 after his aborted bond tour.[20]

The day after Christmas Bradley wrote del Valle:

In answer to your letter dated Dec. 16, 1946 I wish to express the following views. . . .
     As for the field jacket many of the men carried a field jacket along and took them off later in the day, because it got warmer toward noon. Hansen could have done just that. The crossed bandoleers I am quite certain he usually had with him in case he needed extra amunition [*sic*]. The paracute [*sic*] boots I remember he always wore. The man identified as Hansen on the picture could possibly be wearing them. As for the utility cap. Many of the men wore these caps under their helmets. . . .
     Now that I have studied this picture I am inclined to agree with Ira Hayes that it is not Hansen. You see Hayes should remember better than I about Block because he says, Strank, Sousely [*sic*], Block and himself came up the Mt. for that purpose. I was on top of the hill already and

when the flag was to be raised I just jumped up and gave the group a hand. Things happened so fast, I didn't think much of this flag raising until we returned to the U.S. from Iwo Jima. When we made the identy [*sic*] of the men in the picture I, like Gagnon & Hayes, thought the man was Hansen. Now I believe it is not and it could be Block.[21]

Bradley's capitulation apparently had nothing to do with Hayes's clothing hypothesis. It hinged entirely on the fact that Hayes was the only survivor of a four-man patrol (led by Strank) that was sent up Suribachi, allegedly for the purpose of replacing the original flag with a second, larger flag. That was the basis for Hayes's credibility in Bradley's eyes: Hayes was a member of the flag patrol, so he ought to be the authority on the question of who raised the flag. Unwittingly, Bradley relied on Hayes's inaccurate assertion that the purpose of the patrol was to raise the larger flag. Even so, Bradley went no further than to state that the sixth flag raiser *could* be Block.

As the new year began, the investigation into the identity of Rosenthal's sixth flag raiser neared its conclusion. A telegram, dated January 9, 1947, arrived from Gagnon explaining the reason for his tardy response to the investigation board: the documents sent him by the board on December 16, 1946, had been "destroyed by fire." He awaited replacement documents, but in the meanwhile he reaffirmed his earlier position: Hansen was the man "imbedding the base of the flag into the ground."[22]

Del Valle reacted to Gagnon's response by sending him that very day a "certified copy" of Bradley's December 26, 1946, affidavit, as well as the earlier material from Hayes. Del Valle underlined the importance of Gagnon's immediate reply, a reply "now urgently needed." To expedite the matter, the correspondence would be delivered by a Marine NCO from the Manchester Recruiting Substation. Gagnon was told, "You are encouraged to have him aid you in preparing your answer."[23]

Within twenty-four hours, Gagnon made a new affidavit, completely reversing all of his previous statements, including that of the previous day. The first paragraph of Gagnon's statement was copied word for word from Bradley's December 26, 1946, affidavit. The second (and final) paragraph also echoed Bradley's affidavit, not surprisingly, since Gagnon had the statement in front of him at the time:

I was in the same situation as BRADLEY was being on the top of the Mountain when the others came up for the purpose of raising the flag, and being there I gave them a hand. At the time of the raising I thought it was HANSEN but after more thought and studying of the picture I believe that it could have been BLOCK.[24]

Gagnon's sworn statement made no reference to the fact that *he*, not the four-man patrol of Hayes, Strank, Sousley, and Block, carried the second flag up Suribachi. Nor did Gagnon comment on when (or if) he met up with that patrol during its climb to the summit. He simply echoed Bradley's statement.

At this remove, it is fruitless to speculate on why Gagnon abandoned his earlier position on the identity of the sixth flag raiser. The most obvious explanation for his about-face is that he came to the very human realization that "you can't fight City Hall," or, in this case, the Marine Corps. It was perfectly evident to Gagnon that by early January he was the only holdout in identifying Hansen as the sixth flag raiser, and that his position was not satisfactory to del Valle and the investigation panel. Otherwise, they would have accepted his earlier affidavit and his telegram.

Del Valle's investigation board came to a speedy conclusion, embodied in a report to Vandegrift dated January 15, 1947. The board unanimously found that the figure at the base of the flagpole had been "incorrectly identified since April 8, 1945, as being Sergeant Henry O. Hansen" and that "to the best of the ability of the Board to determine at this time, the above-mentioned figure is that of Corporal Harlan [*sic*] H. Block." The report recommended that the Marine Corps records "be corrected to agree with the opinion of this Board." Accompanying the recommendation was the thin sheaf of documents collected by the investigation board in support of its reidentification on the basis of an "exhaustive analysis of all the evidence available." The panel also recommended that "no official blame be assessed any individual in the Naval Service because of the number and diversity of factors found to have been contributory to the original error."[25]

This account of the investigation does not seek to cry "conspiracy!" or to suggest some dark ulterior motives on the part of the three officers who served on Vandegrift's investigation board. All concerned appeared to desire a correct identification of the six flag raisers in Rosenthal's photograph. They were, after all, sufficiently open-minded to consider the possibility that for more than a year the Marine Corps had disseminated misinformation about a matter of the broadest public interest and to shoulder the burden of correcting that misidentification by a public retraction in the national press. Of course, there can be little doubt that Vandegrift was quite willing to accommodate Congressman West's request to look into the possibility that one of West's constituents had raised the flag on Suribachi. Anyone could foresee the positive consequences for the Marine Corps in gaining the good will of a member of the Congress that shortly was to vote on life-or-death issues relating to the future of the Corps. But there is nothing in the record to suggest that evidence was falsified in order to give West a flag raiser from his congressional district.

The underlying problem with the Marine Corps' investigation board was not that it was dishonest, but that it operated *in camera*, with the knowledge that its records would not be open to scrutiny of press or public. This process deprived the board of the usual constraints incumbent on establishing proof "beyond a reasonable doubt."

Regardless of how the board came to think that the Marine in Rosenthal's photograph was Block, not Hansen, this much seems inescapable: the investigation would have been conducted with greater thoroughness had it been known that its procedures and conclusions would be subjected to careful external review. Such knowledge might well have propelled the investigation panel to leave fewer stones unturned in the effort to reach that conclusive result desired by all parties: an identification, beyond any reasonable doubt, of the man at the base of the flagpole. But as Gagnon told the press in January 1947, "Nobody will ever know for sure."[26]

There was one family that felt it *did* know for sure who the figure was at the flagpole's base: the family of Henry Hansen. The Marine Corps' reidentification announcement in mid-January 1947 was tantamount, in the mind of his family, to stripping Hansen of his glory. In stunned disbelief upon reading in the Boston press about the reidentification, Hansen's mother wrote Vandegrift of her "great shock," and cited numerous sources that she felt supported the earlier April 1945 identification of her son.[27]

The day after she wrote Vandegrift, Mrs. Evelley launched a campaign for the open disclosure of the evidence that had caused the Marine Corps to remove her son as one of the six heroic flag raisers. She and her daughter did what all American citizens are taught to do: they wrote their congressmen in Washington and asked for help. Letters went out to the Massachusetts representatives: Senator Leverett Saltonstall, Senator Henry Cabot Lodge, Jr., Congressman Angier L. Goodwin from the Massachusetts 8th District, and the new congressman from the Massachusetts 11th District, John F. Kennedy. All of these gentlemen sent prompt acknowledgments to Mrs. Evelley, and all sent immediate requests to Vandegrift for information about the status of Hansen as an Iwo Jima flag raiser.

The identification controversy was immediately picked up by the local and national press. The Boston papers were quick to report the demotion of their local hero from the ranks of Rosenthal's flag raisers and to cover the Hansen family's defense. One Boston paper printed a facsimile of the 1945 letter from the commander of Hansen's Company E, acknowledging that Hansen "was one of the six men who raised that flag." Accompanying the story was a reproduction of the Rosenthal photograph, a 1945 gift to the Hansen family, signed by Hayes and the other two survivors.[28]

The flag-raising photograph had come back to haunt the commandant of the Marine Corps. In the midst of the uproar, Vandegrift attempted to undo his work of two years earlier when, in the spring of 1945, he had fostered the public misimpression that the Rosenthal photo was of the first flag raising. He now was forced to state clearly and emphatically that there were indeed two flag raisings and that Rosenthal's photograph was of the second. The confusion, he explained in a letter to Mrs. Evelley, was because the flag raising Hansen had participated in "was the first one, using a small flag, and was not photographed by Mr. Rosenthal." "The flag-raising which was photographed by Mr. Rosenthal," he was constrained to admit, "was the second one."[29] This explanation naturally failed to satisfy the Hansen family, who had known since March 1945 that Rosenthal's photograph was of the second flag raising.

Vandegrift steadfastly refused to release the evidence on which the investigation board had based its decision. To the Hansen family's great chagrin, the Marine Corps' official elimination of Hansen from the Rosenthal photograph would stand. What would no longer stand, however, was Vandegrift's attempt to perpetuate the heroic myth. The reidentification episode had forced the open admission that Rosenthal's photo was of a second flag raising. The episode also raised an awkward question: if the Rosenthal photo was of a second raising, where were the photos of the first? Mrs. Evelley's determined effort to obtain a public disclosure of the investigation board's evidence was to have an unintended outcome: the long suppression of former Technical Sergeant Louis R. Lowery's photographs was nearing its end.

The revelations occasioned by the identification controversy in the winter of 1947 brought *Leatherneck* a string of requests for photographs of and information on the first flag raising. *Leatherneck's* besieged editor, R. A. Campbell, wrote a strongly worded memorandum to Marine Headquarters. Campbell listed the requests, ranging from publishers of textbooks to editors of magazines. There was even a threat from *Liberty Magazine* to publish "a story of the first Iwo Jima flag raising whether or not they receive the desired photographs from the Marine Corps."[30]

Campbell's memo contained a reminder of how the Lowery photographs came to be suppressed in the first place. Here was revealed the incontrovertible evidence that the order had come from Vandegrift himself.

Although two pictures of this particular series were released by a Navy Public Information photographic pool early in 1945, the Editor-in-Chief of THE LEATHERNECK was directed by the Commandant of the Marine Corps to withhold publication of the series at that time. It is believed that the Commandant felt that publication at that time would detract from the more dramatic Rosenthal photograph which had been accepted as the symbol of Iwo Jima.

Campbell, strongly of the opinion that full disclosure could only help the Corps, placed his weight squarely behind such action.

In view of the above requests received by THE LEATHERNECK, as well as similar requests received by Headquarters Marine Corps, it is the opinion of the undersigned that publication of these pictures with their attendant story at this time would benefit the Marine Corps by depicting in its proper light a heretofore suppressed subject which arouses journalistic interest by reason of its suppression. . . .

It is further requested that, if permission is not granted at this time to publish this article, the Editor of THE LEATHERNECK be allowed to deny personal responsibility for its suppression.[31]

Campbell's pointed memo was sent to Riley, the Corps' beleaguered director of public information. Riley saw a middle ground between full disclosure "at this time" and continued suppression of the Lowery photographs. Forwarding Campbell's memo to Vandegrift, Riley suggested that in "view of the voluminous requests that the Leatherneck Magazine and this Headquarters are receiving relative to procuring pictures of the first flag raising on Iwo Jima," *Leatherneck* be granted permission to publish the Lowery photographs. Riley did not recommend immediate publication, however, suggesting instead a bit of sleight of hand: that the Lowery "series of pictures be published in the issue of the Leatherneck commemorating V-J Day." Since that issue "will contain pictures of all the important events of World War II, this series of pictures will not be too conspicuous."[32]

So it was that in the September 1947 issue of *Leatherneck* Lowery's photo series of the first flag raised on Suribachi finally saw publication, two and a half years after the fact. It seems entirely appropriate that the last-dated item in the Hansen family manuscripts was a statement of refund from *Leatherneck* for overpayment on an order of three photographs and four copies of that September 1947 issue. Enclosed with the statement was a letter addressed to "Miss Gertrude E. Hansen" from Lowery himself.

Dear Miss Hansen:

It was very nice to receive your letter and it is a great pleasure to be able to comply with your request. The present magazine staff regrets the error of two years ago in not replying to your letter. The times were confused and many things were overlooked.

I am sorry that I did not know your brother, or any of the other men in his outfit. As a roving combat photographer for The Leatherneck I was attached to the Fifth Division for the Iwo Jima operation and was only fortunate enough to be on hand in that particular sector when your brother's platoon was assigned to climb Mount Suribachi. But since that day in 1945 I have heard Sergeant Hansen's name mentioned many times by the men and officers of the 28th Regiment. He was a real hero and a good Marine.

It was through circumstances beyond my control that the pictures I took of the Mount Suribachi ascent were not published before this summer. You can imagine that I, too, did not enjoy having the second flag-raising published rather than the first, which I photographed.

Best wishes to you and your family.
Sincerely,
Lou Lowery[33]

It can only be hoped that Gertrude Hansen found some solace in Lowery's description of her brother as "a real hero and a good Marine." It was, after all, not a bad epitaph for Sergeant Henry O. Hansen, who raised at least one flag on Suribachi.

NOTES

1. J. K. Wells interview with the authors, May 21, 1993.

2. Alexander A. Vandegrift, *Once a Marine* (New York: W. W. Norton and Co., 1964), 307.

3. West to commandant, letter dated September 7, 1946, Investigation File. There is no mention of these events surrounding the identification controversy in either Vandegrift's memoirs, *Once a Marine*, or in his private papers, as filed at the Marine Corps Historical Center.

4. E. F. Block to West, letter dated September 4, 1946, Investigation File.

5. Albert Hemingway incorrectly dates Mrs. E. F. Block's letter to "the fall of 1946." See Hemingway, *Hayes*, 149. Marling and Wetenhall incorrectly state that *Hayes* initiated the contact with Mrs. Block, not the other way around, as is evident in Hayes's letter. Marling and Wetenhall also err in dating the Hayes contact with the Block family as emanating from the Buffalo, New York, anniversary celebration of V.J. Day in August 1946. They are also incorrect in several other respects: the investigation was *not* a "Congressional investigation"; rather, it was an *internal* investigation by members of the USMC, culminating in a report to the commandant, not to a congressional committee. The inquiry panel of three Marine officers was formed on December 4, 1946; it met only three times as a formal panel: December 4, 1946, December 13, 1946, and January 13, 1947, at which time it concluded its work, rendering its final report to Vandegrift on January 15, 1947. This time frame differs from Marling and Wetenhall's "six-month inquiry." See Marling and Wetenhall, *Iwo Jima*, 124, 259, n. 8.

6. Hayes to Mrs. Block, letter dated July 12, 1946, Investigation File.

7. Turnage to West, letter dated September 19, 1946, Investigation File.

8. Hagenah to Riley, memorandum dated September 24, 1946, Investigation File.

9. Ibid.

10. Bradley to commandant, affidavit dated October 3, 1946, Investigation File.

11. Gagnon to commandant, affidavit dated October 17, 1946, Investigation File.

12. Riley to commandant, memorandum dated November 18, 1946, Investigation File.

13. Ibid.

14. Vandegrift to del Valle, memorandum dated December 4, 1946, Investigation File.

15. Vandegrift, *Once a Marine*, 318.

16. Sutter, statement dated December 13, 1946, Investigation File.

17. Hayes, affidavit dated December 10, 1946, Investigation File.

18. A letter, written by Bradley nearly forty years after the investigation, speaks to this question of Gagnon's carrying the second flag up Suribachi:

> While Hayes, Gagnon and I were on the Seventh War Loan Bond Tour, I heard Rene Gagnon say that he was the one who carried the American Flag to the top of Mt. Suribachi. Rene Gagnon was a runner for Easy Co. A battery or batteries went dead and needed replacing, he was on his way to the top of the mountian [*sic*], someone gave him the large American Flag to take along with the replacement batteries. This is the flag that was photographed by Joe Rosenthal on February 23, 1945 (Bradley to Severance, letter dated February 18, 1986, USMC Historical Center).

19. Del Valle to Bradley and to Gagnon, letters dated December 16, 1946, Investigation File.

20. Severance to commandant, letter dated December 16, 1946, Investigation File.

21. Bradley to del Valle, letter dated December 26, 1946, Investigation File.

22. Gagnon to Marine Headquarters, telegram dated January 9, 1947, Investigation File.

23. Del Valle to Gagnon, letter dated January 9, 1947, Investigation File.

24. Gagnon to del Valle, affidavit dated January 10, 1947, Investigation File.

25. Report of Board, January 15, 1947, 3-4, Investigation File.

26. *Boston Sunday Post*, January 5, 1947. For a more complete analysis of the investigation, see Parker B. Albee, Jr., "The Marine Corps' Investigation," paper delivered at the annual meeting of the American Military Institute, March 1991.

27. Mrs. Evelley to Vandegrift, draft of letter dated January 21, 1947, Hansen MSS.

28. *Boston Globe*, January 24, 1947.

29. Vandegrift to Mrs. Evelley, letter dated January 24, 1947, Hansen MSS.

30. R. A. Campbell to director, Division of Public Information, memorandum dated March 6, 1947, National Archives.

31. Ibid.

32. Riley to commandant, memorandum dated March 6, 1947, unsigned carbon copy, National Archives.

33. Lowery to Gertrude Hansen, letter dated September 19, 1947, Hansen MSS.

Chapter 9

D-Day + 50 Years

January 1994. Obituary clippings are scattered like ashes over the desktop. John Bradley is dead.[1] Few recognized his name when the news of his death was reported on radio and television, and in the national press. But his image as one of the six men in Joe Rosenthal's photograph of the Iwo Jima flag raising is part of the American visual vocabulary. This photograph, taken forty-nine years before, made Bradley's death at age 70 a news event, despite the fact that his life during the intervening half century was lived quietly in the shadows, far from the public limelight.

Telephoned at his Wisconsin home in 1990, Bradley politely explained that he did not give interviews.[2] Disappointed at being denied access to the last survivor in Rosenthal's famous photograph, it was nevertheless understandable in that Bradley and his comrades had not been deliberate public figures, like politicians, actors, or sports celebrities. John Bradley, Rene Gagnon, and Ira Hayes, despite the attention lavished on them by press and public, knew they had done nothing uniquely heroic in raising their flag. They recognized that it had taken the courage and sacrifice of thousands to carry the two flags up Suribachi. So after enduring the publicity surrounding his return to the States for the Seventh War Loan bond tour, Bradley deliberately left the stage and returned to civilian life, his duty done.

In 1985, in a rare break in his self-imposed silence on the subject of his role in the Iwo Jima campaign, Bradley described his participation in the flag raising: "I just jumped in and gave them a hand. I just happened to be at a certain place at a certain time . . . we certainly were not heroes."[3]

Bradley's statement cuts across both of the myths that have so persistently enveloped the second Iwo Jima flag raising: the heroic myth that the flag was raised in the midst of fierce Japanese opposition, and the antiheroic myth that the flag was raised as a staged publicity stunt, under conditions as artificial as a movie set. It is tempting to wonder how Bradley tolerated the repeated misreportings of those few moments in his life, how he endured his false representation as either super hero or super fraud.

Any hopes that the press would at last get the flag-raising story straight in Bradley's obituaries were dashed by the publication of Jack Anderson's widely syndicated column on January 19, 1994. Under the promising headline, "The Real Story of Iwo Jima Photo," Anderson, nevertheless, proceeded to perpetuate antiheroic falsehoods about the second flag raising. One misstatement claimed that Secretary of the Navy James V. Forrestal (erroneously described as "back in Washington," when Forrestal was actually on the beach at Iwo Jima) and other "defense officials" were in league with the Marine Corps high command to "pull off" an elaborate public relations hoax: the raising and photographing of a second flag on Suribachi. According to Anderson, these machinations were made necessary by the fact that the Corps and (unnamed) defense officials considered the photographs of the first, "real" flag raising not "stirring enough."[4] Anderson's version failed to take into account that on February 23, 1945, when this plot was supposedly hatched, *no one* had seen Louis Lowery's photographs of that first flag raising. His negatives had not even been developed.

Another falsehood embedded in Anderson's column is one that has unjustly followed AP photographer Rosenthal for fifty years: that Rosenthal staged his famous photograph for Marine Corps public relations purposes and then joined in the conspiracy to keep secret the dirty truth that his photograph was not taken at the time of the "real" flag raising. Anderson claimed:

> So, in the interest of Marine public relations, the AP photographer accompanied a handpicked group of men for a staged flag raising hours after the original event. The second group held the flag in place, and Rosenthal snapped 18 shots of the dramatized event. The flag itself was not the original 54 by 28 banner, but a larger 96 by 56-inch version brought in specially for the occasion.
>
> · The incident was kept secret for decades. Not only the top brass who gave the orders, but the enlisted men who posed with the flag never revealed the truth. For a time, their superiors even forced them to lie about it.[5]

Critical as one might be of the misinformation disseminated in Anderson's column, there was no book in print in January 1994 which he might have consulted for complete, well-documented information on the flag raisings.[6] It could understandably be asked why, after half a century, there was still no definitive account of the flag raisings for the responsible journalist (or the interested general reader) to consult. Equally puzzling is the question of why both the heroic and the antiheroic myths of Suribachi have continued to flourish, side by side, in the consciousness of the American people. But on reflection it becomes evident that over the years there has been ample fuel to stoke the fires of both our national sentimentality and our national cynicism.

Four years after the end of World War II, Hollywood, that proverbial caldron of mythmaking, produced a widely acclaimed manifestation of the heroic myth: *Sands of Iwo Jima.* Starring John Wayne as the consummate Marine, this 1949 Republic Pictures film, made with the cooperation of the Marine Corps (and including cameo appearances by Hayes, Gagnon, Bradley, and Schrier), portrayed the Suribachi flag raising as swashbuckling drama. Although printed mention was made at the beginning of the film that an earlier flag had been raised by Platoon Sergeant Ernest I. Thomas, Jr., the film itself portrayed only scenes from the second flag raising, as photographed by Rosenthal and Genaust. The clear implication was that this flag raising was the one and only, achieved after a raging battle up Suribachi, a battle fraught with American casualties, including the death of the Marine played by John Wayne. For thousands of American moviegoers, *Sands of Iwo Jima* represented reality, not fiction. The film fostered virtually every distortion embedded in the heroic myth, including the misimpression that the flag raising represented America's final victory over the Japanese on Iwo Jima.[7]

Five years after the release of *Sands of Iwo Jima,* at the Marine Corps' 179th birthday celebration in Arlington, a distinguished audience (including President Dwight D. Eisenhower, Vice President Richard M. Nixon, and 7,000 other guests) viewed the dedication of a 100-ton bronze monument.[8] Frequently referred to as the Iwo Jima Memorial, the Marine Corps War Memorial was actually dedicated to all the Marines who had died for God and Country since 1775. But it was Rosenthal's photograph of the second flag raising on Suribachi that served as the model for the gigantic sculpture by Felix de Weldon. So in one sense the monument was a special tribute to the men of Iwo Jima and more particularly to those men in the Rosenthal photograph.

Certainly, "the three surviving members of the flag-raising team," Hayes, Gagnon, and Bradley, were given places of honor at the dedication ceremony, as were the Gold Star mothers of the three Marines ultimately identified as appearing in Rosenthal's photograph. And although Vice President Nixon proclaimed that "the memorial symbolized not only 'the heroism of six men and the great history of the Marine Corps,' but also 'the hopes and dreams of Americans,'" for all intents and purposes Rosenthal's six had now come to represent the Marine Corps' apotheosis.[9] The presentation of the monument "to the American people" by the Marine Corps commandant marked the supreme moment in the heroic myth of Suribachi.[10]

One rather bizarre aspect of this heroic myth has been the number of former Iwo Jima veterans who have sought personal recognition by identifying themselves with some aspect of the Suribachi flag raisings. As Danny J. Crawford, head of the reference section at the Marine Corps History and Museums Division, has written:

Reference historians cringe when they receive another letter or phone call from a former Marine who, overlooked for 40 years, now wants to set the record straight on his participation in the flag raising on Mount Suribachi. BGen Simmons has said that "if all those persons were really up on Suribachi raising flags it must have been a veritable flag pageant!"[11]

Colonel Dave E. Severance, USMC (Ret.), has documented over twenty such fraudulent claims, including the classic case of former Master Sergeant Carl J. Jackel, who began passing himself off as early as July 23, 1945, as the Marine who carried the flag up Suribachi for Rosenthal to photograph. The high point of Jackel's bogus career came in December 1975 when he was honored by the California State Assembly and presented with a flag that had flown over the Marine Corps War Memorial. U.S. Senator Alan Cranston had helped obtain the flag. "This was the first time a flag that has flown over the Marine Memorial was ever presented to an individual."[12]

The excesses of the heroic myth helped to call up its opposite: the antiheroic myth of fraud, exploitation, and deception. A prime example of the debunking of Iwo Jima's glory was an NBC "Sunday Showcase" television drama aired in the spring of 1960. "The American" starred Lee Marvin in the role of flag raiser Ira Hayes, the Pima Marine caught in a web of lies fabricated by his military and governmental superiors. The scriptwriter assumed that the Rosenthal photograph "was essentially a Marine Corps publicity stunt," that the flag raising was "posed," and that the Mighty Seventh bond tour perpetrated a false representation of Hayes and his fellow survivors as heroes.[13] Rosenthal was outraged at the misrepresentation of his own actions and brought a libel suit against NBC, a suit ultimately settled out of court.[14]

Capitalizing on the uproar created by the television production, Charles U. Daly wrote an article titled "The Iwo Jima Camera Shot Heard 'Round the World" for the January 1962 issue of *Cavalier* magazine. Headlining a photo of actor Lee Marvin in Marine combat gear was a quotation attributed to the script of "The American": "They took about 10,000 pictures that day. . . . Everybody knew it was a fake. Everybody on the island was laughing about that phony picture."[15]

The Marine Corps received equal time with a picture and a quote from Lieutenant General Holland M. Smith, who on this occasion lived up to his nickname, "Howlin' Mad": "Those Japs were still all over the place. We were digging them out of caves. Rosenthal was a gallant man and his picture caught a great moment in history, both for the Marines and for the nation. It was no fake."[16]

Daly's article promised an "exclusive report that *should* settle the fight forever." Claiming to have the real story (as Anderson also would claim in his column thirty-two years later), Daly bemoaned that "an unending stream of bull has hidden what really happened atop 546-foot high Suribachi on D-Day plus 4."[17] He then proceeded to add to that "unending stream" with a flow of fact hopelessly commingled with fiction.

Contributing to the antiheroic myth, Daly stated that, while Lowery took an authentic "combat picture" as Japanese "snipers pecked away" at him, Rosenthal's "picture was not a combat shot."[18] Later in the article, Daly erroneously described "Marine publicity boys" combing the sands of Iwo Jima in search of Rosenthal's flag raisers, pursuant to President Franklin D. Roosevelt's command, a command that actually was issued *after* the Marines had already left Iwo Jima.[19] Particularly outlandish was Daly's embellishment of the search for flag-raiser Gagnon (who, in fact, was located undramatically on board the *Winged Arrow* bound for Hawaii):

With only the corpses of Strank, Sousley and Hansen or Block for the President, the PIOs [public information officers] on Iwo got desperate. They almost wept for joy when they encountered P.F.C. Rene Gagnon trudging through the ash, lugging a walkie-talkie battery to a platoon leader.

"They practically rocketed me to a transport," Gagnon, the man behind Bradley in the photo, said when interviewed not long ago. "I was given a shave and shower, and sped by boat to an airstrip, where they bumped a bird colonel to get me and my M-1 on a plane to Washington. Until I was given the story about that flag, I was sure I was getting court-martialed."[20]

From Charles Daly to Jack Anderson, the legacy of journalistic exploitation of the antiheroic myth is passed on, to the disadvantage of the Marine Corps and the American public. But articles in magazines and newspapers have short lives. Like May flies, they buzz about for a day or so and then die. More enduring are the accounts preserved in books, especially those written by credentialed scholars and published by prestigious university presses.

A prime example of just such a book is *Iwo Jima* by Karal Ann Marling and John Wetenhall, published in 1991 by Harvard University Press. One of the first critiques of Marling and Wetenhall's book and its perceived espousal of an antiheroic debunking of the flag raisings was made by Richard Harwood in his review, "The Very Picture of Heroism," in the *Washington Post*. Harwood, himself a veteran of the Iwo Jima campaign, felt constrained to correct what he viewed as the book's distortion of the record:

Marling and Wetenhall tell this story well but their thesis is fragile.

It was not through some conspiracy or public relations campaign that the Rosenthal photograph appeared on newspaper front pages and magazine covers all over the nation. Editors recognized the picture for what it was: a unique, triumphant and accidental work of art.

As for the hero/impostor issue, who is qualified to hang those labels on the men involved? . . . They faced the same hazards and paid the same price for the privilege. . . . Easy Company's third platoon, which raised the first flag, lost all but two of the men it brought ashore.

. . . The Rosenthal picture is not a "phony" and its subsequent exploitation was not the work of "impostors" in Easy Company. They had other work to do and too few lived to see it finished.[21]

Richard Severo, reviewing *Iwo Jima* for the *New York Times*, commented that Marling and Wetenhall in their discussion of Rosenthal's flag-raising photograph "assert that the birth was illegitimate, a fraud, a dark hoax unworthy of men who died in that battle." Severo continued: "The reasons for the subsequent sanctification of the staged flag-raising, the authors say, is nothing more than a mating of unvirtuous photojournalism with an insatiable desire on the part of Marine officers to enhance a history that needed no enhancement."[22]

Unfortunately, *Iwo Jima* caused Severo to question whether the Pulitzer Prize should have been awarded for a photograph of a "staged affair":

> With all the book's research, it does not cover all the questions that arise from the Rosenthal photo. The most conspicuous gap is the question of whether the Pulitzer committee ever reconsidered the award it gave to Mr. Rosenthal, since the circumstances surrounding the taking of the photograph in 1945 are clearly not those for which Pulitzers are usually given. If no reconsideration was ever made, why not?[23]

This sort of conjecture, stimulated by Marling and Wetenhall's ambiguous presentation of the flag-raising events and their aftermath, casts an unwarranted shadow over the reputation of photographer Joe Rosenthal. As Miles Orvell of Temple University wrote in the spring 1992 issue of *Winterthur Portfolio*: "There are some problems and some puzzling uncertainties about what Marling and Wetenhall think they are doing."[24] One of these problems, Orvell pointed out, involved "the crux of *Iwo Jima*," the "authenticity of the famous Rosenthal image."[25]

> If the photograph of the flag raising has become one of the most charged and powerful cultural symbols of patriotism to mainstream America, Marling and Wetenhall, by the time the book is done, have converted it into a symbol of quite a different sort--of antiheroism, of fraud, of all that is wrong with postwar America. We must be clear, however, about exactly what they are saying and what they are not saying, for the issue has already--in the book's reception--been blurred as badly as it was when the photographs were first taken and confused.[26]

Later in his review, Orvell elaborated on the book's problems:

> Unfortunately, however, Marling and Wetenhall are inexplicably vague
> in defining the exact nature of the official distortion, and they even seem,
> at times, to contradict their main point. Thus, they report that
> *Leatherneck,* the Marine Corps publication, suppressed the first image so
> that it would not compete with Rosenthal's, but they do not report any
> source for this assertion or identify who was responsible.[27]

As Orvell observed, Marling and Wetenhall failed sufficiently to document
their sweeping assertions, a failure that substantially undermined the credibility
of their work. But serious as this flaw might be in the eyes of the academic
world (which depends on clear footnoting for a proper evaluation of a scholar's
use of relevant sources), to the world outside the Ivory Tower there were
greater flaws to be found in the text of *Iwo Jima.* To some of the men who
directly participated in the Iwo Jima campaign, Marling and Wetenhall's
questionable documentation paled to insignificance in comparison with the
innumerable errors of fact.

Severance, former commander of Company E (which raised both flags on
Suribachi), had been consulted by Wetenhall for information about events
relating to his company's activities. In a recent letter to columnist Jack
Anderson, correcting errors in Anderson's January 19, 1994, column, Severance
wrote: "In reading between the lines, I am of the opinion that your staff's
primary source of information was the Marling/Wetenhall book. I am
embarrassed to have my name in this publication as a 'reference.'"[28]

At the time Marling and Wetenhall's book was first published and reviewed,
former Time/Life correspondent Robert Sherrod wrote Benis Frank, chief
historian, Marine Corps History and Museums Division, about Frank's
preparation of a rebuttal letter to the *New York Times,* challenging allegations
in *Iwo Jima.*

> If, in writing the Times, you want any more on the Marling Iwo book,
> I can give you a couple of errors. They have Time and Life mixed up,
> for example: It was Life that at first refused to run the Rosenthal
> photograph, partially because of my cable saying it was a phony (on the
> basis of what the indignant Lou Lowery told me--Rosenthal had left for
> the States by the time I got to Guam from Iwo). Marling erroneously
> said it was Time, which did run the picture in spite of my cable because
> it was a great pictorial tour de force. (Both magazines ran Stories of a
> Picture a month later, Mar. 26 editions.)
> The distinction is important because Life was, as you know, the
> world's premier showcase for photography (and it had more than twice
> the circulation of Time). I covered for both magazines, of course.[29]

Not all who had firsthand knowledge of the Iwo Jima campaign responded to the Marling-Wetenhall book with letters to the editors or critical reviews in military periodicals.   Some expressed their negative views more privately. Arthur Naylor, former commander of Company F, commented in a recent interview on the allegations made in *Iwo Jima:* "I would like to confront people who write that kind of stuff, having been there and seen it. It makes me sick to hear it called a publicity stunt. I know how many kids were killed there. I don't understand their purpose."[30]

It is evident from the many responses of participants like Naylor that versions of the flag raising, such as Marling and Wetenhall's, fundamentally fail to comprehend battle conditions on Iwo Jima.   The lives of every man on the island hung in the balance every day.   There was no time or appetite for staged public relations events.   There was time for only the real thing.

Interviewed in December 1992, Major General Fred E. Haynes, USMC (Ret.), who served as operations officer with the 28th Regiment on Iwo Jima, expressed his view: "Marling and Wetenhall missed the point of the whole thing."   For Haynes the point of Iwo Jima was its place in the annals of American military history as "a classic amphibious battle, probably *the* classic."

> I think it was the philosophy of the battle, the strategic importance of it, and the emotional value of the picture Rosenthal took. Because that is part of the symbolism: you've got a Wisconsin farm kid, you've got a South Texas kid, a coal miner's son, you've got an Appalachian kid, and then you've got an Indian. This was a microcosm. I think people have frequently missed the point of this. They were caught up in what was real or not, what was posed or fake.
>
> In my case, it was a real seminal experience. I fought in three wars and I never experienced anything like this. Those who participated--why do you think we get together every five years here in Washington and go to the Cathedral, go to the White House? We go to the Marine War Memorial and have a ceremony. It was an unusual occurrence in human history. Iwo Jima was unique, even for Marines who were veterans of other campaigns.[31]

Several of the Iwo Jima veterans interviewed in researching *Shadow of Suribachi* considered that a correction of the errors in Marling and Wetenhall's book should be the first order of business. To aid in that task, Norman T. Hatch, former 5th Division's photo officer on Iwo, forwarded two densely typed pages of commentary on inaccuracies of fact and interpretation in the Marling-Wetenhall account.   One example from Hatch's critique of *Iwo Jima* will suffice:

Keyes Beech was a combat correspondent and not as stated in this page

[58] "publicity liaison" for the Division. I think that if he were alive today he would either laugh sardonically or be appalled at the effort at put-down the authors continue to strive to insert subliminally all through the book. I know as an accomplished news man he would have resented it. The same applies to the next gratuitous remark that he "bore responsibility for heroics destined for home consumption."[32]

Marling and Wetenhall failed to interview one highly significant participant in the flag-raising story: Joe Rosenthal. Rosenthal remarked that neither of those authors ever talked with him or attempted to confirm the statements they made about him.[33] Rosenthal could have provided considerable assistance of a corrective nature, had he been given the opportunity. Concerning his notations on *Iwo Jima*'s errors, he commented: "I have a copy of their book, and I have little slips of paper stuck in it that make it look like a porcupine."[34] One of the most outlandish misstatements Rosenthal discovered was the description of how he supposedly first saw his flag-raising photo. The text of *Iwo Jima* reads: "It was only when his [Rosenthal's] mother's letter arrived, with the front page of the *New York Sun* stuffed inside, that he learned the truth."[35] Rosenthal commented wryly that he wished he had the letter from his mother Marling and Wetenhall refer to: "If I had that envelope, it would be a very valuable philatelic treasure--a holy post office." (Rosenthal's mother had died some years prior to 1945.)[36] The photographer later concluded his observations on *Iwo Jima*. "Marling and Wetenhall obviously operate according to the old newspaper reporter's dictum: Don't check out a story too closely or you might lose it."[37]

Although spared these unpublished criticisms of their book, Marling and Wetenhall still had their hands full dealing with those criticisms that had found their way into print. In the September 29, 1993, issue of *The Chronicle of Higher Education*, the embattled authors fought back. Claiming to be the standard-bearers of truth, they stated in an essay titled "Patriotic Fervor and the Truth About Iwo Jima": "Our book simply retold the facts of the battle and sorted out the confusion that followed."[38]

Marling and Wetenhall then proceeded to take to task various reviewers and readers for unsympathetic responses to their book. Seizing first on Harwood's review in the *Washington Post*, they claimed he "set us up as straw men for a conspiracy theory--that the deception was planned--that the book overtly disproves."[39]

Lost in the grammatical mine field of the preceding passage, the reader begins to understand how Marling and Wetenhall's book might have left some ambiguous impressions. *Iwo Jima* contains at least one allegation that could lead even the most careful reader to conclude that its authors *did*, in fact, embrace some sort of conspiracy theory:

The careful orchestration of the drive up the mountain on D + 4, the attendance of the Secretary of the Navy, and the large number of reporters shepherded to the scene all suggest that Rosenthal's candid "grab shot" and its impact on the American public were by-products of a conscious manipulation of imagery by the military.[40]

This statement certainly smacks of a conspiracy thesis. It also is an assertion bare of the necessary documentation to support such a position. The charge that "large numbers of reporters" were "shepherded to the scene" represents the major prop for this thesis.   And yet, as far as exhaustive research can determine, there was not one single reporter on top of Suribachi when either of the two flags was raised.   No combat correspondents, civilian or military, accompanied the Marines up Suribachi on February 23, 1945.   Marling and Wetenhall *incorrectly* placed *Newsweek's* William Hipple at the volcano's summit, and even described his actions there, when, in fact, Hipple had taken his leave of Rosenthal, remaining at the base of Suribachi to follow another lead entirely.[41]

Time/Life's Sherrod reported that late in the afternoon of February 23 he and "several other correspondents" walked to the foot of Suribachi, but decided not to make the climb to the top.[42]   In reply to the implication that the Marine Corps staged a public relations event on Suribachi and coaxed the press to attend, one can observe only that *if* such had been the intention, it was a singularly inept job.

The problems inherent in Marling and Wetenhall's book go beyond apparently simple errors of fact and documentation such as those connected with the whereabouts of correspondent Hipple while his friend Rosenthal was photographing a flag on Suribachi.   Such unsubstantiated assertions lead to significant misinterpretations, first by the book's authors and potentially by the book's readers.   To claim that a "large number of reporters" were "shepherded to the scene," while mentioning only one *Newsweek* correspondent, is to build a major thesis on a very shaky foundation.   To fail in documenting the presence of even that lone correspondent on Suribachi (for the good reason that he was not, in fact, there) is to risk the collapse of the entire structure of Marling and Wetenhall's theory of a "conscious manipulation of imagery by the military." Wittingly or unwittingly, Marling and Wetenhall in *Iwo Jima* perpetuated the antiheroic myth and even added to its distortions.[43]

To some readers, the distortions of the heroic myth may seem less pernicious than those of the antiheroic myth, since the heroic distortions at least glorified the courageous conduct of American servicemen in the slaughterhouse battle for Iwo Jima.   It was this heroic myth that first appeared in press accounts dated the very day of the flag raisings.   These first flag-raising accounts came full-dressed with stories of the Marines' herculean assault on Suribachi against ferocious Japanese opposition. This was a saga to lift every American heart: the perfect narrative setting for the Rosenthal photograph dominating front-page Sunday newspapers two days later, February 25, 1945.

Unfortunately, there were *no* reporters present at either of the Suribachi flag raisings. Had there been, accurate reporting might have precluded the emergence of the heroic myth. In that case, there would have been no need for the debunking that helped perpetuate the antiheroic myth.

As it was, news reports shy of firsthand information simply drew on the Marines' undeniably heroic activities from D-Day through D+3, transferring to the climb up Suribachi some of the desperate drama of the four days required for the 28th Marines to reach the base of the volcano. All combat correspondents on Iwo Jima, military and civilian, were fully aware that these were genuinely valorous troops engaged in a bloody fight against daunting odds. In brief, these were no Hollywood Marines. No one, from the officers of the 28th Regiment to the wary infantrymen of the 2nd Battalion, picking a cautious path up Suribachi, could have predicted the undramatic reality: a climb to the crest completely unchallenged by the enemy. The brief firefight that occurred just after the first flag was raised resulted in no American casualties, except for Lou Lowery's broken camera. Japanese resistance was as minimal as it was ineffectual. The actual capture of Suribachi's summit was perhaps the easiest, least costly strategic objective the Marines were to accomplish in the entire Iwo Jima campaign.

Another significant feature in the creation of the heroic myth was the confusion over how many flags were raised and which flag was featured in Rosenthal's memorable photograph. Initially, there was no attempt on the part of anyone to mislead the American public. The conflation of the two flag raisings into one--the one immortalized by Rosenthal--was in large part simply the result of the fact that news stories were received and printed in the States at least two days prior to the arrival of their illustrative photographs. Neither Rosenthal nor the Marine Corps nor the press corps had schemed to misrepresent the photograph as depicting the first flag raising. Rosenthal stated from the first day that his photograph was taken of the second flag to fly over Suribachi.

On Iwo Jima, no one considered the second flag raising a matter of any importance. The replacement of the smaller first flag by a larger flag (the result of two spontaneous decisions) was so insignificant that neither was recorded in the 5th Division's intelligence journals. Some of the embattled American troops had seen and cheered the first flag when it was raised. Only a handful had been aware of its replacement. Those few who knew, including the six men who raised the second flag, attributed no particular significance to the event. It was roughly the equivalent of changing a dim light bulb for one with a higher wattage. The half-dozen photographers present on top of Suribachi knew the second flag raising was militarily unimportant. For them it was just an opportunity to obtain action photographs in a dramatic setting.

Rosenthal's photograph alone gave significance to the second flag raising. Back on the homefront, there was little or no perceived need to check the details of just how the photograph came to be taken. Editors already had their stories about the capture of Suribachi and the raising of the American flag. Now they had a stunning photograph to illustrate this welcome news.

By the time press clippings containing Rosenthal's flag-raising photograph found their way back to Iwo Jima, many of the men involved in the capture of Suribachi had already been killed or evacuated. The survivors were engaged in a brutal battle for the northern half of the island. At this point the six men in Rosenthal's photograph had not even been identified. Rosenthal already had left for Guam, where he would see his flag-raising picture for the first time.

By this time it was mid-March, and the heroic myth had become firmly embedded in the public mind, a myth incarnated in the Rosenthal photograph. Other photographs by Rosenthal's fellow photographers (including Lowery's sequence on the first flag raising) had not arrived as promptly on the scene as Rosenthal's. So his had become *the* photograph of *the* flag raising in the eyes of the American press and public. Timing gave Rosenthal's photograph an unencumbered field until the battle for Iwo Jima was declared won.[44]

Timing was not, of course, the only factor in explaining the national attention accorded Rosenthal's photograph. Even in a field of hundreds, that picture would have ended up in the Winner's Circle. With such a photograph to bet on, why would any photo editor have preferred another picture, even had there been others to choose from?

Rosenthal's photograph gave editors a much-needed illustration of an event that brought the sweet taste of victory to a long and bitter war. Nothing Germany had done to the United States could compare with the treacherous blow struck by Japan at Pearl Harbor. A victory against Japan was a victory to cherish. It was a propitious moment for the publication of Rosenthal's picture: the image of heroic American fighting men raising Old Glory for the first time on Japanese home territory. Here was all the material required to make a heroic myth.

Two of the most glaring errors embodied in this myth--that the acclaimed photograph represented the first historic flag raising and that the scene took place in the midst of death-defying combat--contributed to a second myth: the antiheroic myth of fraud, manipulation, and conspiracy.

In all innocence, and in understandable disappointment at the lack of press attention given his own excellent photographic coverage of the first flag raising, Lowery arrived at Guam from Iwo Jima. There he found Time/Life's Sherrod and dumped his angry story in Sherrod's lap. Knowing that Rosenthal had not photographed the first flag raising and unaware of the circumstances under which a second flag was raised, Lowery jumped to the conclusion that the second flag raising had been staged and passed off as occurring at the time of the original flag raising. Lowery's anger was compounded by his belief that his own negatives had been "held up," with preferential treatment given to those of an Associated Press civilian. In "going public" to Sherrod, Lowery doubtless believed he was both fighting the good fight for Marine versus civilian photographers and gaining legitimate publicity for his own photographs, which he expected to appear soon in *Leatherneck*. He could not possibly have imagined the discomfort his accusations would soon cause *Leatherneck* and the commandant of the Marine Corps, or the dark myth of fraud his story would spawn.

Sherrod believed Lowery's version of the two flag raisings and their photographs. It made sense. It also helped explain the almost inexplicable perfection of Rosenthal's photograph. The photograph had seemed too good to be true. Now here was evidence that it *was* too good to be true: that it was, in fact, a fake.

Sherrod thought Rosenthal had already left Guam for the States, so he did not believe it was possible to check his story. In reality, Rosenthal was on Guam for as long as forty-eight hours after an irate Lowery told Sherrod his grievances. Had Sherrod talked with Rosenthal, the story as Lowery told it would not have been wired immediately back to New York, and "*Time* Views the News" would not have promptly broadcast the electrifying word that America's most popular war photograph was a staged event. The antiheroic myth of a faked flag raising might have been aborted.

Once Sherrod's story was broadcast, however, it was like chasing feathers to restuff a pillow. The truth in that story--that Rosenthal's photograph represented the second, not the *first*, flag raising--was upstaged by a potent falsehood: that Rosenthal had faked his photograph. So it was that the heroic myth of Suribachi became paired with its antiheroic shadow. Lost in the shuffle was the unadorned truth of what actually happened that February day on Iwo Jima.

The contest was soon joined by Associated Press and Time/Life, with AP threatening a lawsuit over the "*Time* Views the News" broadcast and Time/Life insisting that it had a legitimate debunking story. The Marine Corps, in the person of its commandant, Major General Alexander Archer Vandegrift, acted as mediator in a conference with the protagonists. As a result of this air-clearing, *Life* magazine's March 26, 1945, issue ran the Rosenthal photograph, along with the previously unpublished Lowery photograph of the first flag raising. But the *Life* article did not entirely kill the heroic image of the flags raised in the midst of battle: it reported that the second flag was raised while the volcano's peak "was still under fire." Nor did the article explicitly state that Rosenthal's photograph was *not* staged, although it did not allege that it *was* faked.[45]

Ironically, the more-or-less full and frank disclosure in *Life*'s illustrated article on the two flag raisings was not sufficient to lay to rest the ghost of either the heroic or the antiheroic myth. There was apparently something in the American psyche conducive to such hauntings, something receptive to sentimental or to cynical interpretations of the national experience.

It was in mid-March 1945 that the first deliberate attempt was made to shore up the heroic myth connecting Rosenthal's photograph with the first flag raising. Prior to this, all cases of mistaken identity had been the result of happenstance. But now the line was crossed into that ethical mine field, managed news. It was apparently Vandegrift who first crossed it.

The press and public had formed a misimpression that Vandegrift found useful to leave uncorrected. Rosenthal had laid at his feet a picture worth much more than a thousand words. Vandegrift made a policy decision to suppress any photographs that might detract from Rosenthal's. He rightly grasped the fact that Rosenthal's picture impressed on the American mind an image of the Marine Corps' heroic sacrifice then underway on Iwo Jima. The sacrifice was real: the daily toll of casualties was graphic evidence of what the Corps was paying to wrest Iwo Jima from the Japanese. Withholding a few photographs from publication must have seemed a minor matter compared with the high stakes game in which the Marine Corps was involved.

Vandegrift's suppression of the Lowery photographs was temporarily successful. Many people, despite the *Life* article, continued to believe that Rosenthal's photograph represented the raising of the first American flag over Japanese home territory.

Vandegrift's decision would have long-term consequences, however, for both the heroic and the antiheroic myths. In mid-March it might have been possible for him to issue a graceful correction of the public's misconception as to which flag raising Rosenthal had photographed and under what conditions. Had the American public then learned the truth about the 3rd Platoon's unchallenged climb to secure Suribachi's summit, it is unlikely anyone would have thought the less of Iwo Jima's brave Marines, who daily put their lives at risk. And no one could have denied that Rosenthal had taken a memorable photograph. Few at home likely would have cared whether Rosenthal had taken his picture of the first or of the second flag. The picture was its own justification.

But a short month later, by mid-April, the stakes had been raised, and a correction by Vandegrift would have been more awkward to deliver. The men in Rosenthal's photograph, whom Roosevelt had subsequently ordered home, were now back in the States. The Mighty Seventh bond tour would soon be underway, with *these* three flag raisers and their "historic" flag barnstorming the country to raise maximum public support for the war effort. The press and public already were receiving Bradley, Hayes, and Gagnon as bona fide heroes. The operating assumption in Washington was that the greater the public's perception of heroic sacrifices made by the American fighting forces, the greater would be the public's willingness to make financial sacrifices to support the costly campaign against Japan.

So Vandegrift might have thought that it was now too late to confuse the issue with explanations about an earlier flag raised by an anonymous group of men, none of whom were on the scene to make speeches and drum up enthusiasm for the bond drive. The three flag raisers already back for their highly publicized tour had become *the* heroes of Suribachi.

It has been said that the first casualty of war is truth. Whatever the bond tour and its undergirding heroic myth might have gained by Vandegrift's failure to spell out the truth about the flag raisings and their photographs would eventually be offset by the damage done to the reputations of all concerned when the antiheroic myth took the field. As the years marched by and the patriotic fervor of World War II gave way to a period of disillusionment during the Cold War era of the unpopular Korean and Vietnam conflicts, the debunking tone of the antiheroic myth flourished. It fed on the gradually emerging public knowledge that in 1945 the Marine Corps and the federal government had promoted a bond tour that fostered a misconception about one of the most highly publicized events in World War II.

Unfortunately, this accurate appraisal of the deceptive packaging of the Mighty Seventh bond drive cast a shadow over the credibility of many involved in the flag raisings. And among those most frequently targeted over the years by the antiheroic myth was Rosenthal, whose only crime was to take the most memorable war photograph of all time. He is the one who has tried most assiduously to set the record straight.

It has been the work of half a century, this attempt by Rosenthal to correct the record on the Suribachi flag raisings. His efforts began with interviews in the spring of 1945. Ten years later, he co-authored his account published in *Collier's*. The article, "The Picture That Will Live Forever" (a title Rosenthal did not choose and one that even today makes him wince), gave the photographer an opportunity to "tell it all for the record, to recount . . . what I know of what has happened since to those of us associated with that picture who still live."[46]

One of the things that had happened was the disruption of Rosenthal's life. The *Collier's* article detailed some of his trials and tribulations during the decade after Suribachi:

> I have been accused to my face of not having taken the picture and of having appropriated someone else's film, and less than three months ago a Chicago newspaper reported erroneously on page one that I had directed a re-enactment of the first flag raising on Iwo in order to get this shot of the second.
>
> For a time such misstatements angered and depressed me but when,

five years ago, the World Almanac stated in discussing the picture that "Rosenthal also died later," I realized a truth had inadvertently been written. Joe Rosenthal, who is really just another news photographer, who did no more than any competent news photographer would have done and a great deal less than some, no longer lives--at least, not as the unknown private citizen he once was.[47]

The photograph would continue to be both a burden and a glory to Rosenthal, calling to mind the epigram: *Quod me nutrit me destruit* (That which nourishes me also destroys me).

There was one aspect of correcting the record too important and too personal to be dealt with in a news interview: the matter of talking it all out with *Leatherneck* photographer Lou Lowery, who had taken the pictures of the first flag raising.

Rosenthal tells this anecdote about the incident that initiated his long friendship with Lowery, a friendship that lasted until Lowery's death in 1987.[48] In November 1954, just a few days after Rosenthal had attended the dedication of the Marine Corps War Memorial in Arlington, there was a reunion in New York of Marine combat correspondents and photographers. Rosenthal had been invited. It was after midnight on the last day of the conference (and Rosenthal had an 8:00 A.M. flight to San Francisco), but he still wanted to spend some time with Lowery. So he collected a bottle and located Lowery, who was finishing the party off with some fellow Marines. Rosenthal recalls posing with Lowery while some photographers present took flash pictures, including an especially memorable one taken at about 4:00 A.M. when the Pulitzer Prize-winning photographer posed with flash bulbs in his ears. The occasion concluded cordially, with Rosenthal telling Lowery that there might be some debate as to which of them was the better photographer--but no argument at all as to which was the luckier.[49]

Rosenthal still persists in his efforts to set the record straight.[50] But the flag-raising story retains a dark life all its own. As he recently observed: "In 1945 I must have been interviewed at least 20 times about the first flag, second flag. In 1946, similarly, on many, many occasions. Now we are in the 1990s, and I simply cannot understand it. What can I do?"[51]

Rosenthal waxed philosophic in a telephone conversation with the authors in March 1994: "You know that old Greek myth of Sisyphus, where the fellow keeps pushing the boulder up the mountain, even though it always rolls back down? That's sort of how I feel about trying to get this story straight. I push the stone up 10 feet, and it rolls right back 20 feet! Finally, you wonder: what's the point of it all?"[52] After a few moments' reflection, Rosenthal concluded that the point was probably the striving itself, not the success or failure of the enterprise.[53]

Sisyphus is an apt example to illustrate half a century of effort to get the

Suribachi story straight. But when fifty years of encrustations have been stripped away, the facts behind Rosenthal's photograph emerge as a surprisingly simple set of circumstances: a story of ordinary men going about their routine duties under the extraordinary conditions war provides. No one, from the officers in their command posts down at the volcano's base, to the photographers picking their way up the steep slopes, to the battle-weary Marines at the crest had schemed to stage a major public relations event that day. No one, including Rosenthal, had anticipated a rendezvous with destiny at the summit of Suribachi. February 23, 1945, was just another ordinary day in hell for the men on Iwo Jima.

But on that mountaintop when the lives of the photographers briefly intersected the lives of men from the 28th Marines, something memorable occurred. Rosenthal never made grandiose claims for what he had accomplished that winter day. "I did nothing spectacular," he insisted. "I was just at the right place at the right time. Those guys who did the fighting were the ones that were spectacular."[54]

The sole objective of these fighting men was to capture the island while sustaining as few casualties as possible. The Iwo Jima campaign left no time for contrived exercises in public relations. Today, many veterans of the battle remain baffled as to why, after fifty years, there are still journalists and historians who "miss the point."

In the final analysis, more is at stake in an accurate account of the Iwo Jima flag raisings than a correct record of the birth of a national icon. The heroic and antiheroic myths of Suribachi should not distort the reality of how a significant battle was won. Nor should these myths obscure the fact that Joe Rosenthal photographed an authentic moment in the American experience.

The story can now come full circle, ending at the place where it began: the Hansen family home in Massachusetts. In a white cardboard box of correspondence and news clippings two photographs were found. With them was a letter to Henry Hansen's mother.

July 29, 1946

Dear Mrs. Evelley,

Recently I revisited Iwo Jima and had the opportunity to take several pictures and thought you would like to have a couple of copies.

High atop Mt. Suribachi is a fine monument to the boys, yours among them, who made history there.

In the very shadow of this peak is a well kept cemetery where lie the boys who gave their all for their country. Every day the grounds are smoothed and straightened and the markers kept in good order. The appearance of the island is improving, too, as things are beginning to

Return to Iwo Jima. In 1946, Rosenthal visited Henry Hansen's grave in the 5th Division Cemetery in the shadow of Suribachi and the flag-raising monument on Suribachi's summit. Courtesy of Joe Rosenthal. Photographs provided by the Hansen family.

grow again.   The general appearance reflects the reverence for our heroes.

It is difficult to express feelings in a photograph, but I offer these as a salute to the patriots who have made great sacrifices.

Sincerely,
Joe Rosenthal[55]

NOTES

1. Ira Hayes died in 1955, Rene Gagnon in 1979. The sole survivor of the Marines who raised the *first* flag on Suribachi is Charles Lindberg, a resident of Minnesota.

2. Bradley interview with the authors, November 1990.

3. *Return to Iwo Jima*, Arnold Shapiro Productions, 1986.

4. *Albany* (Georgia) *Herald*, January 19, 1994.

5. Ibid.

6. Attempts were immediately made to correct Anderson's account. See Appendix C.

7. *Sands of Iwo Jima*, Republic Pictures, 1949.

8. *Washington Post*, November 11, 1954.

9. Ibid.

10. *New York Times*, November 11, 1954. "Money for the statue was raised by the Marine Corps War Memorial Foundation through voluntary contributions. The cost was $850,000 in pre-inflation dollars. Officially it is the Marine Corps War Memorial but everyone calls it the 'Iwo Jima Monument.' The National Park Service says that the Memorial draws from 2 to 3 million visitors a year, making it one of the nation's capital's most-visited sites" (E. H. Simmons, "The Iwo Jima Flag-Raisings," *Fortitudine*, Vol. 9, No. 2, Fall 1979, 7).

11. Danny Crawford, "Center Treated to Call by Real Iwo Jima Flag Raiser," *Fortitudine*, Vol. 15, No. 4, Spring 1986, 27.

12. Lou Capozzoli, "Orange County Military Beat," *The Register*, December 21, 1975; Severance interview with the authors, October 27, 1993.

13. *New York Times*, March 28, 1960; *TV Guide*, March 26, 1960.

14. Rosenthal interview with the authors, March 6, 1994. William Bradford Huie, author of a short biography of Ira Hayes, *The Hero of Iwo Jima*, also brought suit against NBC. He had sold film rights to Universal Pictures to make a movie, *The Outsider*, about Hayes's decline and fall. See *New York Times*, March 22, 1960.

15. Charles U. Daly, "The Iwo Jima Camera Shot Heard 'Round the World," *Cavalier*, January 1962, 10.

16. Ibid., 11.

17. Ibid., 10, 11.

18. Ibid., 66-68.

19. Ibid., 68.

20. Ibid., 69.

21. Richard Harwood, "The Very Picture of Heroism," *Washington Post*, Book World, August 4, 1991.

22. Richard Severo, "Birth of a National Icon," *New York Times*, October 1, 1991.

23. Ibid.

24. Orvell, *Winterthur Portfolio,* 97.

25. Ibid., 99.

26. Ibid.

27. Ibid., 100.

28. Severance to Anderson, letter dated January 31, 1994, courtesy of Mr. Severance. Severance told the authors that he had been unable to finish the Marling book, its errors being so egregious (Severance interview with the authors, October 30, 1992).

29. Sherrod to Frank, letter dated October 26, 1991. Frank's letter to the *New York Times* called Marling and Wetenhall's allegations that Rosenthal's photograph was part of a Marine Corps publicity scheme "nonsense." See *New York Times,* November 16, 1991.

Frank enlarged on his criticism of the Marling-Wetenhall book in a subsequent issue of *Fortitudine:* "I think that which bothers me most in the book are the snide and throwaway comments of the authors, such as, the statue represented a 'splendid moment [which] had been one among several raisings, that it was second best, somehow, not quite authentic.'" A few sentences later Frank commented: "There are a number of other value judgements and antimilitary put-downs throughout the book which are sadly annoying." See Benis Frank, *Fortitudine,* Winter 1991-1992, 11.

30. Naylor interview with the authors, April 16, 1993.

31. Haynes interview with the authors, December 29, 1992. Rosenthal echoed Haynes's evaluation: "In a certain sense, I'm kind of sorry for Marling and Wetenhall because they don't really appreciate the subject they're handling. They miss the point" (Rosenthal interview with the authors, October 28, 1993).

32. Hatch to Albee, letter dated January 10, 1993.

33. Rosenthal interview with the authors, October 28, 1993.

34. Ibid. As an example, Rosenthal pointed out eight factual errors in the Marling-Wetenhall book on pages 62 to 64.

35. Marling and Wetenhall, *Iwo Jima,* 77.

36. Rosenthal interview with the authors, October 28, 1993.

37. Rosenthal interview with the authors, December 13, 1993.

38. Marling and Wetenhall, "Patriotic Fervor and the Truth About Iwo Jima," *The Chronicle of Higher Education,* September 29, 1993, A52.

39. Ibid.

40. Marling and Wetenhall, *Iwo Jima,* 74.

41. Ibid., 64, 67.

42. Sherrod, *On to Westward,* 193-194.

43. The distortions continue to multiply, even after the publication of Marling and Wetenhall's book, *Iwo Jima.* Referring to Rosenthal's activities on February 23, 1945, Marling and Wetenhall recently wrote in their essay in *The Chronicle of Higher Education:* "Early that afternoon, some combat photographers circumvented security outposts and climbed up to the restricted position. They arrived at the top just in time to witness, and photograph, an impromptu ceremony as the first, historic flag was exchanged for a larger one." See Marling and Wetenhall, "Patriotic Fervor," *The Chronicle of Higher Education,* A52.

Rosenthal responded to this statement with considerable spirit in a recent interview:

There is something serious in their fourth paragraph in which they say that some combat photographers avoided security. I want to know what the hell they are talking about. I have these reactions that are at war with each other: the *silliness,* on the one hand; and yet, it's a serious charge--that we were trying to evade censorship or security or that sort of thing (Rosenthal interview with the authors, October 28, 1993).

When questioned about the Marling-Wetenhall description of "security outposts" that photographers would need to avoid in order to climb Suribachi on February 23, 1945, Severance said there were no such "outposts." His statement corroborates that made by Rosenthal (Severance interview with the authors, October 27, 1993).

44. Rosenthal's "gung-ho" photograph was also published during this time, and the Coast Guard photo of the raised second flag was released for publication on March 9, 1945.

45. *Life,* March 26, 1945, 17.

46. *Collier's,* February 18, 1955, 62.

47. Ibid.

48. Lowery and Rosenthal, according to Lowery's widow, became genuinely devoted friends. Rosenthal flew from San Francisco to Virginia for Lowery's funeral and was seated with the family for the service at Quantico (Doris Lowery interview with the authors, July 19, 1992).

49. Rosenthal interview with the authors, October 28, 1993.

50. See Appendix C.

51. Rosenthal interview with the authors, November 5, 1992.

52. Rosenthal interview with the authors, March 5, 1994.

53. Ibid.

54. Quoted in *Fortitudine,* Vol. 10, No. 2, Fall 1980, 24. Harrold A. Weinberger, NCO in charge of the 4th Division's photo section on Iwo, later said: "It irritates and shocks me when I hear or read that Joe Rosenthal asked the Marines to 'recreate' the flag raising. That statement is an insult to Rosenthal. Joe is a decent, honest and honorable man. He is a modest gentleman who deserves his honors and fame, and he wears his laurels well." See Tom Bartlett, "The Flag Raisings on Iwo Jima," *Fortitudine,* Volume 68, No. 2, February 1985, 21.

55. Rosenthal to Mrs. Evelley, letter dated July 29, 1946, Hansen MSS.

Appendix A

Conflicting Accounts

Difficulties surround the matter of authenticating the composition of the first patrols sent up Suribachi on the morning of February 23, 1945. According to one account by Whitman S. Bartley, in *Iwo Jima: Amphibious Epic*, "At 0900 Lieutenant Colonel Johnson sent out two three-man patrols from Companies D and F to reconnoiter suitable routes and probe for enemy resistance. Surprisingly, no hostile fire was encountered and Marines reached the edge of the crater at 0940." Bartley cites the 5th Marine Division D-3 Journal, Iwo Jima, as his source.

Dave E. Severance, in a letter to John Wetenhall dated July 24, 1989, mentions that Company D sent out a patrol on the morning of February 23, 1945: "The 3 or 4 man Dog Company patrol took a different route, but did not reach the top." J. Robert Moskin, in *The U.S. Marine Corps Story*, remarks on a four-man patrol led by Sergeant Sherman B. Watson and states that "Two other patrols scouted the slopes, but none drew enemy fire." Most other sources including that commissioned by the USMC and published almost contemporaneously with the events in 1945 (Raymond Henri et al., *The U.S. Marines on Iwo Jima*) mention only *one* patrol, the *four*-man patrol sent out by Johnson and led by Watson (Watson interview with the authors, May 28, 1993, and Naylor interview with the authors, April 16, 1993).

Similar difficulties are encountered in attempting to establish the precise time of the first flag raising and the identities of the men who raised that flag. Henri et al. give no specific time but say, "Three men--Schrier, Thomas and Sergeant Henry O. Hansen--actually raised the flag." Howard Conner, in *The Spearhead*, gives the time of the flag raising as 1035 and adds Private First Class James Michels to the list of flag raisers. Robert Leckie, in *Delivered from Evil*, also adds Michels and gives the time as 1030. Bartley gives the time as 1020, as does Bernard Nalty, in *The U.S. Marines on Iwo Jima*. Nalty includes Michels, as well as a new claimant to the ranks of flag raisers: Private First Class Louis C. Charlo, the Montana Indian from Company F who was part of Watson's early-morning reconnaissance patrol. Tom Bartlett, in his February 1985 article in *Leatherneck,* "The Flag Raisings on Iwo Jima," lists the same six names as Nalty. Moskin, in the most recent account (1992), concurs with the Bartlett and Nalty list. In an interview with the authors in 1993, Richard Wheeler expressed some second thoughts about his earlier identification of Louis Charlo as the partially hidden figure in Lowery's photo of the raised flag: "I don't know *where* Charlo came from. He's still a mystery to me. I still think I may have made a mistake in my identification of Charlo. You can't be sure it was Charlo. Another fellow claimed *he* was that Marine--in an article in *Fortitudine.* The other identifications you can count on" (Wheeler interview with the authors, February 5, 1993). That Marine was Gene M. Marshall and the article appeared in the fall 1979 issue of *Fortitudine.*

Bill Ross, in *Iwo Jima,* states that "No one in the patrol bothered to check the time, but thousands of men below, and aboard the ships of the offshore armada, knew to the minute when it happened." Ross sets that minute at precisely 1031. His account drops Hansen from the original quartet and adds Private First Class James R. Nicel, "a replacement who had joined the outfit that morning." The authors have been unable to unearth any other source that lists Nicel. Ross provides no footnote to substantiate either his inclusion of Nicel or his exclusion of Hansen. But the Lowery photographs leave no doubt: Hansen was one of the four raisers.

Samuel Eliot Morison, in *Victory in the Pacific,* gives the time as 1020 and fails to list the other putative flag raisers. He also adds to the confusion by setting the *second* flag raising as being photographed by Rosenthal at 1037. The same error occurs in Jeter A. Isely and Philip A. Crowl's *U.S. Marines and Amphibious War.* They place the time of the first flag raising at approximately 0800 and the second raising at 1037.

This confusion of the times of the two flag raisings (or omission of the fact that there *were* two flags raised that day on Suribachi) was intensified by two Marine Corps official publications. Joel D. Thacker's pamphlet (dated August 15, 1951), *History of the Iwo Jima Flag Raising,* features on its cover a drawing based on Rosenthal's photograph of the second flag raising. The pamphlet does not mention that a prior flag was raised, although the time given for the Rosenthal photo was in fact that of the ignored first flag raising: "Meanwhile, a large flag, measuring 96 by 56 inches, was procured from the nearest available LST, and at about 1035 the flag made famous by the striking photograph snapped by Joe Rosenthal, Associated Press, was flying above the smoke of battle." The exact same information was reprinted eight years later in the Marine Corps Historical Reference Series, No. 14, *History of the Iwo Jima Flag Raising,* November 1959.

The 5th Marine Division's D-2 Journal cites 0947 as the time the first man in Schrier's patrol "went over the top of the summit of Suribachi" and 1030 as the time a flag was "hoisted on Mt. Suribachi." Combat team 28's action report for D+4 states: "A four man patrol followed by a forty man patrol led by 1st Lt. Schrier of LT-228 reached the top of Suribachi on the northeast rim of the crater at 1020 and raised the National Colors." There is no mention of a second flag raised to replace the first one. See Journals and Action Reports, USMC Historical Center.

Appendix B

Photographic Critique

Sergeant William H. Genaust's motion picture sequence demonstrates that if Joe Rosenthal had clicked his shutter a fraction of a second earlier, or later, he would have missed what the great French pioneer of photojournalism, Henri Cartier-Bresson, called "the decisive moment." The classic image of six men raising a flag lasted in reality no longer than the blink of an eye. Then the harmony of symmetrical forms degenerated (as Genaust's footage reveals) into a jumble of awkward gestures in the struggle to raise a heavy flagpole in a stiff following wind.

In a recent interview at his home in Litchfield, Maine, William Hubbell, photographer and author, analyzed the elements that made Rosenthal's photograph so outstanding. Hubbell commented particularly on the choices Rosenthal made, either instinctively or cognitively, in positioning himself at the precise level where his lens would capture the flag raisers silhouetted against the sky. In Genaust's film, taken at a higher angle, the horizon line cuts the figures of the six men above waist level, leaving their lower bodies much less clearly defined than in Rosenthal's photograph.

With Rosenthal the horizon line goes just above the knees. That crucial two feet separates the pictures, whose composition is pretty much the same otherwise. Both photographers were standing on the same plane, looking at the same subject from relatively the same position. Each of their lenses took in the same elements. But it is Rosenthal who, being lower, picked his decisive moment at that instant where the pole left the hands of the last Marine, but where the hands were still visible. That is an important element in the composition.

Rosenthal's composition is greatly helped by the fact that he is lower, so the land [in his photograph] goes right up to the sky at the far right-hand side of the picture. In Genaust's it falls off. It is a weaker image. What happens in the movie frames is that you lose the feeling of a peak, that you are on top of the world, because of the land that shows behind the foreground terrain. Whereas Rosenthal, being a little bit lower, is able to silhouette the rocks against the sky. That gives just that much more of a feeling of being really on the top of the mountain.

It is rare to have a well-known photograph so beautifully documented. Rosenthal's picture of the flag raising is a quintessential decisive moment. It cannot be improved on.

As to the question of whether Rosenthal was an extraordinarily skillful photographer or merely an extremely lucky one, Hubbell concluded: "In that formula of skill vs. luck, Rosenthal's skill transcended. A good photographer makes his own luck" (Hubbell interview with the authors, April 12, 1994).

Appendix C

Correcting the Record

Many efforts have been made to correct recent misreportings of the facts surrounding the Suribachi flag raisings. The former commander of Company E, Dave E. Severance, wrote columnist Jack Anderson on January 31, 1994, that, despite being a fan of Anderson's and believing that, on other subjects, Anderson's previous "revelations were backed by fact," the January 19, 1994, column "would make it appear that your investigators have let you down." Severance continued: "To explain and reveal in detail those errors would cover more space than you may have time to read. I have, however, highlighted those points that are gross errors." Severance concluded: "The 49th anniversary of the Iwo Jima campaign is coming up next month. I have yet to see a newspaper retract any of the many bizarre articles published on this subject . . . you could be my hero by being the first! A column on the 19th or 23rd of February with the facts, and discounting your January story, would delight me, the 115 former members of Company E, and last but not least, Joe Rosenthal" (Severance to Anderson, letter dated January 31, 1994, courtesy of Mr. Severance).

Rosenthal himself wrote Anderson on February 9, 1994, commenting on the "substantial misconceptions and errors of fact which appeared in your [Anderson's] article." Rosenthal closed with this observation: "Year after year the matter has been rehashed in articles almost too numerous to count, and in a large number of books that include long passages about the two flags up there. Rather than 'the incident was kept secret for decades' as you suggest, perhaps too much effort has been devoted to rewriting the event" (Rosenthal to Anderson, letter dated February 9, 1994, courtesy of Mr. Rosenthal).

Norman T. Hatch, the former 5th Division's chief photographic officer on Iwo Jima, wrote Anderson a four-page single-spaced letter pointing out the errors in the January 19 column. Hatch explained: "I first became aware of this particular article through Marine friends from around the country who were so incensed at the multitude of inaccuracies, gross attempts to defame and abysmal ignorance in relation to the facts that I felt honor bound to call these to your attention." Hatch concluded: "The suppositions in your article are just that--suppositions without basis in fact--Marling and Wetenhall notwithstanding" (Hatch to Anderson, letter dated March 29, 1994, courtesy of Mr. Hatch).

In his March 9, 1994, column headlined "Raising White Flag on Photograph," Anderson responded in print to letters such as those submitted by Severance and Rosenthal: "We raise the flag of surrender for a recent column in which we wrote about the historic Iwo Jima flag-raising photo from 49 years ago. Little did we know that writing about this famous event would produce such an avalanche of letters and create a terrible misimpression."

Anderson blamed his errors on the fact that he and his researchers had "relied too heavily on what now appears to be a singularly controversial book and several newspaper pieces about the flag raisings." (It can be assumed from his reference to Marling and Wetenhall in his earlier column that the book Anderson referred to was their *Iwo Jima*.) Anderson then acknowledged two mistakes in his January 19 column. The first was that he had mislocated Secretary of the Navy Forrestal "back in Washington," when Forrestal was actually on Iwo Jima. "The other admission of error," Anderson said, "is owed to the efforts of another Iwo Jima veteran, retired Col. Dave E. Severance of La Jolla, California. He has done extensive research and proven to us that the Marines of that day never deliberately kept the first flag raising secret." These were the limits of Anderson's corrections. See *Sun-Journal*, Lewiston, Maine, March 9, 1994.

In one of his many efforts to correct the record, Rosenthal wrote this letter to Brigadier General Edwin H. Simmons, USMC (Ret.), editor of *Fortitudine*, in response to an article by Robert Sherrod in *Fortitudine's* winter 1980-1981 issue:

> I did manage to get at some notes relative to Sherrod's piece on "Another View of the Iwo Jima Flag Raisings" (Fortitudine, Winter, 1980-1981). I first saw it late in 1981, and, because of some controversial aspects, I recall some slight annoyance that I had no opportunity for comment of my own at the time.
>
> Time has softened its impact, in a sense, though I do have a reaction about Sherrod's possible influence which may lead later researchers astray.
>
> Please don't think me ungrateful for some complimentary remarks therein; but I must point out some trivializations and inaccuracies.
>
> I never answered "yes" to an AP query, "Was the photograph posed?" And Sherrod completely overlooks the fact that the first flag planters were identified in an immediate dispatch from Iwo by AP's Ham Faron among others. My own caption and story never laid claim to being first. . . .
>
> Well, early in March 1945 on a radio broadcast "Time Reviews the

News," correspondent Sherrod was quoted as saying that the Rosenthal photo was "historically a phony . . . that arriving atop Mt. Suribachi too late, he could not resist re-staging the scene."

At that moment I had left Guam by plane headed for San Francisco and New York for reassignment (not lecture tour, as Sherrod put it). At Honolulu stopover the AP bureau chief asked me to comment on a radioed inquiry from AP New York. I was completely surprised because I thought details about my pictures were well known. Nevertheless, I replied that I did not direct the scene in any way. I did not select the spot nor select the men: and I gave no signal as to when their action would take place. . . .

I was at Guam press quarters at the same time as Sherrod the second week of March. When he had his query from Longwell, why did he not ask me about it before I was airborne from Guam about March 15 en route to AP New York? . . .

Murray Befeler, who was photo-pool coordinator on Guam, later told me Sherrod was hassled by other correspondents on Guam. They thought it was not cricket for him to write even ambiguously about the event. . . .

Dear Ed, I find it distasteful to get back into this repeated nit-picking. But there's the funny kind of feeling that maybe, just maybe, some simple language might be helpful for the record. See Rosenthal to Simmons, letter dated December 6, 1984, USMC Historical Center.

Rosenthal's letter was not reprinted in *Fortitudine,* as he had hoped it would be, but it was forwarded to Sherrod. In his cover letter to Sherrod, Simmons remarked: "Having been blamed for Hiroshima, you should be able to shrug off Joe Rosenthal's criticism (enclosed) on your *Fortitudine* article on the Iwo Jima flag raisings." See Simmons to Sherrod, letter dated December 24, 1984, USMC Historical Center.

Selected Bibliography

Bartley, Whitman S. *Iwo Jima: Amphibious Epic*. Washington, D.C.: Historical Branch, G-3 Division, Headquarters, U.S. Marine Corps, 1954.

Blum, John Morton. *V Was for Victory*. New York: Harcourt Brace Jovanovich, 1976.

Chapin, John C. *The Fifth Marine Division in World War II*. Washington, D.C.: Historical Division, Headquarters, U.S. Marine Corps, 1945.

Conner, Howard M. *The Spearhead, The World War II History of the 5th Marine Division*. Nashville, Tenn.: Battery Press, 1987 reprint.

Daly, Charles U. "The Iwo Jima Camera Shot Heard 'Round the World." *Cavalier*, January 1962.

Evans, Harold. *Pictures on a Page*. Belmont, Calif.: Wadsworth, 1978.

Frank, Benis M. *Joseph Rosenthal, Oral History*. Washington, D.C.: History and Museums Division, Headquarters, U.S. Marine Corps, 1975.

Fulton, Marianne. *Eyes of Time: Photojournalism in America*. Boston: Little, Brown and Co., 1988.

Gailey, Harry A. *"Howlin Mad" vs. the Army*. Novato, Calif.: Presidio, 1986.

Haynes, Fred E. "Left Flank at Iwo." *Marine Corps Gazette*, Quantico, Va.: Marine Corps Association, March 1953.

Heinz, W. C. "The Unforgettable Image of Iwo Jima." *50 Plus*, February 1985.

Hemingway, Albert. *Ira Hayes, Pima Marine*. Lanham, Md.: University Press of America, 1988.

Henri, Raymond, et al. *The U.S. Marines on Iwo Jima: The Battle and the Flag Raisings*. New York: Dial Press, 1945.

Hollister, Paul, and Strunsky, Robert, eds. *From Pearl Harbor into Tokyo*. New York: Columbia Broadcasting System. 1945.

Huie, William Bradford. *The Hero of Iwo Jima*. New York: Signet Books, New American Library, 1962.

Isely, Jeter A., and Crowl, Philip A. *The U.S. Marines and Amphibious War.* Princeton, NJ: Princeton University Press, 1951.

Keegan, John. *The Second World War.* New York: Viking Press, 1990.

Kunhart, Philip B., Jr., ed. *World War II.* Boston: Little, Brown and Co., 1990.

Leckie, Robert. *Delivered from Evil.* New York: Harper and Row, 1987.

Manchester, William. *Goodbye, Darkness.* Boston: Little, Brown and Co., 1979.

Marling, Karal Ann, and Wetenhall, John. *Iwo Jima: Monuments, Memories, and the American Hero.* Cambridge, Mass.: Harvard University Press, 1991.

Maslowski, Peter. *Armed with Cameras.* New York: Free Press, 1993.

McCullough, David. *Truman.* New York: Simon and Schuster, 1992.

Millis, Walter, ed. *The Forrestal Diaries.* New York: Viking Press, 1951.

Millot, Bernard. *Divine Thunder.* New York: McCall Publishing Co., 1971.

Moeller, Susan D. *Shooting War: Photography and the American Experience of Combat.* New York: Basic Books, 1989.

Morison, Samuel Eliot. *Victory in the Pacific: 1945.* Boston: Little, Brown and Co., 1975 ed.

Moskin, J. Robert. *The U.S. Marine Corps Story.* Boston: Little, Brown and Co., 1992, 3rd rev. ed.

Nalty, Bernard C. *The United States Marines on Iwo Jima: The Battle and the Flag Raising.* Washington, D.C.: Historical Division, Headquarters, U.S. Marine Corps, 1970 ed.

Newcomb, Richard. *Iwo Jima.* New York: Holt, Rinehart and Winston, 1965.

Parrott, Marc. *Hazard: Marines on Mission.* Garden City, N.Y.: Doubleday and Co., 1962.

Proehl, Carl W., ed. *The Fourth Marine Division in World War II.* Washington, D.C.: Infantry Journal Press, 1946.

Rosenthal, Joe, and Heinz, W.C. "The Picture That Will Live Forever." *Collier's,* February 18, 1955.

Ross, Bill D. *Iwo Jima.* New York: Vanguard Press, 1985.

Sherrod, Robert. *History of Marine Corps Aviation in World War II.* San Rafael, Calif.: Presidio Press, 1980, 2nd ed.

---. *On to Westward.* Baltimore, Md.: Nautical and Aviation Publishing Co. of America, 1990 ed.

Simmons, Edwin H. "The Iwo Jima Flag Raisings." *Fortitudine,* Vol. 10, No. 2, Fall 1979. Washington, D.C.: History and Museums Division, U.S. Marine Corps.

---. *The United States Marines 1775-1975.* New York: Viking Press, 1976.

Smith, Holland M., and Finch, Percy. *Coral and Brass.* Washington, D.C.: Zenger Publishing Co., 1948.

Spector, Ronald H. *Eagle Against the Sun.* New York: Free Press, 1985.

Thacker, Joel D. *History of the Iwo Jima Flag Raising.* Washington, D.C.: Historical Branch, G-3, Headquarters, U.S. Marine Corps, August 15, 1951; reprinted as Pamphlet 14, 1959.

Vandegrift, A. A. (as told to Robert B. Asprey) *Once a Marine.* New York: W. W. Norton and Co., 1964.

---. *Personal Papers 1946-47.* Washington, D.C.: History and Museums Division, Headquarters, U.S. Marine Corps. [PC 578 Boxes 5 & 6].

van der Vat, Dan. *The Pacific Campaign.* New York: Simon and Schuster, 1991.

Warner, Denis, and Warner, Peggy. *The Sacred Warriors.* New York: Van Nostrand Reinhold Co., 1951.

Wheeler, Richard. *The Bloody Battle for Suribachi.* New York: Thomas Y. Crowell Co., 1965.

---. *Iwo.* New York: Lippincott and Crowell, Publishers, 1980.

---. *A Special Valor: The U.S. Marines and the Pacific War.* New York: Harper and Row, 1983.

WW II Time-Life Books History of the Second World War. New York: Prentice Hall Press, 1989.

Index

About the Authors

PARKER BISHOP ALBEE, JR., is Associate Professor of History at the University of Southern Maine. He holds a Ph.D. in history from Duke University.

KELLER CUSHING FREEMAN is a writer, editor and former professor. She holds a Ph.D. in history from the University of Georgia.